Living Religion

Joseph L. Fisher and Margaret W. Fisher

Living Religion

Edited by
George Kimmich Beach and Barbara Kres Beach

Clerestory Press • Arlington, Virginia

Clerestory Press

Clerestory Press books are published under the auspices of
The Unitarian Church of Arlington, Virginia
4444 Arlington Boulevard
Arlington, Virginia 22204

Watercolor painting on cover:
  "Surf on Flint Island," by Margaret W. Fisher.
Cover design by Lynn Goldstein.
Text design by John Shackford.

Library of Congress Catalog Card Number: 92-74995

ISBN 1-56726-950-8

CONTENTS

Part Three: Community and Caring

In September, 1991, Joe Fisher was hard at work in his home office. When he emerged after several hours, he announced with satisfaction that he had gone through all of his sermons and my poetry which we had delivered in various Unitarian Universalist church services over the past fifteen years. He had them all in proper sequence and was surprised and pleased with the quality of their content. He was eager to see them published. Undergoing radiation and medication for spinal cancer which had advanced to his brain, he knew that his time was not unlimited.

Subsequently when our Minister, Dr. George Kimmich Beach, came with his wife, Barbara Kres Beach, to make a pastoral visit, they asked what they could do to help. Joe asked me to bring the collected essays and poetry for them to see and advise us on publication. Kim and Barbara took them home, read them, were excited by them, and later returned with an offer to edit them and help us organize them into a book to be entitled *Living Religion*. Both are writers and professional editors themselves. Joe was delighted!

They would donate their services and with the help of our able church secretary, Barbara Gilligan, would organize the manuscripts on computer. Barbara Beach would then call on the good services of her colleagues in the designing, printing and publishing business to make this book a reality. A Maine coast painting of mine was selected for the front cover, and we went into production. Voila!

The origin of these thirty-one poetry/essay services came at a period of our lives when Joe Fisher had just completed twelve years as Moderator of the Unitarian Universalist Association. He was in his first term as a member of the United States Congress and was full of enthusiasm for both church and state. I was equally enthused, having worked closely with him in a supportive role. I urged him to put in writing some of his thinking as he dealt with the issues and decisions involved in his work.

We started listing topics we might deal with and expanded beyond public affairs to personal issues and philosophical concerns. I happened to be on the Pulpit Supply Committee at the Unitarian Church of Arlington, Virginia, during the time of the sabbatical leave our then minister, Robert Clarke. So a pulpit was readily available, and we launched our services. We continued to deliver them in Unitarian Universalist churches and fellowships across the United States up until January, 1990, when we delivered our last service. I served as lay leader at each service, reading my own poetry related to the topic of Joe's essay-sermon.

These were wonderful, rich years of collegial work for the two of us. We delighted in surprising each other at each service, keeping our writing secret from one another (except for a brief summary statement agreed upon a month in advance). It was always exciting to see how our thought had developed, and we were rarely disappointed.

Cancer finally claimed Joe Fisher on February 19, 1992. On the day of his death I was going over his essay on "Endings and Beginnings." In it he stressed the way in which the life that is lived is of far greater significance than the death itself. And so it has been for Joe Fisher, whose life was full and satisfying. He was my partner for fifty years, and I am proud to combine my words with his in this book, the culmination of our years together.

— Margaret W. Fisher

INTRODUCTION

By George Kimmich Beach

When he affiliated with the Unitarian Universalist faith, Albert Schweitzer characterized it as a way of "faith in action." Joseph and Margaret Fisher—Joe and Peggy, as we have always called them—exemplify what Schweitzer had in mind. Their spiritual and moral convictions have undergirded a life-long engagement in the civic, religious, and professional institutions of their community and world. Religion for them has always meant "faith in action."

Peggy Fisher first used the term "living religion" in her outline for a young people's course on Unitarian Universalist beliefs that she and Joe taught in their home congregation. For a living religion, she suggested, the Unitarian Universalist flaming chalice is an apt symbol: an inner light that inspires caring and active service.

Joe and Peggy Fisher have reflected deeply on the meaning of their activism. In the poetry and the essay-sermons here published for the first time, they have shaped their reflections into a vision of public and personal life. As Peggy notes in her Preface, she and Joe initially outlined the series and set to work. Their outline was enlarged to accommodate new themes as they emerged. The book reflects the Fishers' original plan: to begin by setting forth the theme of the whole series ("Religion and Living"), and to conclude with a review and a call to commitment ("Religion and the Future"). The project took more than fifteen years to complete.

I asked them why they had undertaken such an ambitious project. They wanted, they said, to create together religious services for their own and other congregations. They wanted to draw upon their experience, relating religion to life as a whole. Especially, they wanted to give strong, affirmative expression to their liberal faith. With their rich store of familial, professional, and voluntary experience, none have been better qualified for such a task.

Margaret Winslow and Joseph Fisher met on a blind date, in her home town, Indianapolis, on January 1, 1941. She was a sophomore at Wellesley College; he had begun graduate studies in economics at Harvard University. It was a whirlwind romance: in April Joe proposed; a little more than a year later, on June 27, 1942, they were married.

Joe was then working for the National Resources Planning Board, in Alaska. (From the outset of his career serving "the public interest" was his guiding ideal.) Peggy transferred to Reed College in Portland, Oregon, to be with Joe, whose office was moved to that city following the Japanese attack on the Aleutian Islands during World War II. The Fishers' first year of married life was spent in Portland, where Peggy completed her Bachelor's degree in French literature. Their first son was born four months after her graduation and just two weeks before Joe left for military service in the Pacific theater. At Pearl Harbor Joe first worked on the logistics staff of Admiral Nimitz. When that work was completed, he transferred to the Army newspaper, *Stars and Stripes,* as an editor. He remained in this position until the end of the war.

Joseph Lyman Fisher was born in Pawtucket, Rhode Island, in 1914, one of two children in a Unitarian family. A trim athlete, he was a skillful boxer and an avid wilderness hiker and canoeist. He enrolled at Bowdoin College, in Brunswick, Maine, graduating in 1935, and began his career as an economist specializing in resource management. After the war, the Fishers moved to Cambridge, Massachusetts, where Joe continued graduate studies in economics, receiving a doctorate from Harvard University in 1947. The growing Fisher family then moved to the nation's capitol, living in Falls Church initially and in Arlington a little later. From 1947 to 1954 Joe was Executive Officer and Senior Economist of the President's Council of Economic Advisers. From 1954 to 1975 he worked for a private research and educational foundation, Resources for the Future, Inc., becoming its President in 1959.

Politics was a natural extension of his civic activism. A Democrat and a leader in Arlingtonians for a Better Community, a liberal political coalition, Joe was elected to the Arlington County Board, on which he served for a decade, including two terms as Chairman. During his political career he also served as the Arlington representative on the Metropolitan Washington Council of Governments and as member of the board of the Washington Metropolitan Area Transit Authority; for both he also served as Chairman.

Joe's greatest political triumph came in 1974 when he upset the eleven-term Republican incumbent, Joel Broyhill, in the 10th Congressional District of Virginia. In the House of Representatives Joe soon established himself as a respected expert on economic policy. By 1980 his original political base in Arlington County had been diluted by a burgeoning Republican majority in western Fairfax County; in the year of "the Reagan revolution" he lost his bid for reelection to Congress.

A staunch but never a doctrinaire liberal, Joe Fisher had made a lasting mark on national and state politics. Richard Pearson noted highlights of his career in an obituary article in the *Washington Post* (February 20, 1992):

> Mr. Fisher was named to the powerful House Ways and Means Committee, and soon made a reputation for his work on taxation, energy and budget policy, and he was chosen by his committee chairman to coordinate seven task forces that drafted the energy program that emerged from several congressional and White House proposals.
>
> In 1982, Mr. Fisher joined the cabinet of Gov. Charles S. Robb as Virginia's secretary of human resources, a post in which he was responsible for a $3.5 billion budget and 20,000 employees in 15 agencies. Although he took office at a time of economic retrenchment, he received favorable reviews from critics spanning the political spectrum.

Joe remarked to me that the complexity of social needs and political pressures made being Secretary of Human Resources for the Commonwealth of Virginia the most difficult job he had ever had. Yet far from avoiding large responsibilities, he relished them. The depth of his knowledge of contemporary social problems and his commitment to effective public programs to address them is evident in the chapters of this book. Looking back upon his public career, he took the greatest pride from his contributions to federal environmental policy and his successful role in creating the Bill of Rights for handicapped persons in Virginia.

Education played a large part in Joe's and Peggy's lives, extending their vocational identities. Together they enrolled in a the master of arts in Education program at George Washington University. A 1952 graduation photo shows Joe and Peggy standing with the Dean, Peggy's "second pregnant commencement" barely disguised by her academic gown.

During these and subsequent years Peggy and Joe were raising three daughters and four sons. With a husband so deeply involved in civic life, many of the burdens—and the joys, she adds—of raising the family fell to Peggy. (Joe "uncomfortably" recalls the answer one of their grade-school age daughters gave to a teacher's question to the children about what their fathers did for a living. She said, "My daddy goes to meetings.") Nevertheless, Peggy found time to establish her own career as an artist, an arts educator, and a poet.

When Joe's work took them to the capitol of Virginia, Peggy entered Virginia Commonwealth University, in Richmond. There she earned a bachelor of fine arts degree, refining her skills as a painter and a teacher of

painting. She has taught painting at the Northern Virginia Community
College and the University of Virginia, and in the adult education program in
Arlington. For Peggy teaching art is a humanistic endeavor; in her words, it
is a way to "help people realize their potential for creativity." She adds, "and
people are never too old to learn."

Her own landscapes, figure paintings, and family portraits, in both oil and
watercolor, are vibrant with color and feeling. Her art reflects the places she
has lived or visited—including Greece, Indonesia, Italy, China, Ecuador,
Mexico, and Columbia. Most often they reflect her deep feeling for her
"home base"—in Arlington and at their family retreats in Loudoun County
and Maine. Her poetry exhibits similar qualities: clear, forceful expression of
perceptions and deeply felt values. She addresses the reader in her personal
voice; thus her poetry challenges us and evokes a personal response. She has
received awards from the New York Poetry Forum and the National League
of American Penwomen, in which she has been an organizational leader.

A conservationist in her several communities, Peggy has served as
member and chair, since 1989, of the Goose Creek Scenic River Advisory
Board (to which she was appointed by three Virginia governors), founding
member of the Arlington Beautification Committee, and member of the board
of the Preservation Society of Loudoun County and Keep Loudoun Beautiful.
Her civic and artistic achievements have been recognized in several awards.

The partnership of Joe and Peggy Fisher has also been expressed through
their religious community, the Unitarian Church of Arlington, where they
have been active members and leaders from its inception, in 1947. When
their children were young, they taught Sunday school classes. Joe was
elected Chairman of the Board of Trustees of the church, and later, to the
Board of the Unitarian Universalist Association (UUA). When the position
of UUA Moderator was suddenly vacated, creating a leadership crisis, Joe
was selected by his peers to fill the position. He was subsequently elected by
the national membership to two more four-year terms.

The office of Moderator, normally held by a layperson, is the highest
volunteer position in the UUA. Joe's twelve years of service, from 1964 to
1976, were marked by painfully divisive controversies in the denomination
over the Vietnam War and "black empowerment." In conversation, years
later, he recalled presiding at one particularly fractious UUA General
Assembly, when a young woman in hippie garb approached him at the
podium. What next? he wondered. She placed a string of "love-beads"
around his neck, which he accepted with his broad smile. Suddenly the
Assembly burst into applause, a tribute to his fair-minded and unflappable

leadership under sorely trying circumstances. The tension of the moment was broken; the Assembly regained its confidence and unity.

The associations of which Joe Fisher was a member and a leader are numerous. Some were professional: the National Academy of Public Administration, the Commission on Physical Sciences, Mathematics, and Resources of the National Academy of Sciences, the American Forestry Association. Some were ecological: The Wilderness Society, the Environmental and Energy Study Institute, the Chesapeake Bay Foundation. Some were civic and charitable: the International Hospice Institute, the United Way of Virginia, the Northern Virginia Community Foundation; some were academic: Bowdoin College, in Maine, Meadville/Lombard Theological School, a Unitarian Universalist seminary in Chicago, and George Mason University, in Fairfax, Virginia.

In 1985 Joe's severe back pains were diagnosed as bone cancer. Through treatment he gained remission and relief from pain, enabling him to maintain the extraordinary round of political, civic, recreational, and familial activities that marked his entire adult life.

After Joe and Peggy returned to Arlington from Richmond in 1986, Joe was appointed Distinguished Professor of Political Economy and special adviser to the President of George Mason University. He taught classes and kept up a busy round of engagements until late in 1991. Shortly before his death the University announced the inauguration of the Joseph L. Fisher Fellowship Endowment Fund in Public Policy, to support students in The Institute for Public Policy. Kingsley E. Haynes, Dean of the Graduate School, noted the qualities that had led so many institutions to turn to him for leadership:

> "Joe" Fisher embodied the best characteristics of academic perspective and hands-on public service, both as a participant in the legislative process and as a member of the executive. He has a special combination of calm and stability in very difficult situations as well as a powerful commitment to change and adaptation. He served as an elected and appointed official at all levels of government and was appreciative of the critical role of governmental personnel. He was an outstanding teacher and a skilled adviser in both the analytical and political arenas.

These biographical notes may give the reader a window on the lives from which the works in this volume grew. As Peggy notes in the Preface, after completing his three terms as Moderator of the UUA, she and Joe decided to develop a series of services for their Arlington congregation and others, articulating the "faith in action" which their lives had become. There is no explaining how Joe and Peggy found time to write and present this ambitious series of services—while maintaining their multiple civic and professional interests and being the hub of a clan that includes seven adult children and fourteen grandchildren. Suffice it to say that they both felt impelled to teach, to inspire, to exhort, to recount the fulfillment they had found in their "living religion."

Early in 1991 Joe's cancer returned. In spite of extensive radiation treatments its pace accelerated. During this period Joe broached the subject of assembling his sermons and Peggy's poetry in book form. Barbara and I readily agreed. Joe reviewed the first round of editing, gave his approval, and urged us to complete the project.

He foresaw his death, and spoke of it with Stoic courage and acceptance. Looking back at his life, having "fought the good fight," he saw his personal and professional goals fulfilled. He was surrounded by a loving family, for whom he was deeply grateful and to whom he returned love. He had always been the emotionally reticent New Englander, but in the time after his cancer diagnosis, a daughter confided, his reserve gave way to warmly open expression of feelings between the children and their father.

In his last public address, in October, 1991, as Honorary Co-Chair, with Peggy, of the Building Campaign of the Unitarian Church of Arlington, Joe urged the congregation, "Go for it!" He had given himself the same advice for a lifetime. At Christmastime the family enjoyed a reunion at home in Arlington and the marriage of their eldest grandson, Joseph Nathaniel. The wedding, at the Unitarian Church of Arlington, was one of the last times he was able to leave home. He spoke of his deep sense that, whatever he had accomplished, he had depended on Peggy, his beloved companion in marriage. He died, on February 19, 1992, a few months shy of their fiftieth wedding anniversary.

Joe and Peggy had helped found the Hospice of Northern Virginia; in his last weeks he became the recipient of Hospice care at home. His memorial service at the Unitarian church was attended by an overflow crowd, the largest number in its history. A few days earlier, family members and close friends gathered at Arlington National Cemetery to offer final appreciations—words, music, a brief dance. There his ashes were buried, next to the graves of two four-star generals. The marker reads: "Tech Sgt. Joseph L. Fisher, Member of Congress."

Readers of *Living Religion* can anticipate a feast of ideas and inspiration. Of Joe's essay-sermons we can say: Here are wise and nuanced judgments on the political, practical, and ethical aspects of social policy in contemporary America and the world, a wealth of information about these public concerns of public life, and personal perspectives rich in moral and spiritual insight. Through this running commentary on the contemporary world are woven many delightful stories. Alaska and Maine, Washington, D.C. and Richmond, Virginia, Arlington County and his rich marital and family life figure in these reminiscences.

Of Peggy's poetry we can say: It richly reflects the inner life. Yet her poems also probe the ways in which personal and social experience challenge us to respond to life with feeling and resolve. They are alive with imagery and forceful cadences. Peggy's poetry reminds us, again and again, that there is more to life than preening one's own soul; it invites us into a larger world of courage and compassion, commitment and caring. The acute imagery of her poems complements the broad sweep of Joe's sermons.

For Joe and Peggy Fisher, a living religion has multiple contexts: nature, society, and individual personhood. The world of nature is a constant background in these works. Peggy bids us—

> Within this gentle woodland take your ease
> And give your tethered heart and soul release.

Joe's essay-sermon, "Inspiration from a Pond," is pungent with description of his "special place" of annual pilgrimage. He bids us to find our own places for personal "retreat."

These reflections lead him to call for "an environmental ethic," an ethic drawing its inspiration from "the inter-relatedness and interdependence of all living things in the natural environment." While politicians often set in opposition environmentalism and economics, Joe notes that *ecology* and *economy* share a common Greek root; both refer to care for the household. Care for the earth as our natural "household" evokes meanings and feelings from "the depths of experience," Joe writes, "the necessary forerunner of great thoughts and great actions." This religious awareness is essential to an environmental ethic which is effectively acted upon. In her poem, "Permanence," Peggy rekindles our love for our common household, the earth.

A second context of living religion is social, including a lively sense of community, leadership informed by commitment to the common good, and courageous work for reconciliation between contending groups. In "Gaps, Crises, and Power" Joe discusses the "gaps" between generations, economic classes, and racial and ethnic groups that invite conflicts and rend communities. In the face of these challenges he affirms "the gentler forms of power that arise from understanding the problem, discussing it, and arriving peacefully at honorable compromises." The relevance of his liberal faith to the crises of our age, to steadfastness in the face of anger and threats of violence becomes clear: "What I am suggesting here is that gentle and benign power—the power of love, if you like—is stronger than we realize."

Joe's reflections on politics and "the public interest" bring us to the central concerns of his career. He affirms that values, rather than the quest for popularity or power, must guide political judgment. There are no simple answers to complex social problems, but only those found through the slow workings of a democracy. Confidence in and patient work with the democratic process is required of us. We depend on leaders who have spent time with the disciplines of self-knowledge and are devoted to the common good.

The third context of a living religion is individual personhood. In "Religion and Solitude" Peggy and Joe reflect on solitude as a source of inspiration readily available to all. People deeply engaged with social and political causes—or simply with their own jobs and families—are tempted to become absorbed in ceaseless, outward activity. We need, they say, to invite solitude, deliberately setting apart times and places for ourselves alone.

Although, as Joe notes, solitude is often confused with loneliness, those who attend to their inward needs become capable of a solitude that enriches and renews life. He comments, at one point, on Peggy's well-developed ability to schedule periods of solitary activity into her day, and his own learning to respect these times by not intruding. In her words—

> There is a human need
> for space to grow. . . .

Peggy and Joe practiced what they preached. We see this in their creative and recreative activities, giving themselves "space to grow."

And what of religion itself? In Joe's words, "Religion is the distillation of life's experiences, those received as part of the ongoing traditions of civilized people as well as those coming directly to each individual. . . . Self-conscious and reflective, religion is as natural as waking up in the morning and falling asleep at night, as natural as breathing." Neither ritual observances nor doctrines foreign to daily experience, religion is a dimension of life as a whole. Paul Tillich called it "the depth dimension," the dimension of ultimate concern within life's multiple, immediate concerns.

Moreover, far from "passive philosophizing," a living religion leads to action. It releases the best in us, creative thought and caring deeds. Authentic religion is also deeply personal, he says, making possible "serenity in the face of tragedy, patience in the face of uncertainty, and fortitude in the face of destruction."

Peggy's poem for the concluding chapter asks—

> Is there a way to reach beyond
> the tiny space we have in time?

Her final stanza answers, evoking the sense of urgency we feel when we value life deeply and recall our finitude—

> Perhaps it's not too much to hope
> that life has deathless qualities
> that reach beyond this finite time,
> this precious time we have on earth.

A poignant sense of original blessing and of final transcending pervades these works, Joe's and Peggy's essay-of-a-lifetime in living religion.

A striking feature of Joe's essay-sermons is their short, concluding prayers. The last of these is a lovely, brief exhortation, bidding us to seek new knowledge, to respect life, to care for humanity, and finally, to link "Soul with World." He closes—

> Stand on this ground
> And touch the sky.

Throughout, Joe and Peggy Fisher call us to surpass ourselves and enlarge our humanity. Rooted in the real-world concerns of our time, their writings reach for a spiritual and moral vision that will transform reality, that will "touch the sky."

Part One

Inspiration and Integrity

CHAPTER ONE
RELIGION AND LIVING

Inner Light

There is an inner light that guides our lives
That gives us purpose, hope, and strength
To do that which we must to find —
Fulfillment as we move through life.

Its voice is music, art, and prayer,
Is dancing, song, and poetry.
It seeks out justice in our courts of law
And healing by the doctor's hands.

Wherever kindness, love, and sympathy
And comforting are found, a silent glow
Of inner light is felt. Its gentle pulse
Extends into the universe.

Religion and Living

You've probably heard people say, "Religion is all right, but I can take it or leave it." A recent poll revealed that while nearly half the respondents had no church affiliation, nearly all of them professed a belief in God, if only as a hedge. Meanwhile, young adults look for religion in transcendental meditation, wilderness backpacking, drugs, and other ways approved and not approved. A few are even looking in churches.

The longing and searching for religion, I suspect, is as strong as ever. But more and more people are looking for it in new ways and unlikely places. Those looking most frantically for religion are often the same people who have persuaded themselves they are escaping it.

Several years ago, a friend and I were climbing the White Oak Canyon Trail in the Blue Ridge Mountains. Needing a short rest, we stopped at the top of one of the waterfalls near a group of four young people and fell into conversation with them. The discussion quickly took a philosophical turn. I asked where they were headed.

One of them answered, "In search of the meaning of life."

"What do you expect to find?" I asked.

The responses tumbled out: "Peace of mind." "To be left alone." "Love." "Nothing."

They were pleasant, attractive, college-educated, soft-spoken. One of them carried a two or three gallon jug of red wine in a wicker sling which they drank through a rubber tube. I suggested that each of them might be hiking along the trail trying to find his or her place in the world.

"Something like that," one of them said.

We were silent for a while. One of the fellows opened the stopcock and let some wine run into his mouth. The girl with him got some bread out of her pack and broke off pieces for each of us.

"I think," she said after a while, "we are really looking for a religion, each of us for our own religion, which will be the meaning of our lives."

"Do you think you are more likely to find your religion here in the mountains by yourselves or back home in a job or finishing your studies?" I asked.

"Oh, back home, of course," they said. "But meantime this trip is helping us to sort things out."

Interesting and wonderful things can happen in the mountains while you are resting.

Several years ago I had an instructive encounter with several central city youths. I was going to a meeting of the Board of Trustees of the United Planning Organization, which is the anti-poverty agency in the Washington area. The meeting was being held in the basement of a Baptist church located in a poor section of Northwest Washington. I found a parking place about a block away. It was a warm summer evening. I was early and in no hurry. Two teenage boys, about fifteen years old, were on the sidewalk playing pitchpenny, a game I hadn't seen for years. I watched a while until one of the boys said, "Hey, you want to play?"

"OK," I said, and took a penny out of my pocket. We each tossed our pennies to the crack in the sidewalk. I came closest. We continued playing for a while. I just about broke even. We rested a while and discussed the merits of scaling the coin compared to spinning it end over end—if a coin has an end.

One of them asked, "What you doing here? Where you going?"

I said, "I'm going to the Baptist church down there to a meeting."

"Who else is going?" the other one asked.

"Friends," I answered.

"Ain't no friends there, man; that's a church" he said.

The boys laughed in agreement.

"I have friends there," I said. "Come on with me and I'll show you."

"What you going to do at the meeting?" the first one asked.

"Try to figure out how to help people," I said.

"What kind of people?" He was suspicious.

"Mostly poor people in trouble," I said. "People out of work; people who can't pay their bills; people in trouble with the law; stuff like that."

"Want to go with this guy?" he asked his friend.

"OK," his friend said, "we got nothing else to do."

We walked along toward the church. "What you doing that kind of stuff in a church for? Church is for praying, ain't it?"

"Some people think helping others beats praying—beats pitching pennies, too." I said.

"That so?" he said. "Maybe we ought to try it." They both laughed again.

We went into the church. I introduced them to my fellow board members. The boys sat quietly and attentively through the meeting and enjoyed the punch and cookies that some ladies in the church served afterwards.

Interesting and wonderful things can happen in the central city on your way to a meeting in the Baptist Church.

If there is a lesson to be drawn from these two encounters and many others like them, it is that religion is important to practically everyone whether they stop to think about it or not. In fact, most people spend more time looking for it than they realize. In a sense, searching for religion is the main thing people do in their lives.

Religion, as I am thinking of it here, is not a formal ritual or an inherited set of beliefs accepted without thought. Nor is it a church or any other kind of institution. Rather, religion is the distillation of life's experiences, those received as part of the ongoing traditions of civilized people as well as those coming directly to each individual. It is a man looking at the world and learning to live in it. It is a woman discovering herself, shaping her destiny, and coming to terms with it. It is a man or a woman being with other men and women, learning from and teaching one another, cooperating and competing with one another, paying attention to and caring for one another. Self-conscious and reflective, religion is as natural as waking up in the morning and falling asleep at night, as natural as breathing.

Alfred North Whitehead wrote: "Religion is the vision of something that stands beyond, behind, and within the passing flux of immediate things; something which is real, and yet waiting to be realized . . . something that gives meaning to all that passes, and yet eludes apprehension . . . something which is the ultimate ideal, and the hopeless quest."

Professor Whitehead was on the right track. Religion is all these things. More than being a result of living or a reason for living, religion, I claim, is living at its most profound levels. Religion is living fully, generously, thoughtfully, lovingly, looking back and ahead, looking outward and inward. The quality of religion is measured by the quality of living. The quality of living is raised by the quality of religion. If religion is living, as I believe it to be, it is living in a certain way with a certain style.

I have said that religion is the distillation of life's experiences, life's hopes and disappointments, life's achievements and failures. Like life, religion evolves and changes as one grows. A person's religion sums up what he makes out of life and the world at that moment.

A life experience, from which a person's religion is brewed, is composed of many elements. The proportions differ from individual to individual. For some, nature provides the principal religious element—snow lying quietly on a hillside, the flash of a red cardinal flying through the trees, the grandeur of a great canyon, the marvelous ecology of a pond. For others, art and music, whether viewing and listening to the works of others or creating their own private masterpieces are the basis of their religion. Many find their true source of religion in human relations, in loving and being loved, in doing acts of kindness and receiving them. Still others extract religious experience from suffering and death, both of which are a part of life. For most of us, all of these, and more, make up our living religion.

I told earlier about some young people—on a mountain trail and in the ghetto of a big city—who, at least during the time I was with them, deliberately or innocently searched for religion. Older people also engage in the same search, usually with a sense of greater urgency. Our minister once told of the youngster who, noting how frequently his grandmother went to church and prayed, remarked to a friend that she must be cramming for finals. I suspect most people cram a bit for finals as they begin to number their days, if not by praying, then by spending more time trying to figure out what it all adds up to. No doubt as each of us pushes past 50 and 60, we make a little more effort to figure out what is going to appear on the bottom line. This is a wholesome exercise to be encouraged. I remember my grandfather, never a religious man as far as I knew, even made out a ledger of pluses and minuses toward the end of his life. I found it one day on his desk and was surprised at the number of doubts and shortcomings this supremely self-confident man believed he had.

Religion, though, is more than the distilled essence of life's experiences. It has a more active role. Unless it moves men and women to new thought and stronger action, it is no more than passive philosophizing. At its best, religious reflection leads to action to improve living—for individuals, for those whose lives they touch, for humankind. The effort of a person to make religion out of life, to define a role in the immediate community and in the cosmos, to discover and release our best, is a very human effort. It is also as divine as anything we shall ever know. Religion raised up out of the experiences of living, out of life itself, provides several essentials people can't really live without.

One essential that religion provides is motivation for making our life count for something. It enhances our understanding of the difficulties we all have with preoccupied associates in an indifferent, if not hostile, world. It encourages action to overcome these difficulties. Equally, religion enhances our capacity to understand and cope with our own shortcomings and occasionally misguided tendencies. It energizes us to raise our sights and live constructively.

Religion based securely in human experience also provides a realistic perspective on the possibilities of life and a key for opening the right doors. Religion makes it easier for a person to organize time, energy, resources, and life, and to harness these to worthy purposes of self-realization, service to humanity, devotion to God, living with nature, producing useful goods, penetrating the unknown and raising children.

Growing out of multifaceted life itself, religion makes possible serenity in the face of tragedy, patience in the face of uncertainty, and fortitude in the face of destruction. It permits people to maintain hope for the future and faith that the human voyage is worth the effort. Religion inspires courage in us, in the manner made glorious by Camus' doctor in *The Plague,* to meet with dignity whatever vicissitudes fate can throw at us. With pain, death, and collapse all about him, the doctor was able to persevere in his work with a courage that is the mark of manhood.

An experience-based religion carries with it an honesty that is unpretentious and reliable. It grows out of the ground, not down from the sky. It assumes only life and the world in which life exists, has existed, will exist. Yet by strange and wonderful processes the sperm and the clay together have evolved great structures—of science, technology, and social institutions of law and governments—and religion itself. All of these move ceaselessly, interacting, occasionally exploding into new, unpredictable forms. What a panorama this is! What a history to be a part of! It is no wonder that humans have conceived gods and erected religious systems to cope with grandeur and awe and at the same time to preserve a place for the humblest individuals lest we, lest you and I, be lost entirely from sight, diminished to nothing.

Religion, I say again, is living fully, generously, thoughtfully, lovingly, looking back, looking ahead, looking outward, looking inward. Rooted in life, it seems to transcend life to give people motivation, perspective, courage, honesty, and dignity to deal with, even to master life for a brief time. For a person to say, "Religion is OK, but I can take it or leave it," is like saying, "Life is OK, but I can take it or leave it."

The search for religion, therefore, becomes the most challenging and rewarding of all human adventures. If you like, religion in the sense I have used it can be called God, and the search for it can be thought of as divine.

Do not draw back from the search.
Pursue it through the twilight
of the night and the rose color of the morning.
The search is the reward,
not so much the finding.
The world remains in flux and movement
but always toward purpose,
perchance divine.

Peace of the Woods

Soft breezes brush my face and blow my hair.
They purify my body and my mind.
Forgotten are the glare and noisy grind
Of crowded, smokey streets and thoroughfare.
A chipmunk scurries from his secret lair
With chirping chatter as he seeks to find
Some nuts and berries, seeds of any kind,
Then hurries back to store his winter's fare.
The chickadee darts lightly through the trees
Whose softly swaying branches whisper, "Peace."
Inhale the fragrance of the gentle breeze;
Immerse yourself in nature's fair increase.
Within this gentle woodland take your ease
And give your tethered heart and soul release.

❧

Inspiration from a Pond

Every one of us has a special place to which we can go for inspiration. Most of us have several such places. Usually these spots are outdoors, but not always. I once knew a fellow who had a remote and well protected carrel in Widener Library that provided the quiet seclusion and musty environment he needed from time to time to regroup his forces. He even wrote poetry there. My wife tells me her girlhood inspiration place came when she was leaning up against the family garage, around the corner out of sight of parents and passers-by. I have two such places. I used to have others when I was a boy and young man living in different towns, but now I have two: one for summer and one for all other seasons. My all-other seasons inspiration place is right here in Arlington on the bank of the Potomac between Windy Run and Donaldson Run: a quarter acre between the river and the rocky palisade with a thin waterfall falling over the cliff in the back, several sycamores arching out over the river's backeddies close to shore, and a smooth rock to sit on.

But it's my summer inspiration place I want to describe more fully. Located in eastern Maine—way "Down East"—a few miles in from the coast, it takes about half an hour to hike there from our camp. There is a small pond formed by a beaver dam across a stream, just beyond a height of land so that one comes upon it suddenly. Mountains and rock ledges rise around it leaving only room for the pond and an ample supply of willows and aspen, soft enough for the beavers to gnaw down easily and slide to the water. The beaver lodge, igloo-shaped and well constructed, is at the more protected side of the pond about five rods from the dam (people still reckon distance down there in five half-yard rods.) A few pines too big for the beavers to take down and a few maples too hard for their teeth, provide shade here and there. Blueberry and raspberry bushes have come in plentifully in the parts recently cut over by the beavers. The berries go well with a drink of the cool, fresh water scooped up from one of the pools just above the pond formed as the stream makes its last cascade into the still water.

My special place is on a rock, flat for sitting on, between the dam and the lodge, sheltered somewhat by overhanging alder bushes. Another rock is placed just right for leaning back against. The few sounds become louder as I sit quietly on my rock and gain repose—the water tumbling over rocks as it comes into the pond and as it leaves below the dam, the chirp and chatter of chipmunk, a crow cawing in the distance, the light flutter of a vireo's wings from one of the pine trees, a frog sounding off from somewhere near the bank, the soft and magic quaking of aspen leaves in the breeze, humming insects.

Toward dusk, if I am there then, and lucky, I will hear the noise of the beaver at work and perhaps the slap of his tail on the water, sounding alarm as he dives. Or, if I am very lucky, I will hear a deer breaking through to the water's edge, and then I will see the deer, graceful and alert, camouflaged against the bank. Of course, there are the numerous snaps, cracks, and rustles of unknown origin one always hears in the woods when one is quiet and receptive to nature's voices.

I could go on describing the sights or the smells as well as the sounds; their delight and variety are not less: a fat bluejay on the branch of a tree, a dark trout nibbling on the underside of a floating leaf, the jerky movement of a water spider as it breast-strokes across a still part of the pond, the smell of the hot noon-time sun on the blueberries, the fresh aroma of the early morning dew lifting from the bushes and the grasses, the delicate scent of pines and bayberries.

But that is enough for description; the mood has been established. It is a mood that opens the eyes, ears, fingertips, mind, breast, and soul to new thoughts and old reflections, to the wonders of nature right there all the time, to speculations about my past, your past, the human past, in the whole panorama and process of life.

Without question, the beaver's pond is also my pond. Whether the beaver receives inspiration there, I don't know. I do know that I do. Without question also, being at our pond, the beaver's and mine, is a religious experience for me, a living religious experience in which I am an integral part of nature around me and in me, in tune with its vibrations of sound, its spectrum of colors, its flow of sensations. It is a transcendental experience, not in carrying me out of nature, but in intensifying the feeling of oneness with nature. It is a mystical experience, not of being out of the real world, but of being completely and unselfconsciously in it.

To use a word until recently esoteric for most people, being at the pond is an ecological experience. I am embraced within the natural ecological system of the pond, physically for the time I am there and in spirit when I am away. The miracle is that I only have to be there a few times each year to be able to go there in imagination to recapture its inspiration. I am trying to take you there with me and in a vicarious but vivid way, to share with you this inspiration from a pond.

As I said earlier, I have no doubt each of you has such a place in the mountains, at the seashore, in the nearby park, in your own back yard. Even if you don't go to it often in search of composure, ideas, reflection, peace of mind, new resolve, or whatever you need, you may be comforted by the knowledge it is ready to receive and inspire you. Like home to Robert Frost, my pond, or your equivalent, is a place where, when you go there, it has to take you in.

These experiences that you and I have had in our special natural places are religious experiences. The psychology of them runs deep in us all. Scientists have developed a remarkable capacity to examine nature and nature's forces to uncover their rules and regularities, as though they were outside looking in. On the resulting scientific knowledge, the technologies and trappings of modern day-to-day living have been developed. For the last two or three centuries homo sapiens, with an arrogance that is unique, has sought mastery over nature, and in the present age of science may think fatuously that we have achieved such mastery. Such mastery is a dangerous illusion, a Faustian bargain with the devil; the end can be only catastrophic.

The notion that humanity's challenge and duty is to subdue nature is not confined to America or the West, or even the Judeo-Christian ethos. A modern Chinese poet, Chang Chih-min, wrote in *Personalities in the Commune*:

> Let's wage war against the great earth!
> Let the mountain and the rivers
> surrender under our feet.
> March on nature!
> Let's take over the power of rain and wind.

My quarrel is not with the effort of science to understand nature or the effort of industry to produce useful articles. My quarrel is with the presumption that nature—forests, animals, water, the landscape, the air around us—is to be used, misused, even ravaged with little or no thought of humanity's or nature's future. When it comes to deciding what to do with the natural environment and natural resources, we fall short. Engineering efficiency is not an adequate guide, nor are economic comparisons of benefits and costs or political and administrative feasibility tests. As a guide, even ecological stability falls short unless it includes the needs and aspirations of human beings as well as ecological systems, whether they are small, like the beaver pond, or large like the world's oceans and atmosphere. What is needed, of course, are broad and long-range ethical guidelines within which industry and politics can do their work. Carl Sandburg told the story of the white man who drew a circle in the sand, saying, "That is what Indian knows," and then another around the first saying, "That is what white man knows." The Indian took the stick and drew a circle around both saying, "This is what neither Indian nor white man knows."

Like a number of you, I have been concerned with the environment, and I have been pleased that an insistent environmental movement has arisen in this country during the past seven or eight years. Magazine articles have proclaimed the ecological crisis, have analyzed its origin, and have pronounced doom for the country unless strenuous efforts are made to reverse it. Supporting evidence is easy to find: the air over our cities is often foul; rivers, lakes, and bays are polluted; solid waste problems have become a headache for every city council in the land; congestion and crowding are a nightmare on highways and in cities, and DDT-type pesticides and radioactive materials have polluted the atmosphere and oceans of the world.

The word crisis is not too strong for the present situation, despite the fact that the present day environment, compared to conditions in earlier times, is an improvement. People in this country no longer die from typhoid, and the average length of life has increased rapidly in the past century or two. An astonished visitor from an Asian country recently remarked to me, "Why, you can drink faucet water anywhere in your country with perfect safety." It is undoubtedly true that the modern American urban slum, for all its unattractive features, is a better place to live than most of London in Dickens' time; and that the poorest country town in Appalachia offers more than Goldsmith's deserted village.

Nevertheless, Americans are deeply distressed by the condition of their natural environment. They are convinced that American technology, financial resources, and managerial know-how will substantially improve it. They are impatient for progress to be made toward a cleaner environment. If the objective situation is bad, it strikes most people as even worse when viewed against their legitimate expectation of a clean and healthful environment.

Two other attributes of the present crisis situation give special seriousness to recent forms of pollution: radioactive fall-out and ozone depletion, for example, not only kill people and other forms of life, they can harm the genetic materials and thereby distort, perhaps grotesquely, the evolutionary future of the race. Equally foreboding, other kinds of environmental disturbance, such as uncontrollable plant disease vectors or induced and irreversible climatic changes, can undermine the ecological support system for life on earth in the future. These matters are not well understood nor is it possible to assign precise degrees of risk and danger to them. But it appears that a kind of folk wisdom is at work whereby large numbers of ordinary individuals feel apprehensive, even threatened. The environmental crisis, therefore, goes far beyond the inconveniences and nuisances of modern living—the noise, ugliness, and unpleasantness. It goes to the most profound levels of concern about the future of humanity and the earth.

The story of air and water pollution, landscape disfigurement, congestion, and noise is by now quite well known. The causes, though less well known, include rapid population increase especially in the poor countries of the world; continuing economic and industrial growth which has been built upon gasoline and internal combustion engines, coal and electric generating plants, tin cans and glass containers, plastics and nondegradable chemicals, paper and packaging, and, most basic of all, careless behavior of people as producers, consumers, travelers, and householders. Unless the clean environment message gets through to ordinary people, progress will be painfully slow. In this sense everyone is involved in both the problem and its solution. The range of behavioral changes that will be needed extends from voting for sewage treatment plants and more parks to refraining from driving unnecessarily large automobiles and throwing beer cans out the window.

Ethical principles must be established to support right and good environmental behavior. What actions should follow from better ethics? What are the imperatives? What can be done to set and enforce standards of air quality to provide financial incentives and educational programs to support them? These imperatives are not easy for urban dwellers, barricaded as they are in air conditioned offices, factories, and homes. For them a leap of imagination is required; a beaver pond is needed for inspiration.

It is not easy to crystallize one's thinking on the ethical dimension of the current ecological crisis, but this must be done. It seems clear that humanity's relation to nature needs to be redefined in the light of recent trends both in the objective condition of the environment and in the subjective perception of what it means. The "right" relation may involve a redefinition of relation to other humans as well as to nature. Earlier notions of the human being as opposed to nature or as the exploiter of nature will have to be replaced by the more inclusive concept of the human being in or with nature. We depend on nature for food, shelter, clothing, transportation, and recreation. Nature, now as never before, depends on those of us whose activities determine nature's future. Humanity itself, it has been said, has become a geological force in its capacity to work profound changes in the earth, its waters and its atmosphere.

The idea of spaceship earth, so eloquently set forth by Adlai Stevenson a few years ago, is profound. Perhaps before long we will view the solar system a single space ship. Equally important, is the idea of space ship neighborhood community which also must be a viable unit. Humanity and nature must find sustainable and satisfactory arrangements in capsules of different sizes, ranging from home and neighborhood to city and the whole world. Each capsule has its own integrity, its own dynamic, evolving character. People will have to learn how to be at home not only in their own homes, but in their cities, their countries, and the world.

It seems to me that an ethic more attuned to ecology is called for—an ethic that recognizes the interrelatedness and interdependence of all living things with the natural environment. As human beings we will inevitably focus on man and society, but not on man as the exploiter who strives to dominate nature. But neither do I advocate an ethic that casts the human being in a subservient role at the mercy of nature. Our highest calling in these matters may be to understand the human and social ecological systems in which we are centrally involved, to fashion our aspirations and goals out of this understanding, and then to act so that the quality of our natural environment and our own lives can move to higher levels. In this the importance of policies, programs, social institutions, and modes of individual thinking and behavior can hardly be overestimated. The ethical dimension of our ecological crisis is the important dimension. A new ethic of human ecology needs to be fashioned to go with Aldo Leopold's land ethic in which the protection of the natural environment and a sufficiency of food and other resources will be placed in the perspective of an improved quality of life toward which all persons will strive.

One thing more is needed beyond an environmental ethic, to provide the enthusiasm, the sentiment, and the devotion without which any ethic tends to be dry, intellectual, and unemotional. This is the religious element, the element best found by a beaver pond. Inspiration, the necessary forerunner of great thoughts and great actions, comes out of the depths of experience, out of an awareness of living—in this case the experience of living with and in nature. Emerson advised, "Hitch your wagon to a star." Did he mean aim high or align yourself with nature? I think he meant both; they are one and the same.

Wholesome living requires an appreciation of nature and natural processes and of our part in the whole. Like Thoreau, each of us needs a Walden in imagination if not in fact to comfort us and to inspire us, and to remind us of the seamless web of earth and life of which we are a strand.

God of the winds, God of the rain;
God of the stars, God of the green buds;
God of nature, God of all:
    Guide us to the place
    Where inspiration may be found
    To renew our earth
    And with it, us.

The Artist's Song

Of joy and sorrow I would sing —
   of rain and sunshine, light and dark,
      of black and white, of gray and green,
         of springtime yellow, autumn gold.
Of strength and weakness I would sing —
   of failure and accomplishment,
      of bleak despair and new discovery,
         of glimmering hope and daring faith.
Of sound and silence I would sing —
   of harmony and dissonance,
      of rhythm and cacophony
         of quietude when all is done.
Of art and artlessness I sing —
   of human need to feel and touch,
      to see and thrill, to share emotion,
         to move with purpose and direction.
My song to you is yet my prayer
   that you will listen, see, and care,
      that I may share, and you with me,
         a bond of creativity.

The Art of Living

Of the several strands making up the rich and varied fabric of living, the one most frequently thought of as unnecessary turns out to be the most enduring. I am speaking of art which gives color, form, interest, élan, and meaning to what we think and do, without which our drab days would file past indistinguishable one from another.

In an Easter sermon John Donne once said:

> All our life is but a going out to the place of execution, to death. Was there ever any man seen to sleep in the cart . . . between the prison and the place of execution? Yet we sleep all the way; from the womb to the grave we are never thoroughly awake.

We are never thoroughly awake unless our daily routines are illumined by flashes of beauty, cut through by the sharp knife of truth, sensitized by the giving and receiving of affection, lifted by new insights in life's meaning.

It is the purpose of art, the function of the artist, to awaken these responses in each of us, to distill their essences, to concentrate them—and, I avow, to consecrate them in the deepest religious sense as the trembling, vital force of our lives.

Kenneth Clark, in his book, *Civilization,* which is based on the immensely popular TV series of the same title, cites this famous quotation from John Ruskin:

> Great nations write their autobiographies in three manuscripts: the book of their deeds, the book of their words, and the book of their art. Not one of these books can be understood unless we read the two others, but of the three, the only trustworthy one is the last.

Clark himself goes on to say, "If I had to say which was telling the truth about society, a speech by the Minister of Housing or the actual buildings put up at the time, I should believe the buildings."

In the presence of great art or under the spell of a great artist, each of us has experienced revelations of ourselves and the world that otherwise would never have come our way. Art provides insight into the human condition and the human potential. Further, art is a tool of self-analysis, a means for introspection, a light for discovering who we really are and might become. Art focuses mind, fine tunes sensitivities, quickens emotion, and offers us a new and deeper appreciation of all that is and yet shall be. In short, art can be and frequently is a religious experience to persons who are simply in its presence as well as those who create or perform it.

Poets, painters, composers, dancers, nature worshipers, among others, have expressed or portrayed this transition from art and beauty to the ultimate religious truth. Some years ago as a delegate to a United Nations Conference in Geneva, I went one Sunday, with some others into France to Chamonix where we rode the cable car high up the slope of Mont Blanc. It was a wintry December day. Silently and smoothly we glided higher and higher into the swirling snow and mist. We emerged finally on a platform from which, shivering, we looked higher still to catch intermittent glimpses of the summit as it appeared, faded, and mysteriously reappeared—a frighteningly magnificent piece of Nature's art, in this world and yet beyond it. I thought of Coleridge's lines in his "Hymn Before Sunrise, in the Vale of Chamonix":

> O dread and silent mount! I gaze upon thee,
> Till thou, still present to the bodily sense,
> Didst vanish from my thought: entranced in prayer
> I worshipped the Invisible alone.

Fortunately, experiencing art is open to everyone even though the creation of high quality works of art requires training, practice, and ability possessed by relatively few. An American Assembly conference report on the Future of the Performing Arts had this to say:

> The arts in America are often attacked as elitist and the creation and heritage of a minority. We consider them elitist in the best sense of the word, as a nation's best which can be shared by all. . . . While each of the performing arts may appeal to a particular segment of the citizenry, taken together they appeal to a broad spectrum of the populace.

My concept of art embraces the consumers of art as well as the producers, the enjoyers, and the creators. The relationship is symbiotic; one without the other is incomplete. The painters and dancers not surprisingly enjoy their own work; often viewers in the audience are amateur artists in their own right. Art is as much a way of looking at life and the world as it is painting on a canvas or molding a piece of clay. Thus, we speak of the art of cooking, the art of politics, the art of human relations, the art of love-making. Or, we speak of an artist with a wood chisel, a hockey stick, a needle, or with words.

An old, nearly blind man in the town where I lived as a boy carved whistles out of willow wood. He would select fresh, soft willow sticks about three-quarters of an inch in diameter and cut them in six- to eight-inch lengths or longer if he cut holes for playing different notes. He drove out the soft heart of the sticks with a spike, peeled off the bark except for a few decorative bands, cut back the mouth piece on the bias, cut out the notch for achieving the whistle sound, and smoothed the whole for handling and blowing. Skilled hands, a jack knife, plus love and care transformed a crude willow stick into a musical instrument. Stradivarius himself could not have been more of an artist and craftsman.

If art is primarily a way of looking at life, a way of living, then art does not stop with Michelangelo and Rembrandt, Nijinsky and Caruso, Mozart and Aaron Copeland. It extends to everyone who makes or does something artistically. In this way, art becomes universal, open to all in every age and place.

Having this universal characteristic, art bridges time and space, and reaches across cultures. A number of years ago our oldest son and I went on a canoeing trip into the Quetico-Superior Wilderness Area of northern Minnesota and adjoining Ontario. There, for a week or so we shared the quiet woods and waters with the beavers, the moose, the herons, and the northern pike. We made our way through a string of lakes separated by short portages to Basswood River, which we then followed for some miles. We thought of the early French voyagers who had paddled this route in rhythm with the ballads they sang, trading goods west and pelts east. Suddenly, we rounded a bend and saw crude paintings half way up the high cliffs done long ago by the Chippewa or Ojibway Indians. Artistic forms suggesting birds, animals, and humans in weathered pigments of local origin—rust brown, ochre running to orange on one side of the spectrum to faded green on the other, hints of other autumn-like shades—were still visible. They reminded us that long ago out of a different culture a few artists somehow suspended in air were driven to paint a bit of their souls on the rock where all who passed could see. Did they imagine that centuries later my son and I, out of a western European, white American tradition, would rest on our paddles at that place, gaze up at what they had done, and grope for the message they had painted there? I think they did and that is partly why they made the paintings.

We fell to talking about the near miraculous way that artists could speak across such distances of time and space in a universal tongue. The experience reminded me of another I had years earlier when I lived in Southeast Alaska. I was in Sitka, once the headquarters of the Russian-American Company, where my work for a government agency had taken me. That Sunday morning, December 7, 1941 it was, I attended the old Orthodox church with its icons and long half-log spruce benches, all since burned down.

After the service, which was conducted in a babel of Latin, English, Russian, and the language of the Tlinget, I walked out from the town a mile or two to the Sitka National Monument, which contains the best collection of totem poles in the Northwest. An old native craftsman, one of the few remaining, was chiseling on a of a cedar pole, shaping the head and forepaws of a bear. I stood for a time in the gentle drizzle and watched him. He had all the time in the world; he worked slowly and carefully. I asked him why a bear was to be in the totem. He said, "Bear is strong, patient, and wise. We learn much from bear. But bear not very good to eat; salmon, deer, berries are better. Don't you think so?" He grinned and chuckled softly. I agreed with him. I stayed on a while and we talked occasionally. I began to appreciate a little the style and tempo of his way of life, to see more deeply into the meaning behind the art he was carving into the wood, to feel his contribution to the world.

By the time I walked back to the town there was a dither of excitement. Word had just come that the Japanese had attacked at Pearl Harbor and that the United States submarine base in Sitka harbor might be bombed next. The town was being blacked out and made as secure as possible.

Several days later, partly to escape the confinement of the town and the blacked-out windows, I walked again to the totem pole park. The old man was still carving on the bear, unconcerned about the war and the threat to Sitka and America, as though he had absorbed into his own being the bear's strength, patience, and wisdom.

Art conveys a steadiness of purpose, a permanence, a reliability that transcends the foibles and misadventures of any given time. It is not to be put aside, even for wars. I have chosen to illustrate the universal and timeless quality of art by recounting a personal experience with Native American painting and carving. I have had experiences carrying similar lessons in India in the presence of the architectural perfection of the Taj Mahal or ordinary Hindu and Buddhist temples.

Given the importance of art in the whole scheme of things, why do artists have to struggle so to make a living and sustain their art? With a professional dancer and two musicians, maybe three, in my immediate family, not to mention a painter-poet wife, I have had reason to think about this. Of course, the problem is not a new one. Except for a fortunate few who have found the favor of rich patrons, government or foundation grants, or the market place, artists have always had a hard time making ends meet. What can be done?

In the future there are not likely to be as many families of great wealth, whether named Mellon or Medici. This leaves governments and sales in the market as sources of support for artists. Larger budget allocations by federal, state, and local governments certainly would help. The federal government, in which I now have some responsibility as a member of Congress, does far too little. Appropriations to the National Endowment for the Arts should be increased over a period of years, say five, by a factor of ten, and more after that until the annual outlay reaches $100 million. Most of this money would be used to support individual artists (including, of course, musicians, actors, dancers, and others) as well as groups such as orchestras, opera and dance companies and theaters. Income tax deductions for donations to tax exempt organizations in the arts should be continued. Such gifts should not be made part of any tax reform, on grounds that what people give in support of charity, education, medicine, and art should not be taxed. This obviously is not a tax dodge or loophole and results in no monetary gain to the donor.

A number of artists, art groups, and their supporters have been advocating an option on the individual (and perhaps corporate) income tax form whereby a tax payer can checkoff a small amount, say five dollars for use by the government to encourage the arts. Another version is to provide a box for persons to check if they are willing to pay an additional five dollars for the arts beyond the tax due. Although the first approach is already permitted for checking off a small amount to be used to pay for presidential political campaigns, it does open the door to special interest groups who might like a similar option—groups concerned with mental health, peace, criminal justice, wildlife protection, or what have you. It would be hard to draw a line, and budgetary control and even fiscal integrity might be lost. The more responsible course by far would be to increase annual appropriations for the arts in a direct and open way avoiding, of course, the imposition of artistic standards or loss of freedom of expression.

I would strongly advocate encouragement and matching grants from government to artists and art groups. A few years ago when I was a member of the Arlington County Board, I succeeded in persuading my colleagues to establish such a program through which the county invited proposals from community organizations (service clubs, citizens associations, and the like) for one- or two-year projects in the arts, recreation, education, and other fields. An appointed citizen committee reviewed the proposals and recommended the awards. The criteria specified that the projects should be innovative, not require much hardware, involve people creatively, and show a good chance of being continued and replicated elsewhere. Carrying out of the projects was to be entirely in the hands of private individuals and groups with the local government officials providing advice only when asked. There was to be no red tape except for an evaluation report at the end. The program worked quite well for several years, I thought, before it was unwisely dropped to achieve an insignificant saving at a time of budget difficulties. In my view, the county received more real benefit from this little program, dollar for dollar, than any other expenditure being made, especially in the arts. Fortunately, the idea has been adapted for use in other places.

The American historian, Charles Beard, wrote somewhere that if he could see the government budget of a city, state, or country, he could tell more about its citizens and their life than from all their paintings, poetry, and music. The reverse, I think, is more likely to be true, but how public money is spent reveals a great deal about a people. If the arts are starved of sufficient funding, then the whole society is weakened and spiritless. Art brings joy, not only to those who create and those who partake of it, but to the whole community. Art also holds up standards for the community to strive toward in its homes and buildings, its landscape, its form and structure, its style, and even its soul. Art, therefore, is precious to the community.

Government, which is the art by which a community lives together and finds its way, is obliged to encourage art, accept its messages discriminatingly, and follow its insights when possible. Government must not coerce art or cast it down or neglect it; to do so would be to undermine the very community it aims to serve and whose public expression it is. Government without art will lack style, interest, standards, and ultimately purpose. Government, in short, must lend a respectful hand to art.

Artists not only record the essence of times past, lives already lived, and events that have happened, but they also prophesy the future. The person who has looked up at the ceiling in the Sistine Chapel until his neck was stiff, as I have done, or has crossed over to Mont Saint Michel, or has looked through the trees at Durham Cathedral in the mist, or climbed the stepped pyramids to the Aztec gods outside Mexico City knows something of what used to be. Similarly, a person who has visited an antebellum Virginian plantation house or seen a New England clipper ship, or even a picture of one, knows something of life in those places in the first half of the nineteenth century. In the future, say the year 2000, a person driving or taking the Metro in the late afternoon to Dulles Airport will be thrilled to see Saarinen's gracefully soaring terminal building with the sun lighting the clouds with pinks and purples as it sinks into the Blue Ridge. I like to think that person will think a little better of this generation. Let us hope we don't do anything to spoil the effect.

But art also contains prophetic insights into the future. Think of Dante or Milton with their concern for salvation, or of Shakespeare:

> Tomorrow, and tomorrow, and tomorrow
> Creeps in this petty pace from day to day. . . .
> Life's but a walking shadow . . . a tale
> Told by an idiot, full of sound and fury,
> Signifying nothing.

In Nuremberg about fifteen years ago, I had a chance to see Albrecht Duerer's engraving entitled "Melancholia I." A deep-eyed woman representing humanity sits among the trappings of science and the symbols of enlightenment, staring past them as she broods on the futility of the human effort. Several centuries later science has yielded up nuclear weapons, carcinogenic chemicals, and a pace of technological change that bids to throw us into catatonic shock, and humanity is still brooding. Yet not all prophetic art is grim and foreboding. Handel's "Messiah" celebrates life over death; the "Madonna and Child" portrays the abiding loveliness of birth and motherhood.

Artists, then, work along the creative and uncharted edges of the world expressing their insights in music, painting, sculpture, drama, dance, and poetry until finally they arrive at the center where meaning, truth and beauty are. They have visions; they pursue the grails that are holy to them. Craftsmen, they go beyond craft to the discovery of meaning, truth, and beauty.

Without artists life is humdrum, and there is no lift for the spirit. Nor are the confusions of the world reconciled, the tortures of the mind eased, or the darkest evil penetrated by light except as phrase, line, color, movement, texture, and sound are brought to the task.

Each person of whatever station can choose to receive the artist's message whether gloomy or happy, foreboding or inspirational. The art of living consists in substantial part in opening our minds and hearts to the insights of poets, musicians, and painters, and then perchance to create or perform artistically ourselves. In this way artists and art lovers alike can penetrate to the center where life vibrates most hauntingly and sings most beautifully. Art viewed in this way is an integral part of religion: of putting life in perspective, of harmonizing personality, of respecting nature, of loving others, of releasing creative force, of discovering truth, of enjoying beauty, of grasping meaning.

God of the inner soul,
God of the outside world,
    Speak to us of art:
That we may find truth, beauty, meaning
    In the harpist's chord,
    The sparrow's song,
    The painter's strokes,
    The dancer's flight;
And thereby learn the art of living.

I'll Make the Choice

Two roads I know. The first is paved and wide
And marked with signs and flashing lights,
With trucks and autos rushing by
And drivers mesmerized at once
By sameness, danger, and monotony.
The other road is rough and winding,
Wandering through countryside,
Past cattle grazing, dairy farms,
Past woods of cedar, pine, and oak
Where deer and fox and rabbits run.

To choose the first might save some time.
Decisions would be few. The lights
And signs would tell me all I need to know.
With cars and trucks on every side
I'd grit my teeth and join the pace
And grimly set my course.
The country road would also take
Me where I need to go. Its landmarks
Give a sense of place, of natural identity.

I think I'll choose the quiet road
Unhurried as I go in solitude.
Too often in our worldly haste
We're pressed to choose the faster course
Where quality of life gives way to
Flowing with the crowd, and in the crush

Creative thought is lost and with it
Self-identity and self-respect.
I'll make the choice. I'll take the time
To see the beauty of this world
And choose directions that enhance
The depth and meaning of the day.

What We Choose Is What We Are

A hymn we frequently sing in Unitarian Universalist churches begins:

> Since what we choose is what we are,
> And what we love we yet shall be . . . .

What we choose is what we are. It's interesting to ponder the extent to which this is true. If our critical choices really do determine who we are, we had better make them thoughtfully. They had better be based solidly on values that are the best we can muster. They had better spring from feelings and emotions of generosity and considerateness and, yes, love. The hymn reminds us that what we love, we yet shall be.

In short, our choices must have a religious foundation. Incidentally, the words of this hymn were written by William DeWitt Hyde in 1903. He was President of Bowdoin College, where I studied as an undergraduate.

Of course, not all choices require such a profound treatment. Whether you choose chocolate or vanilla appears to have no religious dimension. Nor does the choice to have neither chocolate nor vanilla—unless controlling your waistline has assumed a religious dimension, invoking rituals such as confession, atonement, and prayer.

No, I have in mind choices carrying larger consequences—moral choices, choices that decide the direction of one's life. It's not so easy to spot the big choices ahead of time, and most of us have a capacity for kidding ourselves as to which are the big decisions and which are little ones, which are profound and which are frivolous. But usually we can tell the difference.

Do you recall the story of the husband and wife who had their decision so beautifully worked out? The husband explained it. "My wife makes all the minor decisions: where we live, whether we have another baby, should we acquire a second car. I make the major decisions: whether the star wars program should be continued, how to balance the federal budget, what U.S. policy in the Middle East should be." I sometimes think how we determine which decisions are major and which minor is the heart of the matter.

A while back when I was still Secretary of Human Resources for the Commonwealth of Virginia, I gave a talk at what was called a Life Cycle Conference made up of public health and social workers, family counselors, geriatrics professionals, and others. The theme of the conference was: "Choice—A Challenge or a Burden." The theme is a fascinating one that threads its way throughout life, from childhood to old age. It is fascinating partly because the "challenge or burden" question has no clear-cut answer.

During World War II the "Sad Sack" cartoon strip of the GI and the potato appeared. It depicted a confused GI with a peeled potato in his hand trying to decide whether to drop it in the pail marked "big potatoes" or the one marked "small potatoes." He is saying to the sergeant who is glowering over him, "I don't mind peeling the spuds, but it's these decisions that get me down!" Some people seem to make decisions easily and rapidly. Others fret and worry over them.

For most people, I suppose, choice is almost always a challenge and frequently a burden. Go/no-go situations are easier than coping with gray-area decisions for which the pluses and minuses are hard to balance out. The latter are the kind that give us trouble. To compound the matter many choices are underlain and surrounded by uncertainties; surely this is true of personal and family choices. We can't know for sure what will be the consequences of career choices, marriage and partner choices, moral choices in dealing with children. In making choices part of the challenge is to be prepared to accept the burden that inevitably follows from the choice.

Choices have to be sorted out to be handled successfully: which ones are important and why are they important; which ones affect other people and which are mainly private; when should the choice be made; how, once made, should it be evaluated so that future choices will be better ones.

I am an economist by profession, a social scientist. Such types deal in choices and construct theories about them—what are the causes that impel individual and social choices, what are the conditions and constraints surrounding them, what consequences follow from them. One of my graduate school professors used to start with two peasants, one with wine and one with corn. How much wine would the first give up to the second for how much corn? With many producers and consumers how would the choices be worked out in establishing a price for corn and a price for wine? And he would always tell about Buriden's ass standing exactly half way between two bales of hay unable to decide which way to go. The ass starved to death. What an ass, you might comment.

No choice, you see, is also a choice that may have severe consequences. As a politician I know the usefulness of putting off a decision; chances are that the issue will go away of its own accord. That is why politicians procrastinate and avoid committing themselves.

Obviously, certain choices each of us makes will determine the course of his or her life. Each of us, however old or young, can look back and see these turning points.

These determining individual decisions are not wholly rational as a rule. Emotions, hunches, subconscious impulses—the whole being of a person goes into them. The heart, the brain, the parents, the teachers, the environment, the gut—all go into them.

In my own case all these have been involved in obviously major choices: college, jobs, life partner, army enlistment, investments. But at least as important are those other choices that come along from time to time and don't appear at all important until later, on reflection. Typically these are moral choices: as a child whether to steal a candy bar, whether to lie about where I went as a teenager with the family car, whether to cheat on the college exam or to report cheating on the part of someone else. You can add to the list and cite examples from the adult as well as the earlier years.

A good many years ago my wife and I taught a junior high class in the religious education program of our church. It consisted of a series of cases of moral choices, or the moral aspects of choices. One, I recall, came from Carl Sandburg's autobiography of his youth, *Always the Young Strangers*. He and some of his boyhood friends on a hot July day in Galesburg, Illinois, couldn't resist breaking the seal on a box car down in the switching yard and stealing some cool ripe watermelons. They were caught. What should be the judgment and the penalty—mild chastisement, heavy reprimand, restrictions under parental enforcement, or a fine that could be worked off. Which would you choose to impose on the boys, remembering the adage, "as the twig is bent, so the tree grows?" Several years ago the whole nation went through the soul-searing experience of the disaster that befell the Challenger astronauts, including Christa McAuliffe, the school teacher from Concord, New Hampshire. She, like each member of the crew made the fateful series of choices that led to their being on that particular mission, beginning with the decision to enter the astronaut program. They were fully prepared to meet whatever the consequences of those decisions might be. "The moving finger writes, and having writ, moves on . . . ."

Choice can be a challenge and a fate as it was for Christa McAuliffe and the others. They did not look upon it as a burden, a chore, or an imposition. Mature wisdom, I believe, is to confront choice, to decide, and to accept the consequences. The daring choice, the unconventional choice, the choice that feels right in the bones—these frequently are the right ones to make. Above all, it seems to me, each individual as a sign of personal maturity and dignity

Usefulness of putting off a decision - most often issue goes away - why leaders procrastinate

Each individual

should make his or her own choices. Advice should be sought and heeded, of course, but the choice itself should be private and as responsible as it can be. Few tragedies are more poignant than to look back on a turning-point choice, especially one that didn't work out, and have to say the choice was really made by someone else. For adults such choices should be one's own.

Robert Frost, himself a self-styled New Hampshireman, said it beautifully in the familiar lines:

> I shall be telling this with a sigh
> Somewhere ages and ages hence:
> Two roads diverged in a wood, and I —
> I took the one less traveled by,
> And that has made all the difference.

I remember hearing Frost read these lines in his New England cadence at the conclusion of a talk he gave years ago in Sever Hall in the Harvard Yard.

In the world of public policy that I have lived in for many years, the policy maker or decider finds it tempting to say: the facts made me do it, the boss made me do it, the folks back home made me do it, the computer made me do it, the poll made me do it, or whatever else. Anything but "I did it because I believed it to be right." A person defines himself or herself, as the politicians say, in making decisions.

I said at the beginning of these reflections that choices, truly significant and life determining choices, must have a religious foundation. This is especially true when the evidence, the analysis, and the arguments don't yield the answer. In such cases one has to reach down deep inside for values which can point the way to go. Usually these values are ethical and religious in nature.

For us the values of liberal religion help to set the norms for choice, identify the guiding principles, encourage and enforce those principles. Liberal religion recognizes the freedom of each person to evaluate the options for himself or herself, adopt this one and reject that one, and help others with their choices. Liberal religion, I affirm, requires that choice be exercised responsibly; that is, in a way that takes into account the effects of our choices on others as well as the effects of their choices on us.

Therefore, we should look upon choice as an opportunity that society, the world, or God, if you like, offers us. Choice is a blessing to be treasured, truly a challenge more than a burden even though its burden of consequences will have to be borne. We should use the choices open to us intelligently, vigorously, compassionately, allowing them to emerge from our best impulses and values. This is the way to live with choice religiously.

Guide to us all — above, inside, wherever —
Three ways, at least, lie open ahead:
Blind, compass-less luck,
Directions pre-determined for us,
Independent, mature, responsible choosing —
The last by far the best for those
Who seek to live free, religiously.

CHAPTER FIVE
RELIGION AND SOLITUDE

A Place Apart

There is a human need
  to be alone at times,
    to find a quiet place,
      a place apart from all
        confusion and distress.
There is a human need
  for solitude and peace
    of body, mind and heart —
      a need to contemplate
        directions we would go.
And there are times when strength
  and courage must be found
    to meet new challenges
      of life, surpassing any
        powers we have known.
There is a human need
  for space to grow, for time
    to think, to dream, to pray,
      to meditate upon
        the meaning of our lives.
There is a human need
  to find identity
    within our own creative
      power—the power of hand
        and mind and yearning heart.

Creative use of time
alone, with space for growth
of intellect, provides
an inner light we crave
to see the way ahead.

Religion and Solitude

A number of years ago my friend Ned Hall, a cultural anthropologist and long time advisor to the U. S. foreign aid program, wrote a most attractive book entitled *The Silent Language.* In one chapter he tells how people in different countries and cultures think of and use space. In our country, for example, you are not really in my office or living room until you cross the threshold. In some other countries you would be regarded as in the room while you are still outside near the door. The sense of privacy, you see, would be different. As another example, we have all had the experience with Latin Americans and southern Europeans who generally find one or two feet to be a comfortable conversational distance while most Americans, Canadians, and northern Europeans require twice that distance. The point is that although the distances vary everyone needs some sacrosanct private space, a place that a person can call ones' own.

The same is true of time. People need an occasional quiet period to rest, reflect, and restore their spirits. Ned Hall's book contains fascinating accounts of how people in different cultures regard time and punctuality. Being an hour late for a private dinner party causes consternation, even havoc, in this country because the food is already cold; in other countries the same degree of havoc may result because the preparation of the food has hardly begun.

In addition to an envelope of space and time, a certain mood is required if the joys and healing powers of solitude are to be realized, especially for busy people. An unwinding of tensions has to be achieved, fretfulness has to be discarded, the right mood has to be established. Mood is the psychological dimension of solitude.

The three—space, time, and mood—are interrelated in subtle ways. We speak of the time it takes to unwind; for me it's usually a couple of days, give or take a little. I unwind more rapidly in the out-of-doors, most rapidly of all in wilderness areas. Others, I gather, successfully find solitude in a long walk through city streets, in a museum, or even at a ball game right in the midst of the "madding crowd" rather than far from it. To each according to his or her taste, I suppose.

My wife, whose habits I have come to know quite well over the years, is able to establish the elements of solitude more rapidly than I. She can even schedule it, which is a rare talent. She has Thursdays reserved for being alone in the house or the garden. She paints, she writes letters to our children or to friends; she day-dreams; she writes poetry and mumbles it to herself. How do I know? Well, once or twice I have had occasion to go home during the daytime on Thursday and have eavesdropped. Then, somewhat ashamed of this performance, I have turned around, slammed the door, and coughed loudly to announce my presence, thereby breaking her spell, of course.

No doubt about it: we each need our own island from time to time, all alone, to get ourselves together. In the university and research world that I have inhabited for much of my adult life, individuals also need islands of knowledge and competence as a basis of self-respect. To know more than anyone else in the world about something, however small it is, provides immense security and confidence for a professor. Of course, there is the case of the scientist who knew all about penguins and his dinner partner who said plaintively, "But I already know more about penguins than I want to know." I'm sure, however, the penguin expert was a secure and happy person.

The benefits-of-solitude bit can be overdone. Many people in the world are alone more than they would like. Apartment houses and retirement homes, even student dormitories, are full of lonely people. One has only to go through an apartment complex as a precinct worker soliciting votes. Many times I have knocked on a door hoping to win over a voter only to have to make my pitch through a closed door to a faceless voice on the other side. Worse still, I realize that I am being scrutinized through a one-way peephole. Many people are afraid, not entirely without cause, I must say, to open their doors even to their neighbors. Such people are shriveling up in their own cocoons, denying themselves the light and warmth of human contacts. Their loneliness is being compounded by their apprehensions. It is sad, altogether sad.

The experience of being alone may come to any one of us from time to time; for example, during the let-down following a disappointment or failure when, at least for a while, all hope seems to have vanished into thin air, all effort in vain, all justice miscarried. At such times doubts rise to their highest level of unreality—self-doubts, doubts about others, doubts about the system, doubts about the worth of values themselves. God apparently is dead, or at least in a deep sleep.

This is especially the case if the failure is, or is thought to be, a moral failure. Sticks and stones can break my bones and names can never hurt me; but moral lapse, recognized and admitted, can cut deeply. In such situations, and we have all been there, we seem to be alone with our innermost doubts. We are then most in need of a helping hand, a psychological lift, perhaps from a friend but more likely from within ourselves, from our own sense of religion and its forgiving, healing, and restoring essence. Something like this, I suppose, is part of the ultimate meaning of confession, of atonement, perhaps to a degree even of resurrection for a Catholic.

There is, of course, a difference between loneliness and solitude. Loneliness is typically unwanted, debilitating, confining, frustrating, profitless, and sad. Long protracted, it can bring on various psychological and behavioral problems. Solitude, on the other hand, is usually welcomed as an opportunity for rest, reappraisal, and renewal. It is a constructive experience. Luis Munoz Marin, the great Puerto Rican governor, used to talk about *serenidad, la serenidat de la isla.* Solitude or the kind I am speaking of yields such serenity. Too much of the space-time-mood combination can mean loneliness, sadness, and ineffectiveness; the right amount of it can mean self-discovery and rebirth. In this sense most of us would like to be born again.

We do best when we have a good balance of solitude and multitude. Emerson, our own Unitarian Emerson, that most judiciously balanced of all essayists, put the matter this way:

> It is easy in the world, to live after the world's opinion; it is easy, in solitude, to live after your own; but the great man is he who, in the midst of the crowd, keeps with perfect sweetness the independence of solitude.

Do you think you can manage that? Not easily, for sure, but it's worth a try. The well integrated personality toward which we strive does contain elements of both self fulfillment and group adjustment. Important though it is, the self part can be carried too far and spill over into selfishness, an ego trip of some kind. "I'll do it my way," was the refrain in the macho song popular a few years ago. On the other hand, the group part, carried too far, leaves a personality made up only of blurred reflections of other personalities, a double or triple exposure on the same film print on which nothing clear comes through. And smack in the middle is the perfectly integrated personality, so well-rounded that it slides off everything with which it comes in contact and leaves not a trace behind. Then, of course, there is the guy or gal who likes solitude as long as there's someone to share it with. Obviously, Emerson had none of these caricatures in mind when he wrote those gorgeous lines with their perfect cadence, and neither do we.

All religions help their followers cope with the problems of loneliness; they all encourage, on occasion, the joys of solitude. Liberal religion no less than the others, copes with loneliness by providing daily services, individual counseling, and emergency help to those who are alone. I was down at a health clinic a few days ago for X-rays of an injured shoulder. There I met two of our members: the younger one was giving over her afternoon to driving and being with the older one. Our church also has retreats, usually in the Blue Ridge mountains, where some solitude may be found.

But institutional efforts will never be enough. Loneliness has to be overcome and solitude gained by an individual's religious approach to living. In the final analysis religion is an intensely individual and private matter, which can be vastly enriched by individual and private contemplation or its possibilities. The quest for purpose and coherence in your life or mine, for a pattern of interest and beauty, for accomplishment, for *serenidad,* is the goal. The quest, the search, is religion.

Insights into this kind of religion for most people are most likely to come in private moments, in solitude, away from noise and distraction. There is most certainly a mystical quality in such experiences. One bumper sticker you see around proclaims: "I Found It!" My bumper sticker would say: "I'm Looking For It!" But then I would want to add: "But As Soon As I Find It, I'm Sure I'll Start Looking Beyond To Find Something More!" Now you know why it would be impractical for me to get into the bumper strip thing—except, of course, for politics.

It is no accident that the great revelations in history have come to single individuals, alone, on a mountain in Sinai, under a bo tree in India, on the shore of Galilee, on the road to Damascus. The most magnificent lines in Shakespeare's tragedies are the soliloquies: "To be or not to be. . . ." The artist works alone. Great poetry was never written in a group-think session. Solitude is, indeed, a sweet source of inspiration.

My plea here is not for loneliness but for solitude as a necessary ingredient of religious living. Let us arrange our lives so that the space-time-mood experiences I am calling solitude can take place. I believe they will enrich our religion and our living.

Good friends —
  Don't be afraid
    To leave the town behind,
    To walk into the woods alone,
    To row out on the sea.

  For there you'll find
    Relationship with deer and oak,
    With clouds and sun and sky,
    And peace within your soul,
    And peace within your soul.

The Fleeting Quality of Time

These things I know —
    The brilliance of an autumn day
    When green gives way to red and gold
    And then to umber and to bronze,
    The cool crisp air and fragrance of
    The earth and falling leaves,
    The migratory chatter of the birds
    Congregating in the trees
    Then rushing off to seek the sun.

These things I know —
    The need for love and tenderness,
    The need for mutual support,
    The give and take of kindness shared,
    The gratitude for friends in time of grief.
    The joy of creativity,
    Of inspiration and a day well used,
    That fleeting time of clarity,
    Of insight that I must record.

These things I know —
    That time moves on relentlessly,
    That as each season's colors change
    So will the opportunities
    To love and serve and to create.
    That days and hours are sacred trusts

Whose value I can scarcely comprehend,
That what I treasure here on earth
Is all the Heaven that I know.

It's About Time

My wife suggested we develop the theme of time. Although the subject looked unmanageable to me, she was enthusiastic, so I went along dutifully. I thought that surely, given a little time, profound thoughts would occur to me. And they did—a series of musings about time and how we deal with it, and then toward the end, remarks on a few issues calling for action before time runs out.

Many of us live in a time-driven world, always in a rush and a sweat. Others of us seem to have plenty of time to smell the roses. A rare few have discovered the secret of accomplishing a great deal without ever being in a hurry. Why these differences? As individuals, whatever our age or station, we must come to terms with time—chronological time, psychological time, or whatever—and learn to pace ourselves, realizing we shall never master time but equally determined not to let time master us. Not to fight time but neither to allow time to run straight over us, not to crack the whip over time or be a slave to it. We fancy ourselves as moving serenely down the stream of time, with a forward pull on the oar here and a backward thrust there, to avoid the rocks. "Time is a stream I go a-fishing in," Thoreau wrote.

For me time moves unevenly. I have never found its "measured groove." In a wakeful period at night five minutes becomes an hour. During a fast game of tennis an hour passes in five minutes. In school when I hadn't prepared my lesson and the teacher was calling on students randomly, fifty minutes was an eternity. Very few of us have a metronome inside our heads.

On the other hand when I work hard at it, I can make a schedule and make a fair pass at sticking to it, at least for a while. And whenever I slip off the schedule, I console myself by thinking that time and motion studies dehumanize us. Recently, I saw a book written for executives that explained how every appointment and chore could be handled in two minutes. The message of the author was extremely annoying to me. I am sure those who follow this advice are insufferable.

Where does this leave us? Of time, Augustine once said, "I know what it is until you ask me." Frequently we are told that "time is of the essence" but the essence of what, I ask. We are told that "time stands still" and that it "races on." In my view it slithers by mostly while I'm not paying attention.

Time, as we all know, can perform miracles like knitting up "the ravell'd sleeve of care." Also it can be obstinate as, for example, "time (not to mention, tide) waits for no man."

Ecclesiastes has it that there is a "time to plant and a time to pluck up what is planted" "a time for every purpose under heaven." Very orderly, very balanced, very comforting. But the last frost of spring and the first frost of autumn are hard to predict, as any farmer knows. Were there "world enough and time" we could probably get to the bottom of the matter, but there's not.

Young people have endless vistas of time ahead of them during which to work out their lives, or so they think. Those in the middle years, as a rule, live in a fairly comfortable time frame, busy but able to manage things tolerably well. Those who don't are headed for frustration, ineffectiveness, a high level of stress, and all too often mental health problems. Older people begin to see the end of the game even though they still can't be sure how it will turn out. For most of us intimations of mortality become more frequent than intimations of immortality. The cruelest reflection on time for older men and women was expressed by Shakespeare: "I wasted time, and now doth time waste me."

Anthropologists shed light on our subject. Edward Hall in his book *The Silent Language* recounts what the hostess in different cultures means when she invites guests to come to dinner at seven o'clock. In a few places she means exactly what she says—seven o'clock on the button. In this country she means absolutely no earlier than seven but not more than twenty minutes after seven at the outside. In Latin countries showing up at 7:00 or even 7:20 would throw the hostess and the servants, if any, into panic. Half-past eight would be quite acceptable. (Actually, the invitation in those countries is more likely for nine at the earliest.) Time, is interpreted differently everywhere. The Plains Indian would have told the white explorer to follow the Missouri river for two moons. Nowadays the road map gives the tourist the distance to nearest mile and the time to the nearest minute.

Physicists are telling us that time in the profoundest scientific sense is not straight-forward as we thought but is caught up in the web of relativity. Even in my lifetime certain fixed reference points in time have been shattered—the four- minute mile, an hour in the oven for each pound, two hours after stoking the furnace for the house to become warm.

At George Mason University, I teach a graduate seminar called Public Policy Process. We aim to understand the twistings and turnings of that mysterious process from beginning to end. One notion that is quite helpful is "the window of opportunity." In order for a policy to become established or enacted—legitimated is the professional term—all the ducks have to be lined up, including the pressure groups, the legislative leaders, and the calendar. Only then is the window of opportunity open so that the policy can move through and be established.

Timing, you see, is everything in the public policy game just as it is in hitting a tennis ball or playing the stock market. You can't pass a tax reform bill just any old time; sometimes you have to wait years until the ducks are lined up. We are still waiting for the ducks to get lined up, for the window of opportunity to open, for a serious effort to reduce the federal deficit and cut down on nuclear weapons.

Another insight on time came to me some years ago when I was in the Council of Economic Advisers to the President. We were trying to establish a procedure for estimating the benefits and costs of various public programs and projects called for by several acts of Congress and executive orders. A conservation program, for example involves dams, land treatment, reforestation, and new farming practices. The heavy costs are incurred in the early years for dams, reservoirs, and altering the land form. The major benefits come later as the soil becomes more productive and the trees are cut. But a benefit received 20 or 100 years later is not worth as much as a benefit available immediately, nor will it offset a cost that has to be paid right now. Why? Because the future benefit may never come, or we might not be here to get it when it does come, or it might not be worth much then.

We had to find some rational way to discount benefits and costs projected for some years in the future. The rate of discount became very important. A high rate of discount made it hard to justify a program with future benefits but immediate costs. A low discount rate would work the other way. You can see that programs that benefit future generations are not likely to be undertaken if the discount rate is high. Since there is no market rate for such items, some rate has to be picked out of the air. This is surely an arcane matter but the political struggles over the discount rate have been fierce. It all boils down to how one values things in the future compared to the present. The stakes are high because billions of dollars worth of projects are determined by such estimates every year.

This digression has a point. How time is regarded works its way into the fabric of government, as it does into just about everything else. And it isn't only in science that time is dealt with in a highly technical manner. People seem to agree that time goes faster when you are busy. Others say the older you get, the faster time goes. When we are sound asleep, time stands still, takes a holiday. Time flies. Time creeps. Time passes us by. We seize the moment. That great constant, time, seems to be elusive and changeable.

We talk about "managing time" and "using it to good effect." Of course, we really mean managing ourselves in a purposeful, useful, satisfying way. This perspective on time appeals to me. If time is a river, it means rowing on it to some destination not just drifting. Perhaps this is why I enjoy rowing or paddling more than float trips. Time, I think, should be dealt with in a positive way, even a bit aggressively, allowing, of course, some time for reflection. A healthy life requires us to live on a schedule, recognizing that life can't be a series of two-minute drills.

Occasionally, time stands still. Time stood gloriously still for me earlier in this service. During the silent prayer when many of you bowed your heads, one of our daughters came forward to the podium and gave her mother a big red rose cut fresh from our garden this morning. And then she went to where I was sitting on the platform and gave me a kiss. I wish that moment could last forever.

I said at the outset that in addition to a series of musings about time I would offer a few words on actions that need to be taken before time runs out. That is to say, certain actions, not taken in a timely way or not taken at all will leave us with such an accumulation of problems that no amount of time will permit us to deal with them. Philosophical speculations must not immobilize us. For example, I am dismayed that in the recent elections across the country half or less of the qualified voters took the time to show up at the polling places. *It's about time* we started voting in larger numbers if we want our democratic system to work properly. *It's about time* we tackled the federal deficit in a serious and responsible way and got it through our heads that we have to pay taxes for the public services we want. Otherwise, the debt will go up, inflation will rise, or something else will happen we don't want to happen. It's another case of where avoiding an immediate cost must not be allowed to take precedence over a much larger future gain.

It's about time we mounted an all-out attack against drug abuse wherever it is present.

It's about time we stopped production and distribution of nuclear arms. And to do this will require both behavioral and moral changes. An affirmative answer will have to be given to the question, Am I my brother's keeper? And people everywhere, not just the political and military leaders, will have to give an affirmative answer. *It is indeed about time* we all decided to live peacefully with our neighbors around the world.

It's about time we determined to practice what we preach about tolerance and respect for the rights of others at home as well as in far away places.

It's about time, in short, we adopted a religion for living peacefully and constructively with all who inhabit this planet with us.

However great the pressures of time may be, fortunately we have enough time ahead of us to deal with these issues. In my view we have only to get started toward solutions, to move in the right directions, to see some progress. The long march does begin with a single step, followed by another and then another. There is time for this approach. But we must begin without delay if we are to feel the exhilaration of progress toward our goals, the surge of morale that comes from joint endeavor.

Time, space, community, one's inner self—these are the contexts of our lives. But only through time can we note progress, growth, improvement. The moral, religious aspect of time is to live with it comfortably, to respect its imperatives, to use it wisely, to enjoy it. And *it's about time* we did just that.

In our Western culture—increasingly in other cultures also—we are taught that time should be used (perhaps should use us) to promote the glory of God, the welfare of humans, the protection of nature, the advancement of art—or all of the above. That is the received imperative, the challenge, the responsibility. It is part of our code and our religion, regardless of any of the philosophical contradictions about time.

"Wherefore" says the old Ecclesiastes, "I perceive that there is nothing better than that we should rejoice in our own works; for that is our portion; for who shall bring us to see what shall be after us?"

> How does one address Time?
>   the great healer,
>   the mischief maker,
>   inscrutable sphinx,
>   the metronome,
>   time past, present, or future?
> Whatever Time is —
>   idea or fact,
>   concept or reality,
>   understandable or not —
> Make it your friend.

Part Two

History and Hope

CHAPTER SEVEN
RELIGION AND CHANGE

Continuity

The poet speaks of leaves of grass that find
　　their origin in ashes of the past
　　　　and germinate in fertile soil,
　　　　　　a miracle of continuity.

And so the changing patterns of our lives
　　will find their continuity
　　　　in building new directions from the past,
　　　　　　new ventures in discovery.

Each new beginning led us to our course.
　　Each friend and teacher who has shaped our lives,
　　　　each person who has cared for us
　　　　　　has helped to make us what we are today.

Upon their confidence, upon their love,
　　their dreams and hopes for us we dare to build
　　　　a new tomorrow and to bravely face
　　　　　　the challenges and changes in our lives.

Living with Change

Most of us resist change. Change tends to be disorderly, unpredictable, discomforting. Occasionally we welcome change, perhaps agitate for it, but even then we don't want too much of it, thank you. No one is a revolutionary in all fields.

Still, change is the rule. Somewhere Plato or his ghost writer stated that nothing endures but change. Darwin and the evolutionists provided a rationale and direction for change. We all know that much as we would like it, things simply won't stay put.

In the great tug-of-war between change and stability each of us is stretched thin from time to time. So is our community and our world. The Metro rail system will bring change to northern Virginia; neighborhoods will resist that change. Emerging nationalism in less developed countries forces change which more developed countries will try to block or slow down. Each of us has sighed "things aren't what they used to be." Yet we know full well things couldn't possibly be what they used to be. The birdsong ends, the tree falls, youth passes.

> The Moving Finger writes; and, having writ,
> Moves on: nor all your Piety nor Wit
> Shall lure it back to cancel half a Line,
> Nor all your Tears wash out a Word of it.

When I go back to my roots in a village in down-east Maine for summer vacation, I will say, "What's new, Than?" He will say, "Nothin' much, Joe." These are the two opening moves in a gambit we both know well. I'll say, "How's old Charlie?" He'll say, "Don't rightly know. Died last winter. Chest tightened up; couldn't breathe." I'll say, "How's clammin'?" He'll say, "Not good, Joe. They been took by the red tide." "Flounders, Than?" "Overfished," he'll say. "H'ain't come back much yet." So it will go. After a while I will find that quite a lot has happened, all manner of changes have taken place with which the community has had to cope.

You could say that living is largely a matter of coping with change; at its best coping creatively with change. To my down-east Yankee friends it may simply mean setting out lobster traps instead of digging clams. It may also mean having to notch down closer to the poverty line, or moving away. More creatively, it can mean providing some new article or service to the summer visitors, the rusticators as they used to be called.

Religion can help people change themselves and their world, especially when they don't want to and don't know how to. I take religion, as you know, to be the process for finding one's way toward a satisfying, useful, meaningful life. Religion provides the setting in which you and I find instruction and inspiration for coping constructively with change so that we can proact as well as react to the mandates it places on us.

I have long been attracted to Bergson's belief in *elan vital,* the creative element in evolution. The religious approach to living, I think, offers the best hope of discovering and responding to the *elan vital* which lies within each of us. To a considerable degree, each of us can be the master of his fate, the captain of her soul—even in adverse circumstances.

When I was a boy, our family had a wind-up phonograph. One of my favorite records was called "No News, or How the Dog Died." It was a real shaggy-dog, Maine-type story that covered both sides of the record. It started out like my story about Than. One old codger asked another one if there was any news. The answer came back, "No, no news of any account" except that his dog died. Well, to shorten the story, it turned out after extensive questioning that the dog had died, along with cows and horses, because the barn had burned down while the animals were in it. And the barn had caught fire because a spark had blown over from the house, which had also burned. Further questioning dragged out of the second old codger the information that his wife had been in the house and had died also. In fact, the whole town had burned down. "No News, or How the Dog Died."

The moral I wish to draw from this particular fable has nothing to do with the taciturn nature of Maine folks, which isn't accurate anyway, but rather that one event, or change, leads to others and then still others, rippling out until the surface of the whole pond is agitated. Moreover, what appears first as a relatively insignificant change frequently is just one piece of a complex pattern of changes with consequences reaching far out in many directions. Assimilating large clusters of inter-related changes, adjusting to them, making the best of them, and coming out of the whole experience with poise and understanding constitute a challenge of the highest order of difficulty. Maturity consists of developing the philosophy, religion if you like, to meet such challenges—and to meet them on a more profound level than the first old codger in the story appears to have done.

Plus la change, plus c'est la meme chose. The more things change, the more they remain the same. But the certainty that the sun will rise tomorrow morning is matched by the equal certainty that tomorrow will be different. The blossom will open more; the bird will sing a slightly different song; the sunrise will not color the sky in the same way; your mood will be happier or sadder; you will think different thoughts. It is not possible to step twice into the same river. Even basic concepts will budge. Newton's laws of motion are just a hair off the mark, Einstein demonstrated. Religions don't remain the same either. Most religions tend not to admit changes in basic propositions. They stake too much on a particular doctrine of infallibility, immortality, revelation, grace or atonement. Conventional religious persons, especially those of a fundamentalist persuasion, are reluctant to open their minds and hearts to the evidence of behavioral as well as natural science.

To be sure, some propositions survive for a long time. A dear friend and teacher of mine used to say that if a group of people from the early centuries of the Christian era could be with us today, most of what they saw would be strange and inexplicable to them: modern technology, TV, airplanes, processed foods, electrified houses, whole professions, even languages. But the teachings of Jesus and Moses would be as relevant as ever: the Ten Commandments, the Sermon on the Mount, the leadership of Moses, the example of Jesus.

I see no contradiction here. Great teachings are timeless because they are hospitable to change. Matthew recounts parables of men and women who, having broken commandments and rules, mended their ways and were accepted again as worthy individuals. Equally significant, the basic teachings themselves were left open to new insights and interpretations. "Thou shalt not kill" and "Blessed are the peacemakers" now have to be extended far beyond the tribes of Israel of ancient times and far beyond the nation-states of our times to embrace the whole world. Jesus, of course, would approve.

The profound sense of changelessness in the midst of change, of permanence in passage, of durability during destruction, is strikingly captured by T. S. Eliot in *Four Quartets:*

> Time and the bell have buried the day,
> The black cloud carries the sun away.
>
> .   .   .   .   .
>
> After the kingfisher's wing
> Has answered light to light, and is silent, the light is still
> At the still point of the turning world.

Living wisely with change requires a religion that invites change into its house. Unfathomable change will be invited to stay longer for further discussion. Evil change will be turned out of the house. Unnecessary change will be asked to leave, perhaps to come again later. Helpful change will be given a room and a seat at the table. Inevitable change somehow will be accommodated.

I worry about religions that insist on eternal verities. It is comforting, I suppose, to have fixed points of reference for your compass. But even the north pole is over a hundred miles from where it was when I had my first Boy Scout compass. Better to study change, learn its laws and probabilities, and anticipate it. If there is any certainty in the universe, it is to be found along these lines.

Change is mysterious and awesome enough to link it with what is religious. However imperfect and changeable are the laws governing change, they are majestic and long-lived. As I sit writing on our porch in the early morning, I catch sight of a male cardinal in the trees. Its beauty, gives joy to my spirit. The sheer wonder of it derives as much from its flight from branch to branch, its motion and change, as it does from its color and form. The grand though unpredictable processes of evolution and change in human beings, nature, and society contain the elements necessary, in James Luther Adams's phrase, for living religiously. The religious aspect becomes more compelling when one contemplates employing human intelligence, will, and action to influence the direction and pace of change in mature and responsible ways.

In our century we have flown by other planets in our solar system and observed; we have learned to delay the disintegrative force of cancer; we have built a social security program however trouble-ridden its finances may be; we have probed the human psyche and found new modes for treating mental illness; we have created a United Nations that is fumbling at the door to peace. These changes call for changes in our religious values, certainly in their priorities, and in the way we worship.

When we see a young person after a long time we say, "My how you've grown." The child is proud to have this pointed out; the teenager winces. In both cases growth and change are noteworthy. I would not make a god out of change, but I would incorporate change in my concept of God or, if you prefer, in my religion, just as I incorporate change in my concept of living.

In our church we like to sing the hymn with the words that only Tennyson could have written: "Let the great world spin forever \ Down the ringing grooves of change." This may be a bit reckless for you and me. But it does express the significant excitement and awesome quality of change; it places change clearly in the category of the religious, just as the statement "My, how you've grown" places change in the category of ordinary living. Change, therefore, is an essential feature in both religion and living, which themselves must change as time goes on.

God of all
That lives and moves and is,
And yet may be:

Do not confine yourself,
Or allow yourself to be confined,
Within a room of three dimensions.

Instead, reach farther out,
Bring time and change and unpredictability
Within your general scheme,

That we may live with change, religiously.

The Spirit of America

America lives
From coast to coast — Atlantic and
Pacific shores with pounding surf
And plaintive seagull cries and hidden
Coves and grasses bending with the wind.

Between these shores
The panorama moves through mountains —
Appalachian, Rockies, great Sierras —
From East to West, they loom from North to South.

And in between
Great plains and valleys stretch across the land,
Rich farmland, teeming orchards, scorching deserts,
Spring fed lakes and winding rivers nourish life.

Upon these waters
Cities came to be as men and women
Learned to till the land and harvest bounty
That would help to feed the world.

They came —
Nomadic tribes whose life and worship focused
On the earth and stars, on moon and sun and rain,
On harvesting and bounty of the hunt.

They came —
Explorers seeking new domain;
They came in ships and plied the shores,

Men and women seeking
Liberty to worship in their way.

The Pilgrims came
And built communities, and governments
Were formed and churches built;
And laws were made, and independence
From the mother lands would soon prevail.

The people
Slowly spread across the land,
In caravans they moved in search
Of homesteads and resources in
An endless land of opportunity.

The spirit of America
Was born in this mobility,
Resourcefulness, and love of space
And sheer discovery.

On through the years
Our country grew. From hamlets
Grew our cities and our towns;
Our states were formed from colonies,
And territories were absorbed.

Town meetings set
A pattern for evolving government,
And politics became a democratic art,
Town councils formed,
And Congress and our Presidents
Were chosen in our democratic way.

Debate —
The right to question and defend,
Respect for justice and for civil liberty
Became American ideals.
Not always realized, the dream was there.

The right to choose —
To win, to lose, to run for office,
The rights of working men and women won,
As unions and the civil service grew.

And industry
And science changed our lives,
And engineers designed new modes
Of transportation — autos, ships, and trains,
Balloons and planes and rockets
To the moon and on beyond to Mars.

The power of
The atom and of fossil fuels,
The power of the water and the sun,
The power of the wind, the power of the brain
Frighten us, yet give us hope.

Discovery
Is still the force on which we build.
Communication in this land has grown;
The telegraph, the telephone, the radio,
And television bring the universe into our homes.

Our folkways
In America are deep-ingrained.
The Yankee Doodle spirit marches on —
Parades and marching bands and majorettes
And gaudy floats and clowns and beauty queens.

We dance
To bluegrass, country rock and jazz,
The square dance and the turkey trot.
We've campfire songs and barbershop quartets.

Hallowe'en
And tiny spooks bring tricks and treats and comic dress,
And birthday parties are a ritual;

Little leagues grow into major leagues
And cheering crowds enliven stadiums.

Thanksgiving
Since our country's earliest days
Has been a time of feasting — turkey, stuffing,
Sweet potatoes, pumpkin pies —
And friends and families gather round.

We gather
Thanking God for harvest bounties and
For loved ones and for hearth and home:
This is the spirit of America.

May we the people
Keep the faith with those who went before;
May we thank God for all we have,
And make this world a better place to live.

Depth Perception
Through a Wide-Angle Lens

From time to time each of us should look back at the past, survey the present, and probe the future to regain perspective on our lives and the life of our country. In Abraham Lincoln's words, "we should examine whence we came and whither we are tending."

The purpose of reassessment is to rediscover the values we cherish. Usually they are values cherished by our forefathers and mothers, adapted to conditions of the present and the prospects of the future. Understanding and respect for the future is the place to begin. Identifying where we are being faithful to the best in our historical tradition and where we are not being faithful to it is the next step. Finally, we need prophetic insight into what the future can be, what it must not be allowed to become and how we should move forward toward our destiny.

What we need is a new patriotism, matching the old patriotism in fervor, emphasizing social and economic goals as well as political ones, having an international as well as a national dimension, and appealing to youth as well as to old timers.

We need a patriotism that kindles the hearts of the *now* generation along with the *then* generation—at least now and then.

This Bicentennial Year, 1976, provides the timely occasion for reflecting on these matters. The Bicentennial panorama is a wide one. During the Fourth of July weekend in the Washington area alone, according to Friday's *Washington Star's* special issue in the style of 1876, you can enjoy plays and operas of historical interest; a festival of American folklife; a sound and light show at Mount Vernon; parades without number (Peggy and I took part in three or four yesterday); a show called "Music '76" at the Sylvan Theater; aerial and military demonstrations; Bicentennial dress balls; a 200th birthday party on the steps of the National Archives building; the "Pageant of Freedom" on the Monument grounds; an address by the Vice President preceding the great fireworks display; special Bicentennial church services throughout the area; a 200-pound birthday cake; picnics everywhere; the Singing Sergeants, Johnny Cash and the Tennessee Three singing country and western songs; the National Symphony orchestra at Wolf Trap with an astronaut starting a countdown to Independence Day a few minutes before midnight; puppet and magic shows at the Polo Grounds with free balloons for the children; a program at the Kennedy Center with Bob Hope, the Reverend Billy Graham, and Sammy Davis, Jr. and the Mormon Tabernacle Choir; and at 9:15 Sunday evening, July 4, the grand fireworks—a 62-minute display to tell the story of America, set off from eight barges in the Tidal Basin and ending with 200 peals of a replica of the Liberty Bell and a laser light from the top of the monument spelling out 1776-1976. And as if this were not enough, the Bicentennial Grand Parade Saturday along Constitution Avenue has nine divisions, including Birth of a Nation, Westward Ho, Land of Opportunity, The Spirit of America, and Exploring the Universe.

The panorama of events in Washington extends from the Atlantic to the Pacific over 200 years of our national history. The lens is a wide angle lens all right, but does it afford depth perception? It will if we hold the lens steady and take the time to look through it long and carefully. The Bicentennial Year affords the occasion for looking backward at the course of our country's history and forward for re-establishing our sense of direction as individual Americans, as a nation, and as citizens of the world. Out of this exercise can come a rededication to the best of past traditions and to future goals.

The changes from 1776 to 1876 and 1976 in our country have been tremendous. A small group of colonies on the Atlantic coast with a few million inhabitants have grown to a giant-sized world power of more than 200 million persons stretching nearly half way around the globe. The nation of farmers, idealized by Jefferson, has become a nation of industrial workers, service employees, technicians, and professionals. Farmers now make up considerably less than 10 percent of the work force. A traveler now can go from Washington to San Francisco by plane in less time than it would have taken to make the trip by stage to Baltimore 200 years ago. The average length of life has doubled and infant mortality, a tragedy experienced by nearly every family in the late 18th century, occurs rarely. Most young people now complete high school and more than half go on to college; in 1770 except for a few persons, a few years of schooling are all anyone could expect. Work, which used to run from sun-up to sun-down has compressed into an eight-hour day and a five-day week. Material and cultural accoutrements have multiplied: automobiles, radios and TVs, central heating and cooling, refrigeration for food, books that are cheap in price, attractive, and widely available, hospitals in all cities of any size, electricity for all, paid vacations, and old age security for most.

Accompanying these gains have been many new problems and some old ones. The extraordinary natural wealth of America made some greedy. Until

recently the frontier with its inviting opportunities made it too easy to leave
behind worked-out farms and cut-over forests. During most of our history
insufficient attention has been given to the poor, the handicapped, and the less
fortunate among us. Quantity typically has been emphasized over quality.
Emerson put it accurately: "Things are in the saddle and ride mankind."

As with all people, our defects are born of our virtues. Freedom has led
frequently to irresponsibility; enterprise to exploitation; mobility to
insecurity; wealth and high incomes to profligacy and even sloth; competition
to a lack of compassion; haste to waste; and occasionally patriotism to
jingoism. In addition a tendency to self-righteousness and moralistic pose has
drawn us as a nation into a number of unwise ventures ranging from
prohibition to the Vietnam war. We are not always as right as we, a
self-proclaimed god-fearing people, like to think we are.

A case can be made that Americans are slowly adjusting to the realities of
their own character and place in the world as a strong, energetic people with
generous impulses but with no monopoly on wisdom and virtue. The trauma
of the Great Depression of the 1930s, the victory in the second World War
that led immediately to a protracted cold war plus several hot ones, the slack-
ness of the Eisenhower years, the over-promises of the Kennedy-Johnson
years, the strange and seemingly ungrateful youth rebellion of the late 1960s
and early '70s, the unfathomable combination of inflation and economic
recession in recent years, the national helplessness against the OPEC oil
monopoly, the soul-searing and wretched mess of Watergate—these may result in the chastening and ultimate maturing of America. I don't know, but I
hope so. At least I hope that we stop lurching manic-depressively from crisis
to crisis and learn to regulate and steady ourselves, at least to stay in one phase
long enough to extract the lessons it can teach us.

Our great national hymn, the one we shall sing in a few minutes,
proclaims this lesson: "Confirm thy soul in self-control, thy liberty in law."

In the kaleidoscope of change that has marked two centuries of our
national history, certain principles have remained fixed. Freedom still rings
out for the world to hear. Our political democracy, despite setbacks, continues. Ambition for self-improvement is unabated. Neighborliness and sharing
are still the predominant mode of daily living. We press on toward full economic and racial justice. Equality of the sexes, comes closer to realization
year by year. We make gains toward a more humane, compassionate society
despite occasional retrogression and certain criminal acts.

The Bill of Rights, our basic charter of individual freedom incorporated
into the Constitution nearly two centuries ago, is as fresh today as it ever was:

freedom of religion, speech, press, assembly; the right to be secure against unreasonable searches and seizures; the right not to be deprived of life, liberty, or property without due process of law; the right of trial by jury, to be confronted by one's accusers, and to have legal counsel, a right deriving from England's Magna Carta; the right not to be compelled by torture or otherwise to testify against oneself. These precious rights are guaranteed to Americans whatever their station. We thrill to their recitation. They invoke our deepest loyalties and most profound passions. They steady our ship; they provide the compass to direct us on our historic course. They give us dignity, confidence, and purpose. They make us a nation with a destiny.

Perhaps what we Americans most need as we pass the 200-year mark is a refreshed patriotism. My prayer for our country today—July 4, 1976—is for a new patriotism embracing the best elements of the old patriotism of our forefathers and mothers but including new elements to fortify us for the future. We loved the old patriotism, but it makes us a little uncomfortable now. It was more boisterous, uninhibited, uncritical, uncomplicated, unself-conscious. It was accompanied by overblown patriotic speeches and aggressive flag-waving.

The new patriotism is more subdued, controlled, sober, complex, self-conscious. It is characterized by family excursions to Boston, Philadelphia, and Washington, by local essay contests in history, by "The Adams Chronicles" on television, by carefully planned Bicentennial events. The old spontaneous parades and firework displays in which nearly every kid burned his finger setting off a firecracker have given way to scheduled parades and controlled firework displays.

Fourth of July orators used to thunder: "My country, may she ever be right; but, right or wrong, my country." Now it is enough to say clearly, positively, but quietly: "My country."

Without deprecating the old patriotism that I grew up with and I love, let me delineate new elements to add to the old so that our patriotism will thrill and motivate us for the next century as it has in the past.

The new patriotism will have an international as well as a national dimension. National fulfillment will be thought incomplete in the absence of progress throughout the world toward peace, freedom, justice, and economic development.

The new patriotism will be concerned with social and economic justice as well as with political and legal justice. Minority rights, fair taxation, equal treatment in jobs, better health care, acceptable standards of nutrition and housing, equal access to education and training, security and a decent living for elder citizens and all who need help—these concerns the new patriotism will embrace.

The new patriotism will be concerned also with a cleaner natural environment, with the improvement of cities and the preservation of an attractive countryside, with humanizing technological advances in chemical engineering, nuclear energy, space exploration, genetics, transportation, and communication innovations.

Finally, the new patriotism will be critical when we claim or moralize too much. For example, John Kennedy's assertion about "helping every friend (in the world) and opposing every foe" and Woodrow Wilson's statement about "making the world safe for democracy" will be moderated in their sweep and scope. A more modest and realistic goal would be to try simply to help every friend and make the world safe.

The challenge, of course, is to join the best of the traditional patriotism to the new patriotism, adapting to present perceptions of our country's mission and preparing us all for future perils. I trust a new and invigorated patriotism will help.

The old and the new patriotism were symbolized for me last Fourth of July in Falls Church when I spoke to a gathering in the Community Center. The traditional Spirit of '76 group was there—the fife player, the flag bearer, the drummer looking fiercely independent, dressed up in regalia of the Revolution. An ancient cannon fired several blank charges, a nerve-wracking procedure for cannoneers and spectators alike. And while *this* ancient pageantry was being played out, my eye caught a young man slouching against the building nearby. He happened to be a black youth, but he could have been any young person. He was paying close attention to the pageant while, in the manner characteristic of his age, trying to look as though he had not the slightest interest in it. But it was his dress that drew my attention: blue jeans, white tee shirt, and a red bandanna around his head. The red, white and blue of his costume was juxtaposed with the red, white, and blue of the fife player, the flag bearer, and the drummer: past and present, the old patriotism and the new.

Santayana wrote: "He who ignores history is condemned to repeat it." I commend this insight to you; think about it long enough to work your way through its implied discouragement to a determination to learn from history. This, I believe, is Santayana's deeper message.

The inscription on the U.S. Archives buildings reminds us that "The past is prologue." In a sense the reverse is also true: "The prologue is past." The past sets the stage for the next act of the play, just as that act in its turn sets the stage for the next one. Each generation plays its part and prepares the stage for the next. This is the meaning of history, ours or any other.

I hope these reflections on this occasion of the 200th anniversary of our nation will recall to you some of our heritage, our present problems, and our future promise. The national Bicentennial encourages depth perception through a wide-angle lens, and it will yield insights into the religious aspect of history.

> God of our Parents:
>> Grant us the wisdom to respect
>>> the experience of the past.
> God of our Children:
>> Grant us the greater wisdom
>>> to reshape the present,
>>> to improve the future,
>>>> and thus
>>> to realize our dreams.

Of War and Peace

Human nature has a way of dimming memories
    of cruelty of wars, of families thrust apart,
    of weeping lovers futilely clutching,
    of parents sending off their sons and daughters,
    plagued by doubt and guilt and fear.

Human nature has a way of screening out
    the horrors of the holocaust,
    of mass destruction in the cities and the country,
    of art and architecture turned to rubble,
    and human minds and bodies shattered in the ruins.

Human nature has a way of shutting out these memories
    and sinking into apathy.
    The peace so dearly won is soon presumed to be
    our daily fare as we indulge
    in tunnel vision turning inward with complacency.

Turn, then, outward, humankind,
    beyond the horrors of the wars,
    beyond the loneliness and mass destruction,
    beyond the sacrifice of generations past,
    beyond the clouds of doubt and fear.

Turn the vision outward, then,
 to all the possibilities of peace,
 to opening communications,
 to sharing knowledge, art, and thought,
 to build respect for all humanity.

Of Spears and Pruning Hooks

Since the beginning of history war has alternated with peace such that few people have lived out their three score and ten years without at least one war. In my lifetime, for example, the United States has fought in two world wars, plus a major war in Korea and another in Vietnam. And we have been on the verge of war a dozen times.

More than ten million Americans now living have served in the military forces during wartime. A larger number have worked in war industries. Americans killed in war during my lifetime exceed the number killed in all our previous wars. Although this country is not at war at the present time, I voted last week in the House of Representatives for the largest peacetime defense appropriation in our national history—not happily, to be sure, and not without first supporting amendments to reduce the spending.

Most other major countries have suffered more years of war in this century than has the United States and have lost far more soldiers, sailors, air force personnel and civilians. War-caused problems in Britain, Germany, the Soviet Union, Japan, China, and in smaller countries will continue for several generations. The losses have been staggering in economic and human terms.

The brutal depravity of war was brought home to me shockingly on a pilgrimage I made in the early 1960s to the Nazi concentration camp of Auschwitz, now a national shrine in southern Poland. In addition to the gruesome exhibits of fillings from the teeth and hanks of hair of thousands of murdered Jews, there was a large barracks almost completely filled with small cardboard suitcases in which victims had packed a few personal belongings. One suitcase caught my eye. Crudely lettered on it in white paint were the words:

KLEINKIND FISCHER
Geboren 1943
Sterben 1945

It hit me with the force of a sledgehammer.

Against the fact of war, we have yearned for peace. This timeless yearning for peace is proclaimed by political leaders everywhere, by educators, by preachers and prophets, even by military leaders. Surprisingly, Napoleon once said that war is the business of barbarians. We are not surprised that Dwight Eisenhower said, "After my experience, I have come to hate war. War settles nothing."

The terror and destruction of war give rise to a stronger desire for security and peace. Both individuals and nations yearn for peace, but they do not prevail. Why is this so?

The argument has frequently been made that war is inevitable; that it follows from man's inherent combative nature, from his animal inheritance. Fighting, so this argument runs, is the ultimate test of survival, whether in the jungle of wild animals or of modern nation-states. Others have claimed wars are deeply set in ancient, unremembered territorial and tribal allegiances. Or that they arise out of the vanity of machismo, the glorification of the man on horseback, or the mental-emotional abnormality of a charismatic leader.

No doubt the roots of war go deep into economics, psychology, biology, and philosophy. Cheap imports of raw materials or markets for manufactured products are thought to be necessary. Security for families, property, or national sovereignty are thought to be threatened. Pre-eminence for a particular political and social philosophy is thought to be essential. Ignorance and fears are played upon so as to magnify differences and transform remote contingencies into imminent dangers. Wider concepts like the family of man, international law and order, and an integrated world economic system—concepts upon which peace can be established—tend to be overpowered by narrow, outworn concepts.

The central question is clear: how do we, companions on this particular spinning globe whirling around its particular sun, find our way out of a war-filled past into a peaceful future?

Answers are where you find them. I found one on a poster on the wall of a church bathroom recently. It was taken from the writings of Thomas à Kempis: "Keep thyself first in peace and then thou wilt be able to bring others to peace." This quote expresses quite well my central theme.

Peace, I assert, has to begin in a person's heart to be based there, firmly and confidently. Without this disarmament other approaches to peace will not succeed, nor will war end.

Diplomats wave no magic wand over countries of the world to bring forth peace. International conferences, however helpful, can't do it. Multinational corporations, for all their need of a peaceful world, can't manage it. Cultural exchanges of artists and scientists, though useful in breaking down some barriers, are insufficient. Tourists visiting back and forth frequently irritate their hosts as much as please them. Certainly wars can't bring peace beyond a temporary period; in the long light of history it would be fatuous to think they can.

This is not to say that the diplomats and political leaders cannot be helpful. And it is not to say that organizational efforts for peace are futile. On the contrary, without determined action along these lines peace within a person's heart might die aborning or never find its proper outlet in world affairs.

The two—peace within the individual's heart and peace among nations— intersect. Peace in one sphere encourages peace in the other. Therefore, governmental and group efforts are worthwhile, as are individual efforts. Both the individual and general efforts will require education, practical demonstrations, and much perseverance. Most of all the building of peace, internal and external, will require religious effort, religious leadership, religious concentration of the highest order.

The great religions of the world have tried to deal with war and peace but, thus far, have not been successful. Buddhism advocates renunciation of struggle, person against person, group against group. But it has emphasized inner tranquility, peace of mind, and the prospect of reincarnation in a more favorable form. Such a religion, deeply believed, ought to constitute a promising start toward peace. Unfortunately Buddhism has been limited in geographic scope; countries espousing its meek and fatalistic doctrine have easily fallen prey to marauders from outside. It seems also to lack the positive and energetic attributes without which a combative world cannot be transformed.

In Judeo-Christian development one finds schizophrenia: some of the loftiest testaments to peace and love along with arrogance, exclusiveness, and warmongering. We associate with Jesus such statements as love your neighbor, go in peace, turn the other cheek, and the peace that passes all understanding. Rejecting the invitation to enter Jerusalem as a conquering hero, Jesus in death, even more than life, gave the most profound, dramatic witness for peace and love in our religious tradition. But ironically, sadly, tragically, countless battalions since the crucifixion have marched in his name.

The same division is found in the stories of the Old Testament. As the spiritual recounts, "Joshua fit de battle of Jericho, and de walls come tumblin' down." Yet Micah called out to the chosen people: "Beat your swords into plowshares and your spears into pruning hooks." War and peace were glorified in the same religious teachings.

The American psychologist and philosopher William James, advocated what he called "the moral equivalent of war." The idea still seems to have promise today. What are the possibilities? Hard and challenging work, rewards based on cooperation and avoiding conflict, enforcement of international law, the building of world government.

Notable attempts have been made to erect a structure of world peace. Alexander, Julius Caesar, Charlemagne, Napoleon, and even Hitler tried to establish peace through war; sooner or later, each failed. Prime ministers, foreign ministers, and presidents have tried: Metternich and his Congress of Vienna, Kellogg and Briand with their post-World War I pact, Wilson with his magnificent idea of a League of Nations, Franklin D. Roosevelt and the other founders of the United Nations. Each of them had high motives and expectations, but the results have fallen short. Philosophers, poets, and prophets have described the world of peace. Plato, Augustine, Thomas More, Rousseau, Milton, Isaiah, and Micah who preached about spears and pruning hooks. But lasting peace continues to elude our grasp.

Perhaps having these disappointments, in mind, William Butler Yeats poured out his pessimism, using the metaphor of war:

> Things fall apart; the centre cannot hold,
> Mere anarchy is loosed upon the world,
> The blood-dimmed tide is loosed, and everywhere
> The ceremony of innocence is drowned;
> The best lack all conviction, while the worst
> Are full of passionate intensity.

In our twentieth century now moving insecurely and unpredictably toward its close, war clouds hang dark over the world. Southern Africa struggles toward an uncertain future. Nearly everyone grants the moral inevitability of black control of government there but hardly anyone knows how to navigate the passage to it without bloodshed. And no sooner than the black dream is achieved, it may be outdated by onrushing events which will call for submission to a continental or world order. In the Horn of Africa another struggle proceeds, less profound and traumatic for Americans, but of great concern because of its proximity to the Middle East oil countries.

Undoubtedly the most dangerous part of the world right now is the Middle East, centering on Egypt and Israel but including Lebanon, Syria, the stateless Palestinians, Saudi Arabia, Libya, Iraq and Iran. The problem of securing peace there is so complex and mystifying that it can hardly be described, much less solved. Our own country has launched major initiatives with Egypt and Israel to pluck from the nettle a solution, or at least an approach to a solution. Yet at the same time in the name of peace, compromise, and harmony, the United States has continued shipments of arms to those two countries and to Saudi Arabia, as well as sent military supplies to Iraq and Iran. How much better it would be to promote peace in the Middle East by scaling down United States arms shipments instead increasing them.

Out of despair one is tempted to cry out for a new messiah, a new prince of peace, to sweep away the worn out policies of the past and put things in a new perspective. But we know deep inside ourselves that progress will have to come from our own efforts to listen, and understand, to have patience, suppress unrealistic expectations, and to persist in leadership.

What are the principle conditions for peace, not only in Southern Africa and the Middle East, but throughout the world? I believe these are important ones:

First, a broad set of values and objectives for living shared among the peoples of the world. Fear of one another or of the horrors of war are not enough, even in an age of nuclear bombs. All agencies of society—education, politics, science, commerce, and, most of all, religion—will have to work on this.

Second, a system of international law based on shared values that has general respect and support and can be enforced by economic sanctions, political pressure, and ultimately, police power.

Third, vigorous and dedicated leadership for peace in the countries of the world moving toward the concept of world citizenship with its rights and obligations.

Fourth, peace research in psychology, economics, sociology, ecology, natural and life sciences, and even military science devoted to enforcing peace, to demonstrations of war prevention and peacekeeping, and to education for peace.

Finally, concern for the essential religious component of peace. Niebuhr's insight is prophetic: the dictum of "moral man in an immoral society" has to be enlarged to "moral man in a moral society." In that most magnificent of all historical novels, *War and Peace,* young Rostov, wounded on the field, cries out, "Can they be coming at me? And why? To kill me? Me—of whom everyone is so fond?"

To achieve these conditions will require a "positive affirmation of peace," in the words of Martin Luther King, Jr.

> It is not a question of peace at any price; obviously a person should not give up his soul for peace. But the price of peace is sacrifice, hard work, devotion, willingness to see the other side in a controversy.

In his jeremiad delivered at the Harvard Commencement, Alexander Solzhenitsyn said, "We have placed too much hope in political and social reforms, only to find that we were being deprived of our most precious possession: our spiritual life." He had in mind Americans, Russians, everyone. It would be a mistake to think that a black majority government in Zimbabwe or a settlement of the Palestinian homeland issue, or a non-proliferation treaty, or a successful conclusion of the SALT II talks, or all of them together, would guarantee peace. Dr. Johnson asked:

> How much of all that man endures
> Is that which courts or kings can cure?

Personal change of heart is the essential and overiding condition for peace.

During the second World War after serving as an infantry soldier, I was assigned to the Army Newspaper, *Stars and Stripes,* as a reporter and later as an editorial and feature writer. Not long ago I was reminiscing with my old scrapbook. On May 22, 1945 I used my editorial to address the men and women gathered in San Francisco to write the charter for the United Nations—an organization devoted to the peace and security of the world. I wrote:

> Yours is the difficult task of translating the aspirations of common people everywhere into a workable scheme for the preservation of peace. Yours is the job of bridging the gap between vague, half-formed ideals and hard, political reality; between past disappointments and future hopes. Yours, too, is an unmatched opportunity to earn the everlasting thanks of the human family. You have our prayers.

And on August 15, 1945, the day after V-J Day, I wrote in another editorial: "The end of war is not the end of responsibilities. United Nations plans for world peace must be made to work. And that's the business of each individual who would be a world citizen, just as much as it is the responsibility of prime ministers and generals."

Then as always, individuals' control of themselves is the answer. We need a guidance system to keep the human ship on a peaceful course. Neither a ship of fools nor a ship of angels, we are ordinary men and women who must become extraordinary if we are to survive in peace.

The greatness of Tolstoy's *War and Peace* lies in his bringing together hundreds of individuals and thousands of separate actions into one grand experience. Only by taking an infinitesimally small unit for observation (i.e., the tendencies of the individual) and attending to the art of integrating them, can we hope to arrive at the laws of history. The task of establishing a durable peace will require the integration of individual hopes and actions into the larger, but not more important, policies of governments: harnessing the micro and the macro to the same task.

War has been a part of living for many people in our country and in virtually all other countries. It has certainly been a part of my life and that of my wife. A religion for living must address the evil of war and the hope of peace with moral fervor tempered with analytic insight into what is practical and achievable. Spears can be beat into pruning hooks so that "nation shall not lift up sword against nation . . . but they shall sit every man under his vine and under his fig tree, and none shall make them afraid."

>Give us, God of peace,
>   Not so much peace itself
>   As the will to seek it,
>   persistently and patiently,
>   Until at last it possesses us
>   And we it.

CHAPTER TEN
RELIGION AND POWER GAPS

Respect for Diversity

Great men and women find their strength
In self-respect and through respect
For others whom their lives may touch.
Their greatness lies not in conceit
That they are better than the rest.
They do not boast of greater wealth,
Superior race, age, sex or faith,
Or tout their origin of birth,
Though proud they are to be themselves.
They find their power in acceptance
Of and by humanity
With all its diverse qualities.

Great men and women meet the crises
In their families, the nation,
And the world, not with arrogance
Or violence, brutality,
Or hate, but with compassion and
Respect for human dignity
And differences. The power they gain
Does not intimidate. It is benign,
Conveying strength and pride to those
Who need it most. Unhampered by
Myopic, ingrown prejudice
They bring our lives diversity.

Gaps, Crises and Power

This is the day of gaps—there is the age gap, the education gap, the wealth and income gap, the racial gap, the foreign policy gap, the peace gap, the credibility gap, and the gender gap. Most of these gaps have long been with us. I am sure that grandfather and grandmother thought their children were running wild and going to the dogs, and their parents thought the same a generation earlier. But nowadays there is a heightened and widespread awareness of the gap phenomenon; we all suffer from "gaposis." It weighs upon our conscience. We think gaps are bad and should be removed, or at least reduced. We look about us and see problems everywhere; being human and somewhat rational, we look for explanations. We see misunderstandings among different groups in the population. We express these misunderstandings in the shorthand word, *gap.*

Most of us don't have to look outside our own family to see at least one gap. The teenage-adult gap is perhaps the most visible and most poignant. The high school son, fumbling with the need for status, individuality, and independence, experiments by growing a fuzzy beard. Or a girl takes on a style that parents perceive as rebellious or comic. The natural desire for teenage independence also can be expressed in more serious ways: through experimenting with marijuana, cocaine, and other drugs, through psychological and behavioral withdrawal from the normal groups and activities of teenagers, or through some other form of the "dropout and turn-on" syndrome. This particular gap—call it the age gap or the youth-adult gap—leads directly to family crises. It produces alienation and even family breakdown: the teenager runs away or the parents separate. More typical is the showdown, the knock-down and drag-out confrontation between youth and parent. Sympathies are played on, conscience is rubbed raw, and threats are hurled. Youth wails, "You don't understand me." Age replies, "Show some respect." Youth charges, "You're stupid." Age replies, "You don't understand how it is in the real world." Youth says, "If *your* world is the real world, *I* don't want any part of it." Age answers, "How do you think you can improve the world, if you opt out of it? Total absorption in rock music, basketball, cars, or clothing is no substitute for education, hard work, and discipline." And so goes a nondialogue leading nowhere.

Moving outside the family into the urban community, one meets a new set of gaps. In our cities, certainly in the National Capital region where I have lived for many years, the gaps have become exacerbated to the point of extreme social disorder. Beginning with the landmark desegregation decision of the Supreme Court 20 years ago which set in motion public school desegregation under the enigmatic "all deliberate speed" formula, the region has made progress in legislation, judicial interpretation, executive direction, and other legalistic solutions to the racial problem. Unfortunately individual attitudinal and social practices have not moved forward in parallel with the legal gains. For example, *de jure* desegregation of public schools in our cities has, in many instances, led to even greater segregation *de facto.* To escape integrated schools in the central cities, the whites in large numbers move to the educational and social segregation of the suburbs. Efforts to break down this new segregation by intra-metropolitan bussing of school children have been tried here and there, with less than full success. The next move was to pass laws at the federal level—in the District as in many states and localities—for open housing. The rationale was to enable Blacks and other minority racial and ethnic groups to find homes in the suburbs and thus, at a more basic level, to integrate suburban white society. This sounded plausible, but ways were found to circumvent this legal and a logical solution. The gap still persists in the psychological, ethical, and probably religious sense.

Integration will work when it is present in the hearts and minds of people, and not until then. I do not mean that statutory gains are not important; I mean they are not enough. I do not mean that significant improvements have not been achieved; I mean they still fall short of an integrated community.

The movement of African Americans toward a better life was greatly aided by the voting rights legislation of the mid-1960s and the wider enforcement of civil rights. These plus the establishment of national programs for better health care (Medicare for the elderly and Medicaid for the poor), financial aid for educating disadvantaged youth, housing assistance for low-and middle-income families, food stamps, the Older Americans Act—in short, the Great Society program of the Johnson presidency—together these set the socio-economic agenda the country has been trying to cope with ever since.

In 1964 and early 1965 I chaired one of several task forces that President Johnson set up to prepare legislative proposals for the term to which he had just been elected by a landslide. At the conclusion of our work the several chairpersons were invited to dinner at the White House. In the course of a long evening's discussion the President said with great force and conviction,

"I'm going to put so much long-overdue social legislation on the books that it will take the Congress and the country a generation to digest it!" Talk about prophetic.

Incidentally, four years later I participated in a similar exercise at the behest of President Nixon. In a similar gathering at the outset of his ill-fated presidency, he suggested he wanted to modify and fine-tune these programs, chew and digest them, and not regurgitate them. As you can see, what I have characterized as the racial gap is intertwined with what can be called the economic gap, or more broadly the social gap. Closing one gap enables us to see other gaps. Armed with guaranteed voting rights and better educated constituents, minority leaders with the support of many mainstream leaders are on a vigorous campaign to register more voters and give minority items higher priority on the national agenda. They aim primarily to close some of the economic gaps in unemployment, income, and material well-being. Minority unemployment has been running at nearly twice the rate of other workers. The more convincingly these gaps can be portrayed as crises, the more effectively power can be organized to produce action.

I could go on and talk about other gaps. I could turn to foreign affairs, for example, and cite a number of gaps or sub-gaps, each of which leads to its particular set of crises. One gap about which George Kennan has written a good deal is that between the moral ideals of the American people about democracy, peace, and helping poor nations on the one hand, and our military, economic, and political capacity to sustain programs which can achieve what we desire on the other hand. Long ago Walter Lippmann warned of the danger of allowing our foreign policy commitments to outrun our military capacity, economic resources, and especially our morale. Then there is the defense gap which is highlighted every four years by presidential and other candidates who may be trying to oust an incumbent. They point to the gap in military and defensive strength between the United States and the Soviet Union even though it may not exist.

In fact, the "credibility gap" has become a code term for a situation in which a leader says something that may well be true, but which his hearers refuse to believe. These credibility gaps also lead to crises, as most recent presidents have found to their dismay.

A recent *New York Times*/CBS news poll gave new evidence of the gender gap. It showed that the difference between men's approval of President Reagan and women's is 21 percent, with the women giving the President a hard time. Congresswomen, Democratic and Republican alike, are vying with one another in castigating Mr. Reagan. In perhaps the most generous remark, Olympia Snowe, Republican from Maine, said, "He's just not capable of understanding the problems of today's women." All of this boiled over at a recent meeting of the bipartisan National Women's Political Caucus in San Antonio. Patricia Schroeder, Democrat from Colorado, said, "It all goes back to the realization that women view the world differently from men. Women see the whole picture. Women still worry that unless we change the old cave-man rules, we will all be blown up." A Republican woman member of the Federal Trade Commission characterized the Administration's reaction to the women's demands as "benign bewilderment."

The gender gap is composed of the differing views that prevail between women and men regarding the Equal Rights Amendment, the one-third less pay women receive for the same work as men do, inadequate funding of day-care programs, discrimination in obtaining credit, unequal contribution in raising children, abortion, job promotion to the higher ranks, and so on. Of course, all men don't oppose the women's rights position any more than all women support it. But a significant gap does seem to exist. As local, state, and national elections approach, it is important to note that women make up 52 percent of the voting population mainly because they live seven or eight years longer than men, and in the 1980 presidential election for the first time a higher percentage of women voted than men.

Becoming aware of these trends and reacting to the gender gap crisis, the Reagan administration launched a counter-offensive which stumbled a couple of weeks ago over Barbara Honegger, designated by a White House spokesman as a "low level munchkin" from the Department of Justice. She, you will recall, had been assigned the job of drawing up a list of specific legal and regulatory provisions that discriminate against women. Along the line she resigned in a huff because she came to the conclusion the administration wasn't going to do anything about them, and she was wasting her time. Whether Barbara is guided by legal analysis or inner voices is not clear, but she has succeeded in elevating further the gender gap issue.

This particular gap obviously is related to the age gap, the economic gap, and others. It is not likely to go away soon, although public interest will rise and fall as it usually does. And the attendant crises—political, legal, family, moral, whatever—are not likely to go away soon either. However many gaps may be identified, and however many crises may be associated with the gaps, one wants to find solutions—ways of preventing the crises by reducing the gaps. Power will be required to do this—power used by some group in some way. And the power may range from the power of persuasion, to the power of an idea whose time has come, to power and influence through advertising and salesmanship, to political power, to the more brutal forms of power. I say that power is not the only avenue toward the resolution of problems.

Like most of you I happen to be devoted to the gentler forms of power that arise from understanding the problem, discussing it, and arriving peacefully at honorable compromises. But I have to say that for the immediate future I anticipate that many of our problems will be dealt with by rougher applications of power. Parents resort to a sterner use of power even when they try to overpower their children psychologically not physically. This leads to two possible results: first, the youth is brought back into line and the difficulty is repressed for a time; or second, the youth rebels by dropping out, running away, or escaping into a fantasy.

At the community and social level, power can be applied from several directions. I have already mentioned the black power approach. The white power approach under the name of law and order or common decency, has been exposed. The overt power solution is dangerous because advocates follow strategies in which each side masses its followers and deploys its forces so as to beat down the other side. The so-called American radical, Saul Alinsky, who played a controversial part a few years ago in the Unitarian Universalist Association General Assembly in Denver, advocated the approach of the small, militant, highly disciplined minority that polarizes the situation, expects individuals to be entirely with them or against them ("Are you with us or against us?"), and deliberately precipitates confrontations. Superior discipline and a willingness to be militant, he argues, will carry the day. He regards traditional liberals as innocent bystanders whose consciences can be worked on to extract their support.

For me, this concept of power and how it should be used is unacceptable. I concede its inevitability in certain instances and its utility in a few cases. But on the whole I reject it; certainly I reject any quick and easy recourse to it. I vastly prefer the approach of tolerance, understanding, mutual adjustment of competing positions, constructive compromise, peaceful persuasion—power in its gentle and benign forms.

Down through the years the practitioners of benign power have been notable: Socrates, St, Francis, various kings called so-and-so The Just, The Good, or The Kind, and Jesus. Our own religious tradition has been strong for this kind of power. But an objective appraisal of history hardly convinces us that gentle leaders have predominated or that they will in the future. We shall continue to hope for a change. A while back in one of our Virginia college newspapers, a "Man Wanted" notice appeared in connection with Christian emphasis week: "Young man wanted, fugitive from justice;

preaches overthrow of law and established customs; advocates love, freely given. Mid-twenties, has beard wears sandals. Attracts young people. This man is dangerous. Reward for information regarding his whereabouts. Goes by the name of Jesus."

A number of years ago when the youth rebellion was in full cry, I was presiding as Moderator over a UUA General Assembly of 1,500 or so highly involved delegates. In the midst of an emotional outburst on youth issues—the youth-age gap if you like—when tempers had been stretched to the snapping point, four or five youth leaders came to the platform. They were long-haired, sloppily dressed, sandal-footed, disheveled—in the accepted uniforms of the period. One of them, a young lady, took a string of love beads—remember them?—from her neck and placed them around mine. She knew I had been having an emotionally draining time of it, trying to control an unruly Assembly. She said, "Here, I want to give you these love beads to transfer our love to you. You need them more than I do. And some day, some place, when you find someone else who is having a hard time and needs them more than you do, then take them from your neck and give them to that person. That's the way love can be shared and expanded in the world." What a symbolic and powerful witness this was for closing a gap and averting a crisis. For me and, I think, for everyone present this was a religious experience.

What I am suggesting here is that gentle and benign power—the power of love, if you like—is stronger than we realize. We should have confidence in its efficacy; we should rely on it; we should apply it at all levels to the crises of our times. I am thinking of a positive, constructive direct use of benign power, not a submissive "turn the other cheek" variety. If the understanding gap and resulting crisis is in your family (or in mine), then try an extra measure of patience which is a form of power. If the gap relates to race in your community (or in mine), then how about an extra measure of humility and sympathy; these also are forms of power. If it is the income, wealth, or poverty gap that needs closing, then we can turn to taxes, special grants, and just plain sharing, for much potential good resides in these very practical applications of power.

I plead for a little benign power employed early before the gaps become so wide, the voltage differential so great, that only a lightning bolt can bridge across.

A religious group, religion itself, can serve as a "gap reducer" and "crisis averter" by turning explosive forces into constructive projects. In fact, religion can make connections across the racial gap, the age gap, the income gap, the peace gap, the gender gap—to make the benign revolutions so that the ugly, destructive ones will be unnecessary. Every person, every group, is plagued by one or another of these gaps. Each is accompanied by its own crises. Persons and groups suffering from "gaposis" seek to find their way out of the resulting crisis through the exercise of power. Let the empowerment be achieved, but let the use of power be constructive and benign. This is our challenge and our opportunity. Basically, I believe, it is a religious challenge and a religious opportunity.

> Universal Healer:
> Give to us all a full measure
>> Of humility and determination
>> To bridge the gaps and avert the crises
>>> That plague our times;
>> And thus to restore to ourselves and our society
>>> Civility, understanding, and peace.

Truth Beyond Reckoning

There is a truth beyond all reckoning
That reaches out beyond the universe.
Great minds have sought to penetrate its depths,
To bring it definition and proclaim
Its origins, its laws and purposes.
Copernicus and Galileo bravely
Challenged ancient myths and ignorance
About the orbits and the origins
Of stars and moons, of planets, earth and sun.
Defying doctrine, Darwin traced the origins
Of man and beast. Some called it heresy —
Contempt for scripture and for God.

Yet search for truth through science would prevail.
The work of Newton, Currie, and Pasteur,
And Einstein lead the way to man's dominion
Over earth and space. Nobel, VonBraun,
And Oppenheimer opened doors they wished
That they could close, for they unleashed the seeds
Of devastation of the earth and man.
"Beware," they cried, "we know too little of
Too much. The hour grows late, and we
Cannot afford the luxury of error
But must try to comprehend
Our powers and use our knowledge for the good."

There is a truth beyond all reckoning
That reaches out beyond the universe.
The search goes on for true enlightenment,
The thirst for knowledge never satisfied.
May wisdom parallel that search, with love
And reverence for life its motivating
Force. Let goodness and unselfishness
Determine ways in which our new-found powers
May be used, and may we learn that strength
Is not the use of brutal force, but use of insight,
Judgment and restraint to guide the way
We spend the little time we have on earth.

The Lessons and Limits of Science

Science is at the peak of its influence yet we view it with skepticism and growing distrust. It seems incapable of coping with basic human problems. It has released powerful forces for material progress but has not revealed ways to direct these forces to benefit us. We seem unable to live without the fruits of science while, at the same time, bombs and toxic chemicals threaten to kill us. Poverty remains; famine and death still take their toll. No wonder most of us both love and fear science. It is Prometheus bound and Prometheus unbound.

It has been said many times that the concern of science is solely the objective examination of natural phenomena, of facts and relationships among facts. Its tools of analysis have been sharpened for this work. "Yet it is equally clear," Einstein has pointed out in *Out of My Later Years,* "that knowledge of what *is* does not open the door directly to what *should be. . . .* Objective knowledge provides us with powerful instruments for the achievement of certain ends, but the ultimate goal itself and the longing to reach it must come from another source. . . . Here we face the limits of the purely rational conception of our existence."

I don't need to take much time here to remind you of the benefits of science and its offsprings medicine and engineering to human welfare. The newspapers recently carried a story about Californian Donald D. Hollister who has invented a light bulb that will last ten years, thereby saving electricity, materials, and labor. Some of us can remember the fat, clear glass bulbs of our youth that often sputtered out after relatively few hours. Less than 100 years ago Thomas Edison, after experimenting with thousands of possibilities, hit upon the carbon filament for the first electric light. His invention was possible because in the preceding several decades, electric generators had been developed based on Michael Faraday's discovery that an electric current could be made to flow through a copper wire by moving the wire near a magnet or by moving a magnet. And before that, a steam engine had been developed to furnish the necessary movement.

Many other stories illustrate the contributions of science to health, comfort, and well-being. Alexander Fleming in London in 1928, more or less by accident, noticed a mold growing on a culture of common germs seemed to dissolve the germs. From this observation he proceeded to develop penicillin. Production in 20 thousand gallon tanks runs to many hundreds of tons a year in this country alone. As germ strains become resistant to specific antibiotics, new ones are produced in the continuing battle between the survival capacities of germs and the wits of biochemists.

Equally well known to you are the liabilities of science. Chemists and chemical engineers can make napalm; physicists and nuclear engineers can make atomic bombs; and geologists and metallurgists can find and produce materials whose residues include harmful sulfur, mercury, lead, asbestos, and radio-active elements. The rate at which the experts are discovering how harmful, even lethal, an increasing number of rather ordinary items are is most alarming. Who knows what will be next on the dangerous items list? What food additive, garden spray, cosmetic lotion, laundry soap, child's toy, water-proofing chemical, seafood? Most of us have to draw the line somewhere. I drew my line a few years ago by refusing to give up swordfish which had been placed on the forbidden list.

If the results of science are a mixed bag are scientists, medical doctors, and engineers amoral and not responsible for either the good or the bad outcomes of their efforts? Or should society, should we hold them accountable? This is a profoundly difficult and disturbing question to scientists as well as the rest of us. It especially has been a mind and soul searing question for scientists. Only a few weeks ago, several scientists resigned from important positions in their company to protest publicly against its nuclear reactor program. Some of their colleagues look on their behavior as romantic and immature, unjustified by the facts. Tensions divide the scientific community.

I believe we should be slow to judge in this matter. The power of scientific research is enhanced by freedom to pursue ideas and hypotheses wherever they lead. Imagine Ben Franklin having to get a permit from the Occupational Safety and Health Administration before running the key up his kite string during the lightening storm! Or imagine Louis Pasteur having to deal with a French Food and Drug Administration in the 1880s. On the other hand, we cannot release scientists from taking responsibility for the massive and wide-spread consequences of their discoveries. The ancient common law principle "let the buyer beware" needs to be matched by another principle: *let the maker take care.*

Toward the end of the Second World War, I was assigned as a reporter to the Army Newspaper *Stars and Stripes*. There I got to know another soldier, Jerry Siegel, who had been brought on to create a comic strip. Jerry, a sweet, unassuming, unathletic, Charlie Brown type fellow, was the creator of

Superman. He has been in the news recently. Now a five thousand dollar a year clerk in southern California, he was awarded a modest annuity in belated compensation for the fact the publishing company had long ago euchered him out of royalties on the fabulously remunerative Superman enterprise (comic strip, comic books, toys, T-shirts). Anyway, Jerry thought about his assignment to create a new comic strip suitable for a newspaper read by several million soldiers, sailors, and marines. He discussed the problem with me and finally came up with a plan for a comic strip to be called "Super GI." He thought the psychological appeal of Superman could be transferred to the military. He argued that what the Sad Sacks of that war, the lonesome, discouraged, pushed-around GIs, needed to boost their morale and egos was a Super GI, possessing every advantage science could offer: invisible cloak, lethal ray gun, speed-of-light motion, Herculean strength, and mind reading power. All of these Jerry contended, would be employed to extricate GI Joe from extreme danger, usually in such a way that Joe got the girl, the enemy got dumped in the ocean, and some poor officer ended up with the short end of the stick. The strip lasted about six weeks before the flood of indignant and obscenely critical letters from readers made it necessary to cancel the whole venture. Jerry served out his Army time on the copy desk writing headlines and trying to figure out what went wrong with Super GI.

If there is a moral to this story, I suppose it is that in certain situations, even the most lavish employment of science and technology won't get you anywhere. Is America, is the world, approaching a time when science will be unable to rescue us because we will not want it to, presumably because it will create more problems than it solves raising our hopes only to dash them? Are we losing faith in science? Have we expected too much of scientists? If the answer to these questions is yes, then why is this? Perhaps science and at least some scientists are unable to cope with the dilemma posed by the scientific ideal of the free pursuit of knowledge on the one hand, and the need for limits on the scientific enterprise in the interests of human values on the other hand. Has the renaissance of free scientific inquiry released from the intellectual bondage of the Middle Ages finally run its course? Must it give way to another great struggle to bring the powerful engines of science and technology under a more benign and purposeful regime, in which human values such as cooperation, peace, stability, and social equity have higher priority. The main thrust of the scientific revolution, beginning four centuries ago with Copernicus in Krakow and Galileo in Padua, was surely toward freedom to examine the universe and explain how it worked. Freedom of thought provided the foundation for aggressive, relatively unrestrained institutions and activities of a political and economic nature.

During the modern era other strands have been brought together that support a transition to a science that acknowledges the need to place scientific enquiry in the service of human values. Copernicus removed the earth from the center of the universe and relegated our planet to a modest size and orbit. Newton, for all the mastery over nature his laws of motion led to, established that man and objects alike obeyed the same laws. In exposing the underlying principles of mutation, competition, selection, and survival, Darwin turned the spotlight away from man toward the evolutionary process for all species. Einstein propounded and later verified his theory of relativity supported the intuition that fundamentals—time, space, motion—could be understood only in relationship. And Heisenberg, who died just a few weeks ago, emphasized the uncertainty and unpredictability of individual events while recognizing the stability of large numbers of events in the probability sense. All of these strands of scientific thought, it seems to me, lead away from a pretentious, over-confident, man-centered view and support a scientific outlook in which the spirit of free investigation is accompanied by ultimate responsibility for preserving nature and enhancing of human values.

The dilemma of individual freedom versus social responsibility is not new, and it plagues more of us than scientists. After all, unlike Dr. Faustus who made a pact with the devil in exchange for knowledge and power, scientists are not really supermen and superwomen. They are very much like the rest of us, but their dilemma is especially acute. As the pace of military competition among the countries of the world is quickening, nuclear energy and atomic weapons offer a case in point. A half dozen countries have at least a few atomic bombs and some capacity to use them effectively. Without continued major effort to improve the destructive capability of atomic weapon systems, our country will inevitably fall behind and endanger the safety of its citizens. Scientists and technicians are needed for this work. But the end result may be catastrophic. The only way to avert tragedy seems to lie in continuing negotiations with the Soviet Union for arms reduction. But it will be a slow, difficult, risky process, and we had better proceed with utmost caution.

The peaceful development of nuclear energy, not entirely separate from military uses, poses difficulties also. Meltdowns in reactors can occur, transportation of fissionable materials is subject to accidents and sabotage, dangerously lower safety standards in some other countries and final disposal of radioactive residues with a half-life of many centuries conjure up problems of unimaginable complexity. Yet increasing production and use of nuclear energy seems to be the only way of meeting our likely demand for electricity in the next couple of decades unless people tolerate much higher utility bills and restrict the number of kilowatt hours they use. The electric utility that serves Northern Virginia already produces one quarter of its energy from nuclear reactors and is on its way to producing one-half. Despite increased use of coal, electric rates would probably go even higher if the company did not pursue this course. In the more distant future energy from direct solar radiation and from fusion may rescue us. Both of these sources are clean and potentially plentiful, but they require long research and development lead times and won't help much for two or three more decades.

Scientists and engineers are not much different from the rest of us. Some see great danger; some see little. But most of them, I believe, understand that citizens generally deserve some say in dealing with the problems. This represents progress and bodes well for a future in which everyone's view is given weight. The effort to deal intelligently and maturely with both the peaceful and the military uses of the atom may move us closer toward a new necessary view of science within limits and guided by human values. Thus, the scientific elite and the humanists, as depicted in C. P. Snow's novels, may be brought together.

During the last ten years, I have been active in the effort to establish processes within the federal government for evaluating the likely consequences of new technology. Progress has been made. An Office of Technological Assessment has been established as an arm of the Congress, and it is preparing comprehensive studies of new transportation systems, solar energy, and ocean resource technology. In the executive branch, the Council On Environmental Quality is analyzing numerous environmental impact statements prepared for all major projects from the trans-Alaska oil pipeline to new interstate highways. Earlier, the Council of Economic Advisers was set up to track the course of the economy and to recommend measures to promote maximum employment, production, and purchasing power. I have argued for a Council Of Social Advisers charged with examining the health, education, welfare, crime, consumer, and related problems people face. Thus, there has arisen a broad and concerted effort in government to take heed of the good and bad consequences of new proposals and projects, most of them stemming from science and technology, and to measure their ecologic, economic, health and safety, and social effects. All of this represents an advance in responsible government.

But to move in the direction of a human control of science which recognized the strength of science and holds it within limits, will require more than intellectual analysis. It will require religious commitment. In a sense the scientific quest in its deepest essence is a religious quest. In *Out Of My Later Years,* Albert Einstein wrote:

> Whoever has undergone the intense experience of successful advances made in this domain [science] is moved by profound reverence for the rationality made manifest by existence. . . . This attitude appears to me to be religious in the highest sense of the word. . . . The situation may be expressed by an image: Science without religion is lame, religion without science is blind.

At the very end of his monumental work, *The Origin of Species,* Darwin was reaching for much the same thought:

> There is grandeur in this [evolutionary] view of life, with its several powers . . . whilst this planet has gone cycling on according to the fixed law of gravity, from so simple a beginning endless forms most beautiful and most wonderful have been, and are being evolved.

The modern world of the last few centuries has been and still is a world of science. Copernicus, Galileo, Newton, Darwin, and Einstein achieved breakthroughs more significant by far than those of great generals and statesmen. Yet science has not abolished war or poverty and has only postponed death. For every new thing learned from science, two others come dimly into view; for every problem solved, two others cry out for solution. For all its strength, science is powerless to reveal ultimate truth, beauty, or goodness. The greatest lesson one can learn from science is to respect its limits and control its engines. Otherwise those who employ science are likely to destroy it and all else. Religion that goes beyond the limits of science must teach the lessons of restraint and benign use.

Teach us, God —
>To respect science when it is human
>>and freedom when it is responsible
>And to depend on religion
>>to undergird them both.

>Great is the gift of life
>>for we are the beneficiaries
>>>of freedom and scholarship.
>May we never lose our sense of wonder
>>or our dreams for a better world.

CHAPTER TWELVE
RELIGION AND THE GLOBAL FUTURE

Out of the Shadow: A Prayer

Out of the valley of the shadow,
    out of the shadow of wars past,
        out of the shadow of feuding peoples
            whose bitter struggles cast a pall
                upon our dreams of peace —

We seek some greater power
    to lift our sights, to give us wisdom
        to pursue a course of justice,
            equity, and human dignity,
                of beauty and tranquility,

Out of the valley of the shadow,
    out of the shadow of our fears,
        out of the shadow of pain,
            uncertainty and grief,
                the legacy of human frailty —

We pray for vision
    and for energy to so direct
        our lives that precious time
            shall not be lost, and peace,
                not war, shall rule the world at last.

                      Amen

Religion and the Global Future

Through history prophets of gloom and doom have drawn larger audiences than prophets of milk and honey. The magnificently pessimistic Old Testament prophets—Amos, Isaiah, Ezekiel—spoke vividly of what the wrath of God would bring down unless people mended their ways. In our own time those who dramatize the horrible possibilities of nuclear war, toxic chemicals, overpopulation, or social disorder and crime gain a wider hearing than those who portray a cornucopia of plenty, a land of opportunity and promise. Cassandras outnumber Pollyannas, that's for sure. More people see through a glass darkly than through rose-colored glasses.

The recent *Global 2000 Report* is in the time-honored catastrophic tradition, but it is in the modern idiom, not the Biblical. It is heavy with projections, statistics, and econometric models. Ezekiel didn't have the advantage of computers and data banks, but he certainly was no slouch at peering into the future on the basis of existing conditions, moving trends, and spelling out the inevitable results unless the circumstances were changed. In this last respect the *Global 2000 Report* also points to impending disaster unless things change. The disaster pointed to is not moral collapse, but an environmental collapse during the 21st century caused by over population, shortness of food, water, and energy and pollution of the air, water, and land.

Done at the direction of President Carter, the *Global 2000 Report* was prepared by the Council on Environmental Quality (CEQ) and the Department of State and issued to the public. Since then it has occasioned much comment, more commendatory than critical, and has given rise to a Committee on the Year 2000 made up of leading citizens concerned with the subject. Largely under the leadership of the Chairman of CEQ, an imposing list of recommendations for action, primarily by the U. S. government, has been prepared.

Similar messages have come from study reports from the World Bank, the International Union for the Conservation of Nature and Natural Resources, the United Nations World Model, the Brandt East-West Report, the Club of Rome's Studies on the Limits to Growth, plus others. Furthermore, during the past decade the United Nations and several of its specialized agencies have held so-called megaconferences on population, resources, and environmental issues in Stockholm, Bucharest, and Vancouver. There will be one in Nairobi this summer. I have been a part of this ferment both in and out of government.

Actually the population-resources-environment set of problems is not new. Malthus gave classic definition to it a century and a half ago: population tends to outrun the means of subsistence. It does so even faster, we would now add, if the environment is seriously harmed in the process. The English economist Jevons in 1865 predicted the cessation of industrial growth in Britain by 1900 for lack of fuel. Since World War II in our own country successive waves of books have projected, the end of economic growth. Each wave seems bigger and more threatening than the one before. Some observers believe that the recent breakdown in productivity increase plus the erosion of incomes due to inflation has at last brought us to a no-growth economy. After many times of crying, "Wolf, Wolf!" the wolf has finally appeared according to this view. Other observers disagree.

A few major findings and conclusions of the *Global 2000 Report* give its flavor:

If present trends continue, the world in 2000 will be more crowded, more polluted, less stable ecologically, and more vulnerable to disruption than the world we live in now.

For hundreds of millions of the desperately poor, the outlook for food and other necessities of life will be no better. For many it will be worse . . . unless the nations of the world act decisively to alter current trends.

The world's population will grow from 4 billion in 1975 to 6.35 billion in 2000, an increase of more than 50 percent. . . . Ninety percent of this growth will occur in the poorest countries.

World food production . . . from 1970 to 2000 . . . translates into a global per capita increase of less than 15 percent . . . the real prices for food are expected to double.

During the 1990s world oil production will approach . . . maximum, even with rapidly increasing petroleum prices.

Regional water shortages will become more severe. . . . Development of new water supplies will become more costly.

Growing stocks of commercial-size timber are projected to decline 50 percent per capita.

Serious deterioration of agricultural soils will occur worldwide, due to erosion, loss of organic matter, desertification, salinization, alkaliniza- tion, and waterlogging.

Atmospheric concentrations of carbon dioxide and ozone-depleting chemicals are expected to increase at rates that could alter the world's climate . . . significantly by 2050.

Extinctions of plant and animal species will increase dramatically.

Assuming the outlook is bleak and we are running headlong toward certain destruction, what can be done to prevent the calamity? The general directions are fairly clear: support family planning; encourage conservation, efficiency, and better resource management; protect the natural environment of soil, water, and air, and all life-supporting eco-systems; shift to using renewable rather than non-renewable resources and manage them carefully; educate and train people for earth-keeping; engage in cooperative approaches to resource development and environmental protection with other countries; allocate sufficient investment funds to these tasks.

None of these actions will be easy; each will require profound behavioral changes, improved communication and understanding, major institutional and policy alterations, and innovative leadership. Resistance will be stubborn. I have only to mention the response to family planning, gasoline conservation, or cleaning up spills of toxic chemicals. It seems clear to me that progress toward a cleaner environment and more efficient management of natural resources will be slow unless it is undergirded by a resource and environment ethic with the and sanction of a religious principle.

It should be pointed out that many experts find the *Global 2000 Report* to be far more alarmist than a careful interpretation of the evidence would warrant. Critics of the report fault the methodology by which the gloomy projections are made as well as some of the data used. About this, one critic in a recent issue of *The Public Interest*, refers to G I G O (garbage in, garbage out), and P I P O (prejudice in, prejudice out). He also notes that according to fairly reliable statistics, per capita food consumption has been going up, slowly nearly everywhere in the world; the real cost of many materials, copper for example, has not been rising; and, most significant of all, length of life has been increasing, especially in less developed countries.

We continue to underestimate advances in technology, according to this view, as well as the cleverness and adaptability of people in the face of dire problems. The difficulty they say, is not that the cost of oil production in the Middle East is high, but rather that the OPEC cartel is able to charge monopoly prices by restricting production. Far from the world going to hell in a handbasket, it is muddling along about as usual. H. G. Wells had a neat counter to this last point: the last of the dinosaurs, he said, no doubt thought it was muddling through nicely.

In fairness to the *Global 2000 Report* we should recall that its dire projections are based on the assumption that national policies regarding population stabilization, resource conservation, and environmental protection will remain essentially unchanged through the end of the century. More likely, however, policies will change under the lash of rising prices, new ecological crises, and the perception of technological and institutional opportunities. The *Report* itself notes:

> In some areas forests are being replanted after cutting. Some nations are taking steps to reduce soil losses and desertification. Interest in energy conservation is growing, and large sums are being invested in exploring alternatives to petroleum dependence. The need for family planning is slowly becoming better understood. Water supplies are being improved and waste treatment systems built. High yield seeds are widely available and seed banks are being expanded. Some wildlands with their genetic resources are being protected. Strong efforts are being made in a few places to check the use of highly toxic materials and clean up such spills as have already occurred.

In fact, a major purpose of projections based on present policy is to expose future problems before they occur so that preventive actions can be taken. It is a sad fact of politics that frequently dangers and consequences have to be painted as much worse than they are likely to be, in order to gain support for unpleasant restraints and other actions. A fine point of ethics is involved here: how far and in what instances is it right to stretch the truth to achieve a desirable action? The question is even more perplexing because we don't know what is true and what is speculative about future population, resource, and environmental problems.

The insurance principle, it seems to me, is useful. A prudent individual or family, if financially feasible, will take out an insurance policy against the costs of illness and accidents. Insurance to cover unemployment, old age needs, and disability are provided through social insurance. Even though we hope we will never be sick or have an accident or become unemployed, we are pleased to be insured against these risks. We are willing, with some grousing, to pay the premiums.

It is the same with resource and environmental risks: we should be willing to insure ourselves, our country and our world, where that is possible, against soil losses, water contamination, and air pollution. We should be willing to take out these policies even though we may never need to draw on them. Just as for an individual, there are limits to the amount of insurance a country can carry, but the limits are quite high for a rich country such as ours.

These resource and environmental policies are not typical insurance policies; they contain elements of prevention as well as of cure in them. Most of them involve cooperation among the several levels of government and between the public and private sectors. They include soil conservation programs, water supply and pollution abatement, clean air, control of toxic substances, and ecological preservation. Each of these can be promoted through such measures as tax incentives, direct public outlays and loans, research activities, and education as well as more conventional insurance.

A special word needs to be said about the population, resource, and environmental problems in the economically less developed countries (LDC) of the world. By 2000 four-fifths of the world's population will be in the so-called LDCs. The gap in per capita incomes between the more and the less developed countries will widen from about $4,000 in 1975 to about $7,900 in 2000. At the end of the century 800 million or so persons will have inadequate diets. LDCs are hurt by high oil prices and must use other precious sources of fuel such as wood and dung. Meanwhile, leaders in the LDCs expect their countries to advance economically, as do those of hundreds of millions of ordinary people for whom radios and films have provided a glimpse of the material comforts available in the more developed places.

Obviously a world tinderbox is in the making. Our own country, it seems to me, should address itself vigorously and generously to the matter. Ethics and practical politics dictate such a course. The United States, for all our wealth and income, is near the bottom of the list of countries in the amount of foreign aid it provides relative to per capita income, way below the percentage recommended by the United Nations. My own preference is for greater U.S. contributions through international agencies like the World Bank and the several regional banks and for separation of bilateral economic aid from military aid.

Many specific problems come to mind on which our country could help: soil and agricultural stabilization plus relocation of people in the Sahel, better management of tropical forests, improving irrigation in Pakistan, water purification and pollution control in thousands of places. I spent a week in a small village in the Andes a few months ago. The entire water supply came from one irrigation ditch which carried water for an hour every couple of days. The ditch was used for washing clothes, as a sewer, for crop irrigation and for drinking water. There were several other villages higher up on the ditch. There was no water purification or sewage treatment whatsoever.

The problems are severe and numerous. The trends are foreboding. Utter devastation by 2000 is hardly likely but the eventual outcome is clouded by uncertainty and danger. We wonder what people and governments will do to help the world deal with its population, resource, and environmental problems. I have no doubt solutions, or at least policies can be found, that will keep us ahead of the problems. The real need is for will and determination to settle upon programs of action and pursue them.

Something more than intelligence, political skills, and social discipline are needed. A world outlook is needed: a generosity of spirit, a feeling for the desperate plight of people in faraway lands, a respect for the forces of nature, a willingness to be concerned about the life of future generations.

In short, a religious approach is needed in which human beings, natural resources, and the whole environment are taken into account. Such an approach offers the best promise for a world made livable, enjoyable, fulfilling for all.

Part Three

Community and Caring

I Must Let You Go

Dear little child whose life is still so new
Whose eyes see only light and dark, whose lips
Are parted, searching for your mother's milk.
I love you tenderly, and wish that I
Could hold you every hour, absorbing warm
Security and shielding you from harm.

One day you will be standing up and bravely
Taking steps and falling down
Then standing up again you'll try once more
And you will climb and fall and climb again,
Surmounting fear of hurt and injured pride.
I cannot shield you. I must let you grow.

The day will come when you will go to school
Your mind and body subject to your teacher's care
In competition you will win and lose,
And children will be cruel, and you will cry.
My heart will ache for you, and I would shield
You from the pain, yet I must let you grow.

Then as the years go by our time together
Will be less and less, for you will go
Into the world to find your own identity,
To steer your course on independence bent.
I yearn to shield you, but I know that I
Must cut the apron strings and let you go.

There Is a Bridge

There is a bridge from life to life,
    a common bond of love and trust,
        a tie that reaches over space and time
            and guides us in directions yet unseen,

In times of loneliness it's good to know
    that there's a friend out there who cares —
        a gentle neighbor who would come
            in time of need or just for tea,

It's good to have a friendly place nearby
    where we can go and feel at ease
        with kindred spirits whose concerns
            are sympathetic with our own.

And when we think upon the past —
    on those we loved, who loved us in return,
        we know they helped to shape our lives
            to make us what we are today,

There is a bridge from life to life,
    a common bond of love and trust,
        a tie that reaches over space and time
            and guides us in directions we must go.

Am I My Brother's Keeper?

When Cain brought an offering of grain to the Lord, and his brother Abel brought a lamb, the Lord "had regard for Abel and his offering, but for Cain and his offering he had no regard." This so upset Cain that he went out into the field and killed Abel. When the Lord asked Cain where his brother was, Cain answered, "I do not know; am I my brother's keeper?" The Lord let Cain off easy; his sentence was to be a fugitive and an wanderer on the earth. Perhaps the sentence wasn't so light.

The question "Am I my brother's keeper?" is profound and eternal. Morally and religiously, I assert, the only answer is *yes*.

The question is relevant at two levels: the personal and the social. Am I my brother's or my sister's keeper? In what degree should I be responsible for them and in what situations? At the broader, social level what should be the measure of my concern for the poor, the ill, minority groups, those disadvantaged for whatever reason, wherever they live?

If I am not my brother's or sister's keeper, then I cannot expect him or her to be my keeper. And if neither of us is responsible for the other, nor will take responsibility, are not both of us condemned to be fugitives and wander the earth, rootless, going nowhere—or, as the Book of Genesis tells, dwelling in the land of Nod somewhere east of Eden?

The brother's keeper question is somewhat easier to deal with at the strictly personal level than it is at the broader, social level. Parents do bear major responsibility for their children, or at least they should. For babies the responsibility is almost total; it diminishes thereafter but never to zero. The problem is to loosen the apron strings gracefully as the child matures. This is not an easy assignment for either parents or children. The large number of abused and abandoned children and the small army of runaway teenagers testify to the difficulties many families face.

Children, it is frequently said, owe respect to their parents who in turn owe understanding and assistance to their parents. But the problems associated with the intergenerational web of intimate relations and reconciling the need for dependence with the urge for independence are minor compared with the problems that arise when there is no web at all. One has only to spend a few hours in a domestic relations or juvenile court or make the rounds with a social worker to see the devastation brought about by a break in primary group ties. To the question "Am I my brother's keeper?" a negative answer has been given.

Literature offers numerous examples of both the comic and the tragic aspects of the brother's keeper issue. A couple of weeks ago I went to a production of Eugene O'Neill's play *Ah, Wilderness!* It depicts with love and tenderness the web of relations within a turn-of-the-century American family: episodes as the high school son comes of age; the impossible courtship of the old maid aunt and a bachelor friend who drinks too much; and the dilemmas faced by the parents trying to cope with the personalities around them. Recently O'Neill's *Mourning Becomes Electra,* which portrays another family group in an entirely different vein, has been shown on public television. In this play the web of relations involves love and hate, incest, murder, and deceit: a classic Greek tragedy in an American setting. In the first play each person accepts responsibility for each of the others; in the second play each is bent on destroying one or more of the others. There is no doubt as to which family says yes to the question the Lord put to Cain, and which says no.

The central message is clear: within the relevant social framework—the family, the intermediate neighborhood group, the small bunch of boys or the women's club—each person has the responsibility of accepting, supporting, loving, paying attention to the others, of simply being there when needed. Beyond this is the willingness to help in times of trouble, to sympathize in times of disappointment and defeat, to rejoice in times of success. But being your brother's keeper also carries the obligation of not overdoing the sympathy, the praise, or the help. Otherwise the pride and satisfaction of self-reliance may be sacrificed to the detriment of all. Too lavish an application of love gluts the recipient; too little starves.

Being your brother's keeper at the person-to-person level is basically a religious matter although it often seems like a psychological or educational issue. Honor your father and your mother; love your neighbor as yourself; be kind to your children. Such commandments distill ages of folk wisdom embodied at the heart of religious and ethical teaching of Jesus, Confucius, Mohammed, and Buddha.

The broader, social aspect of my question asks what obligations each of us should feel toward people in our city, our country, or the world? These obligations are harder to define and harder still to discharge. It is more difficult to be a good Samaritan to a stranger. Reinhold Niebuhr has talked about "moral man and immoral society," and how difficult it is for most of us to deal with people in economic and cultural groups other than our own.

I live in a metropolitan region of some three million persons; the number continues to increase rapidly. I live in a country of some 220 million, also growing but less rapidly. I live in a world of slightly more than four billion individuals growing so rapidly that the number will probably reach six billion by the year 2000. If I live until 2000, the population of the world will have increased to more than 3.5 times what it was when I was born in 1914, just before World War I. Like all of you, I want to be a good citizen of my metropolis, my country, and my world. I would like to take some responsibility for the well-being of my fellow citizens wherever they live. But how can I do that in a sustained and practical way? How can I extend the sphere of my concern from my small group of family, neighborhood, and close associates to the globe itself, the whole of spaceship earth? In particular, how can I bring within my concept of brotherhood my responsibility as keeper of those who don't look like us, don't think quite the way we do, eat and dress differently, occupy different economic and social stations, have a different set of prejudices, go to different schools, and may even not like us?

I mentioned earlier the trend in world population, two billion more persons by around 2000. Nearly 90 percent of this increase is expected to be in the developing countries. At the end of this century almost eight out of every ten persons in the world will live in those countries. In most of Latin America, Asia, and Africa even small gains in per capita food production and consumption will be hard to achieve. Improvements in the nutritional quality of diets there will be even harder to attain. The International Labor Office has estimated that 30 percent of the labor force in developing countries will be unemployed or underemployed by 1980 and may be no better in 2000. Difficult economic conditions in rural areas will continue to drive peasants and their families to the shanty towns in the urban areas. Medium-level projections show a two- to three- fold increase by 2000 in the population of Calcutta, Bombay, Cairo, Jakarta, Tehran, Bogota and Lagos. The United Nations estimates an unbelievable 31.6 million population in Mexico City. Public services of all kinds—water supply, waste disposal, electricity, transportation, schools, public health facilities—will be severely taxed. Good housing will be scarce and the natural environment will have to absorb much pollution.

In the face of these all but overwhelming population-resource problems in the developing countries or the world, what can be done? The two broad lines of attack are clear: increase the industrial plants and equipment to produce food, energy, and water supply on the one hand, and check the growth in population on the other hand. Neither will be easy. The first will cost lots of money; the second will require profound behavioral changes. As citizens of the United States, fortunately one of the developed countries, we can help. We can support population and resource development programs of United Nations agencies like the United Nations Fund for Population Activities, the Food and Agriculture Organization, and the World Bank. We can also support aid programs of our own government as well as activities of non-governmental groups including private business firms involved in overseas trade and investment. Through such organizations headway can be made in extending family planning, increasing agricultural productivity, improving public health and education, and training managers for new enterprises.

At the U.N. World Population Conference several years ago in which I participated, a gentleman from Sri Lanka with whom I was having tea one afternoon suggested that in return for his country and other developing countries agreeing to check their population growth, my country and the other developed countries should be willing to check our increasing consumption of energy and other resources, and stop polluting of the oceans and atmosphere of the world. A reasonable bargain, you might say, but not an easy one for either party to keep. The same point was made to me by one of the panchayat, or elders, of an Indian village I once visited. We were standing by the village well talking while my Indian companion translated. Dozens of lively children were in the scene, playing games and running around. Taking it all in, the old gentleman said, "If we in this village had more of your wheat and machinery, perhaps our families would not have to have so many children."

Should we in rich countries feel obligated to help people in poor countries with private and public dollars? Should we respond generously whether or not it increases our national security, makes good business sense, or is appreciated by the recipients? If we believe in the brother's keeper ethic, we will be forthcoming in our response and lean to the side of generosity, striving to see that the aid is delivered to those who need it.

Within the United States poverty is still a condition of life for many. In 1977 some 24 million persons, one in nine, were below the poverty line—$6,157 for a family of four—according to the Census Bureau. Poverty tends to be concentrated in families with quite a few children, in central cities, among blacks and most other minority groups, and among older people. A news release the other day noted that, after taking into account the cost of living, Maine not Mississippi is the poorest state. Although the number below the poverty line has decreased since the early 1960s when statistics were first gathered, but has not decreased during the past five years. Of course, the poverty line is not very high. It affords only a minimum level of living even when the funds are carefully managed.

Most poor people receive welfare assistance. In 1977 the average monthly number of recipients in the Aid to Families With Dependent Children was about 11 million; Supplementary Security Income for the blind, aged, and disabled came to 4.5 million; Food Stamps, 17 million; Veterans Pensions, 3.5 million; Medicaid, 9 million; Public Housing, 3.3 million; General Assistance from state and local governments, 1 million; and the Earned Income Tax Credit for low income families, 15 million. The total cost for that year was about $50 billion. In addition to all of this are the numerous private charities, such as the Red Cross and the Salvation Army, that minister to the poor. Welfare in this country is a farflung and confusing array of organizations and programs.

The difficulties with our welfare system, are numerous: exclusion of millions of needy persons from eligibility for benefits, inclusion of many others who don't deserve or even need help, wide variations in benefit levels ranging from meager to generous, unintended penalties against marriage and family stability, work disincentives, high error rates in determining both eligibility and benefits, a certain amount of fraud and abuse, lack of coordination among the numerous programs, high costs, administrative complexity, and occasional harsh treatment of some recipients. In short, we need welfare reform.

As a member of the special Welfare Reform Committee of the House of Representatives, investigating welfare programs in New York City, I concluded that most Americans would be willing to support welfare programs with their taxes, and support them quite generously, but they first had to be convinced that welfare could be administered fairly and efficiently. And this requires reform to correct the inequities and maladministration. Tax payers want to be assured that ineligible people should not get them, and that those who need them do. This implies efficient administration, streamlined programs, strong incentives to move people off welfare roles into jobs or job training, and limits on the total cost of welfare. Private programs for poor and needy people can be encouraged by permitting taxpayers to deduct charitable contributions from income subject to tax. I have proposed this in Congress.

Citizens should insist that their elected legislators and leaders reform and improve the welfare and other programs that those who live in poverty assist. Once these changes have been made people everywhere will respond generously with their financial and moral support. Taking responsibility for your "brother" means political and private group action as well as the old-fashioned, one-on-one approach.

Being your brother's keeper calls for accepting a range of individual and social responsibilities, and pursuing actions from voting and paying taxes to volunteering and making financial contributions. But most of all it requires a religious commitment that people can become better, and make their world better when each person cares for others, assumes a responsibility for others, and will be his brother's keeper both at home and abroad.

Recently, my wife took from our library shelf a copy of our dear friend A. Powell Davies's book of sermons, *The Faith of An Unrepentant Liberal,* including one titled, "Am I My Brother's Keeper?" Dr. Davies, who had a distinguished ministry during the 1940s and 50s at All Souls Unitarian Church in Washington, D.C., developed his sermon along quite different lines.

> . . . for the hour has come when all the earth must face the most
> persistent question of the ages, and answer to the future and to God:
> I am my brother's keeper.

The task of religion is to provide perspective on problems of poverty, ill health, racial and national minorities, over-population, and lack of enough food; to provide perspective for the people problems in their full ethical as well as their social, economic, and psychological dimensions. The task of religion is to support the application of personal problems others immediately at hand as well as to broader social conditions in ways that yield progress, that give the persons involved a sense of purpose and direction and a confidence that comes from realizing he is not alone. Each person can find greater self fulfillment through helping others and, in return receiving help from them.

Surely I am my brother's keeper and you are your brother's keeper, but you and I will do a better job of it if each of us keeps his own house in order. Caring, like charity, begins at home with your self, your family, your friends and neighbors. With this foundation our caring can grow outward to embrace city, country, and the world—everybody, everywhere.

God of all people, hear our statement:
   To love, to care, to pay attention —
   That is what is required of us,
   If *yes* is to be our answer
   To the profound and timeless query,
      Am I my brother's keeper?

CHAPTER FOURTEEN
RELIGION AND VOLUNTEERING

A Special Wealth

Each of us has much to give
If we but search within ourselves.
It may be talent in the arts
That others can enjoy and share.
We may be skillful with our hands
Or with ability to speak in foreign tongues,
Ability to heal, to teach,
To listen and respond,
To show compassion and to proffer
Strength and genuine concern.
This is a very special wealth
To share, a wealth that grows as it
Is spread about and multiplied,
Returning home a thousandfold.

The Volunteering Tradition

It is customary to begin a discussion of volunteering in America with a reference to de Tocqueville, the remarkable Frenchman who travelled here 150 years ago and wrote *Democracy in America,* in which with keen insight he characterized the purpose, style, and direction of life on this continent. He noted the disposition to "constantly form associations" and to solve community problems through voluntary citizen action.

Volunteerism has built churches and schoolhouses, raised barns, started hospitals, established law and order, and stitched quilts. It harvested crops, set up labor unions, and organized almost any enterprise you can think of. Recently many people have thought the volunteering tradition was dead. I disagree, even while I am sure it could stand an infusion of new blood.

A few weeks ago I gave a talk at the annual meeting and fair of the New River Community Action in Christiansburg, in Southwest Virginia. This coalition of public and private agencies, carries on community betterment programs. Several hundred people came from surrounding towns. It was a grand occasion. When the time came for awards and recognitions, a beautiful white-haired lady presented me with a quilt made by a group of quilters which included, I was told, a few men. The group meets two or three times a week. (There used to be a bumper sticker: "Old Quilters Stitch Together.") Anyway the quilts, which are works of art, are donated and sold to New River Community Action, which uses the proceeds for health, education, and other activities. Thousands of dollars are raised each year.

The volunteer tradition is not dead. A recent issue of *Voluntary Action Leadership* gave examples:

- Long Island's Northshore University Hospital is one of six Human Milk Banks operating around the country. More than 500 women have registered to be volunteer donors of milk for newborn infants that require human milk but whose mothers are unable to provide it.

- Earthwatch, based in Belmont, Massachusetts, matches volunteers with scientific expeditions around the world. This year, some 1,300 volunteers will be involved in 65 expeditions to every continent except Antarctica. Volunteers pay up to $800 plus time and travel costs for the privilege of spending two to three weeks living in tents.

- In Columbus, Ohio, over a score of nursing mothers offered to provide live demonstrations to teach female gorillas at the Columbus Zoo how to breastfeed their infants. The zoo practice of separating mother and baby gorilla may have contributed to the spread of an intestinal disease among infants that may be prevented by nursing.

- AirLifeLine is an organization of pilots who fly for a hobby and provide free airfield-to-airfield transportation service in medical emergencies. Chapters are being developed in 18 states.

- In Chicago, volunteers annually staff the Yule Connection, a telephone hotline service for those who suffer special problems during the holiday season. Last year more than 2,000 volunteers handled calls from those who were alone, felt isolated, or had special needs for food and shelter.

- The St. Bernard Parish, Louisiana, Deputy Corps includes 120 citizens who volunteer to assist the sheriff's office for duties ranging from front-line patrols who answer calls to controlling crowds at parades and high school sports events. In Los Angeles a shortage of paid clerks was endangering the police department's ability to maintain current, useful information. Retired police officers, including an ex-deputy chief, volunteered with civilians to serve as file clerks.

- Also in Los Angeles, organizers of the 1984 Summer Olympics involved as many as 10,000 volunteers in all phases of the games, both as a means of holding down costs and to help build community spirit. Volunteers made up almost 80 percent of the total Olympics staff.

The volunteering tradition is not dead, not by any means! But it needs to be adapted to modern circumstances and given a shot in the arm. And I will argue that the religious impulse for volunteering needs to be reestablished and reinforced.

Sociologists have pointed to trends that have led Americans away from its volunteering tradition. The old-fashioned quilting bee survives with difficulty in an industrial society with its impersonal cities and more women in the labor force. The automobile and the TV set—those two technological contraptions of immense social force—have contributed heavily to the declining influence of family, neighborhood, church, and other institutions in which volunteerism has thrived. The country is still suffering fall-out from the self-centered "me generation," which flowered in the late 1960s and 1970s. The essence of that curious period was captured in the defiant popular song, "I'll do it my way." Many citizens seem to have concluded that government has over-extended itself in taking responsibility for community and social problems. "We must get the government off our backs," Ronald Reagan said in one of the most effective one-liners in the history of American politics. To back up his program, he eliminated government regulations and cut government spending on social programs. This, along with tax reductions, he said, was the way to the promised land of individual responsibility and fiscal sanity.

In accepting the 1980 Alexis de Tocqueville Award from United Way of America, Theodore M. Hesburgh, President of the University of Notre Dame, said:

There is a spirit here that needs to be rediscovered, cleansed from over-regulation, and reinvigorated in modern America. This spirit is the antithesis of the attitude: "Let government do it." This spirit transcends the meddling of excessive and irrational federal regulations and nitpicking bureaucrats who pile up mountains of meaningless reports. This spirit surmounts the single-issues zealots, unmindful of the common good of the nation and the world. This spirit springs from free citizens who prize and use their freedom to touch humanity in its basic needs and anguishes, by dedicated service, freely given. Voluntarism, in its variegated manifestations, is America uniquely at its best.

The Republican Party Platform of that year developed a similar theme: "The American ethic of neighbor helping neighbor has been an essential factor in the building of our nation. . . . Government must never elbow aside private institutions—schools, churches, volunteer groups, labor and professional associations—in meeting the social needs in our neighborhoods and communities."

Let me say, as a Democrat, there is truth in what the so-and-so's say; so much truth, in fact, that the Democratic Party makes similar professions. Of course, it isn't an either-or matter, either public action for community and social improvement or private action. Both are needed, but especially more private, voluntary action. How can more private, voluntary action be motivated and stimulated? How can volunteerism be encouraged as the expression of, in Father Hesburgh's words, "America uniquely at its best"?

Several years ago while in Congress I became interested in using the tax system to encourage private donations to charities. We developed an amendment to the tax code permitting those who took the standard deductions on their individual income tax returns to list and deduct charitable contributions separately. Known as the Fisher-Conable amendment and subsequently enacted, it will mean $4 or $5 billion more a year flowing to hospitals, churches, educational institutions, and community fund organizations.

As Secretary of Human Resources for the Commonwealth of Virginia I supervised a new neighborhood assistance program through which business firms are awarded state income tax credits for money they donate to community improvement projects for health, youth, job training, and recreation. A furniture factory, an architecture firm, a group of accountants, and an undertaker participated.

Through our Division of Volunteerism we developed a legislative proposal whereby the state would put up one dollar for specific kinds of community projects if local governments would also put up one dollar and private sources would subscribe two dollars of new money. In this way the Division would be able to tease private money to do public good.

Some years ago when I was a member of the Arlington County Board, we worked out a program called Citizen Initiatives for County Improvement (CICI) by which the county government offered to match funds up to $5,000 raised by local nonprofit groups for innovative community improvement. It had the potential of being carried on without government support after a year or two. This local program was a forerunner of the mini-grants for community projects.

A little public money can stimulate private, voluntary action for the community or move responsibility toward the private sector. There are many ways to do it. We should experiment along these lines, taking care not to over-estimate the capacity of the private sector. I believe there is a religious element in this going beyond social conscience and citizen responsibility. The positive desire to volunteer to help others, to help one's community, must ultimately be a matter of deep personal conviction if it is to be done freely and generously. It is a sharing and caring, a sharing of oneself and a caring for others, that goes beyond any tax advantage or investment in business good will.

No doubt there are subtleties about giving and volunteering. Altruism and self-interest are mixed in fascinating ways, not all of them commendable. Years ago when I was living in Southeast Alaska, I learned about the Indian potlatch. This was a gathering of people from far and wide, a fair, at which goods and gossip were traded. Much was made of giving gifts.

Anthropologists who have looked into this custom have concluded that frequently a gift placed the recipient under obligation to give even more generously in return. Giving became competitive. One-upmanship abounded. A gift would be calculated to elicit a particular gift in return. If I wanted your fish net, I would give you my canoe paddle if that would turn the trick. The potlatch must have been a psychological field day, with each giver seeking group approval and self-approval as well as a sought-after return gift. Perhaps here as in other cultures, the true giver is the one who gives until it hurts. The psychological tracery of giving and receiving seems never to end. The Indians enjoyed the potlatch as the big event of the season and usually paddled off home at the end thinking they had done well in this unusual kind of trading.

So it is with the volunteers gift of time and effort. Motives may be mixed, but if the results are good I am not inclined to probe the motives. "Give that you may receive" is good advice. Neil Karn, director of the Virginia Division of Volunteerism and a national leader in this field, drew my attention to a Gallup survey done for Independent Sector, a new coalition of nonprofit organizations. The survey reported that the value of volunteer activities in 1980 came to $64.5 billion. Someone has said, "Statistics are like bikinis; they reveal what is interesting, but conceal what is essential." Neil says the essential that is concealed in $64.5 billion, is the intangible benefit of a volunteer program—the "volunteer differential," he calls it. In *Money Talks: A Guide to Establishing the True Dollar Value of Volunteer Time,* he says:

> Although admittedly difficult to measure, these benefits probably constitute a significant portion of the volunteer product. . . . Big Brothers and Big Sisters provide positive role models for troubled youth. Recovered victims of debilitating diseases bring to new sufferers a special empathy and understanding of the experience. Hospital auxiliaries engender an environment of caring and concern and improve patient morale. Mental health volunteers hasten the resocialization and ease the reintegration of patients preparing to return home. Volunteers in prisons build trusting relationships with offenders that elude correctional staff. Citizen involvement in public agencies improves community relations by debunking myths and exposing the public to the real problems confronting the agency. Volunteers afford sanction . . . volunteers are the best advocates and fund raisers . . . volunteers. . . .

Challenging volunteer opportunities exist in government programs such as VISTA (Volunteers In Service To America), the Peace Corps, RSVP (Retired Seniors Volunteer Program), and ACTION, among others. In these programs the pay is minimal but the contributions are large. Three of our own children have served in one or another of these programs. They have benefitted greatly, those they served have benefitted; and the United States as a country has benefitted. Returns on the dollars spent are high, due primarily, I believe, to the enthusiasm and dedication of the volunteers—the volunteer differential.

A few years ago I visited one of our sons who was a Peace Corps volunteer in a small village in the altiplano of Ecuador. One day I went with him to help a peasant family construct a beehive oven in the corner of the main and only room of their house. It was an engrossing project: packing of the clay, scooping out of the interior, and affixing the chimney. The entire family was involved, including the dog and the chickens underfoot. The potential gains from using an oven rather than an open fire inside the room were immense: no suffocating smoke in the house, a saving of at least half the wood; no singed eyebrows. After the work was done, Jim and I were treated to a meal of chicken stew and bread. The heads of the chickens were placed in my bowl as a special honor. This was volunteer help at the grass roots of a society where good relations between countries and people truly can be built.

On another occasion my wife and I had at least a glimpse of the work our VISTA daughter was doing to help Cuban and Haitian refugees in the Miami area. Her job was to recruit volunteers to assist with the programs. The recruitment and training of volunteers is fast becoming a profession itself.

The American military tradition calls for a volunteer army, navy, air force, and marines. The proposal for extending military service to community and national service generally has merit. The chief bone of contention is whether or not to require such service of all young people for a year or so. It is hard for me to imagine an America without volunteers. Like you, I hope the volunteering tradition can be reaffirmed and strengthened. It is one of the most precious elements in our national life. It makes living in communities satisfying; it gives meaning to neighborhoods; it enables people to feel good about themselves. Volunteering lifts the human spirit. Undeniably there is a religious aspect to volunteering when it is done freely and generously. The more of it, the better, I say.

Protector of the human spirit:
    God, man, woman, whatever —
    Accord a special place to those who come forward on their own
    To do the life-restoring, spirit-building work
    That makes the whole adventure of living
    Religious in the deepest sense.

Monuments

These are the city's monuments —
a gleaming dome, an obelisk,
a slab of stone, a carillon,
a simple cross, a jeweled mosque,
a temple carved from ancient stone.

Upon the city's pedestals
we see a soldier standing guard
or scholar with a manuscript
or statesman who has left his mark
or prophet poet who was heard.

These are the city's monuments —
the growing universities
and halls for music, song, and dance,
and halls for drama, galleries for art,
museums, schools, and libraries.

The city's parks are monuments
to love of nature and of peace,
to beauty and the soul's release
where birds and squirrels come to share
a crumb of bread that we can spare.

These are the city's monuments —
the caring homes for handicapped,
and homes for those whose work is done,
and homes for homeless and abused,
and halfway homes for troubled youth.

Throughout the ages monuments
have symbolized the human need
for beauty, peace, and dignity,
for pride in sacrifice and deed,
and worship's inner sanctity.

What Makes A City Great?

Years ago when I was a student in London, I used to roam in that sprawling, colorful metropolis along the Thames, into the deserted financial district called the City, into the posh Mayfair or the down-at-the-heels Bloomsbury with its students and eccentrics, around Piccadilly Circus, back into Soho for a cup of coffee, down to the East End and the wharves, perhaps by the Underground out to Chelsea or Hampstead. It was a marvelous way to absorb the kaleidoscope of London. For an impressionable young American who had lived the preceding few winters in a small Maine town and summers in the Maine woods, it was a "totally new experience" as the TV commercial says. Incidentally, I never gave a thought in those days to safety in the streets.

Since then I have come to know other cities quite well in Europe, Latin America, and especially in North America. Each is different in certain respects yet they are the same. The pace of life is faster in cities. People jostle one another for jobs, for a seat on the bus, for recreation, for ideas, even for solitude. Change comes faster in the cities. New people wash in like waves. A potato famine drove the Irish to Boston. Escape from political oppression in other countries continues to bring freedom-loving people to our cities. Others have come seeking better jobs, better schools and health care, a release from traditional restrictions. Many of the immigrants to northern cities in this country, including Washington, have come from the rural South. Like the earlier immigrants from Europe, they come first to the central cities, then spill into the suburbs, impelled by dimly understood economic, social, and psychological forces.

Each American family has had its own Odyssey beginning from roots in West Africa, Central Europe, Japan, or Scandinavia to some American city.

Cities have become home for most Americans. Seven out of ten Americans live in metropolitan areas and nearly three of them live in central cities including Washington. The remaining three-plus live in nonmetropolitan areas. For the entire period of our national history until the last few years, cities have been losing population. Washington has fewer inhabitants now than eight years ago. People have been moving out from downtown and are no longer coming in from outside. The close-in suburbs are not growing, either. Only the outer suburbs and the ex-urban countryside beyond are growing. The tidal wave of migration from the farms to the cities has stopped. Cities are no longer a powerful magnet.

At the same time urban problems worsen, especially in the central cities. Air pollution is worse; traffic congestion causes loss of time and patience; water and sewage disposal increase in cost; decent affordable housing is not available; street crime and white collar crime abound; taxes are high; industrial firms move out of cities; and government is deplorably inefficient. Whether people leave cities because conditions are worsening or whether the conditions are deteriorating because people are leaving is debatable. In any event many of our cities spiral downward. Young people used to go to cities for jobs, for better public services and housing, and to escape boredom and loneliness. Now they leave cities for the suburbs and country for the same reasons.

How can cities become again preferred places to work and live? What are the obstacles? Who will take the lead in restoring the quality of urban life? How can federal and state governments help? What can private agencies and churches do beyond what they are already doing?

In a recent issue of the *Wall Street Journal,* Irving Kristol wrote:

> It was always a more squalid than gracious city, but it used to be a place of opportunity for its teeming population. In the last quarter of a century, however, it has fallen on hard times. Its manufacturing base has steadily declined; unemployment has skyrocketed; the welfare rolls have been increasing inexorably; the municipal treasury is effectively bankrupt; whole areas have been vandalized and abandoned; crime, alcoholism and other species of social pathology have reached quite incredible heights.

The national government has not been inattentive. It has poured hundreds of millions of dollars into subsidized housing and subsidized employment. But the only visible consequence of such a compassionate policy has been to increase the size of the dependent population and further to demoralize it. The entire city today seems on the verge of becoming a violent slum, and the policy makers are at their wits' end as to what to do about it.

The city in question is Glasgow, Scotland, inhabited by a people famous, if not for their sobriety, then at least for their diligence, thrift and self-reliance. And this should give us pause for thought as we await President Carter's new urban program. For it suggests how intractable the problems of a declining city can be.

This harsh characterization also applies to New York City and to other American cities. Well-meaning efforts to improve urban conditions have not met expectations. Erosion of the quality of urban living cannot be countenanced. Troubled cities mean troubled people, a troubled country, and a troubled world.

Revitalized cities provide enough jobs for people out of work. Manufacturing operations can be carried on more efficiently where cheaper, plentiful land can accommodate spread-out, one-story plants and the large parking lots for workers. Downtown, however, remains an advantageous location for banking, insurance, trade, government, entertainment, and other services that thrive in high rise buildings in close proximity. New job creating efforts should move with the tide: government tax credits, low-cost, long-term guaranteed loans broader monetary and fiscal policies to stimulate central city investments, and appropriate zoning and building codes. The important thing is to move harmoniously with economic forces and not to buck them. The argument between moving people to where jobs are, or jobs to where people are is not fruitful. Some of each will be needed.

Unemployment remains at an intolerably high level. But the rate for minorities is twice as high, and for youth 16 to 19 years old it is two and one-half times as high. For minority youth in central cities the unemployment rate climbs to nearly 40 percent. This could be social dynamite. The economic cost of unemployment in terms of output of goods and services is great; the human cost in terms of individual dignity, family strength, work habits, and feeling right about your country is incalculably greater. We should give principal attention to encouraging private hiring, improving learning-on-the-job programs, and creating additional youth corps, short-term differentials in minimum wages for youths, and public service jobs. We need an all-out attack.

The physical and social environment of cities also must be improved. The so-called built environment of our cities is old and worn out. Some can be restored; others will have to be and replaced. Each city will have to chip away at a monumental task. Planners, and builders will have to lead the way, with citizens providing sustained financial support. There will be no easy road back for most American cities even with stable or falling populations and the most efficient designs possible. Cities need pinpointed housing assistance, urban homesteading, back-up mortgage support, mass transit, better program coordination, community block grants, attention to smaller neighborhoods where people really live. This is a tall order when taxes and inflation are high, and competition for public spending keen. I suggest a ten-year urban rebuilding plan. People will be surprised at how much they can do in ten years of well directed effort.

Cities have a natural as well as a built in environment. More than steel and concrete, asphalt streets, and utility pipes, cities are backyards and parks, lakes and rivers, trees and gardens. Looking out of my study window yesterday while writing this, I saw a rabbit, several squirrels, fish in my fish pond, cardinals, blue jays, morning doves, sparrows, a tufted titmouse, one robin, and two sea gulls. And I live in an inner suburb of the nation's capital ten minutes away from the White House by car.

Air and water pollution, solid waste disposal, noise, congestion, and landscape disfigurement are also of concern to city folk. Many of us who live in cities, find urban living almost too complicated to cope with. If we crave a drink of cool, unchlorinated water, we can't just go to the well. If we want a breath of sweet fresh air, where is it to be drawn? If we need an hour to be alone, where do we go? If we want to stroll on a hot evening, what safe street or park do we walk along? Taking better care of the natural environment in our cities is a good way to improve them. A better cared for park, a cleaned up neighborhood, a program for protecting birds, the cultivation of small garden plots, and the beautification of river and stream banks can change the nature of urban living. Many programs to bring cities back to life can be started by small groups of concerned people: a scout troop, a church group, a community action program.

In one of his ballads on city life, Tom Lehrer sang:

> Of just two things you must beware:
> Don't drink the water, don't breathe the air.

To prevent this dire catastrophe, or anything approaching it, all levels of government and all urban citizens must get on with the job of setting and enforcing tough but realistic standards for air and water quality, for noise and congestion, and for land use. Where possible, tax, penalty, and other incentives should be employed to induce industries, government agencies, and people generally to stop abusing the natural environment of cities.

Third is the need to reorganize city and metropolitan finance if urban living is to become satisfactory once again, and to make the administration of urban affairs more efficient. New York City, for example, has sunk into a financial morass of escalating costs, declining tax base, welfare cases, loss of potential leaders, rigidities and inefficiencies, throughout. In varying degrees, other cities exhibit the same dreary syndrome. How can these engines of decline be made to reverse direction, or at least be slowed down?

In a real sense, the financial plight of so many of our large cities is simply the dollar and cents result of the other problems I have been considering: the physical decay, the environmental deterioration, and the erosion of the economic base. Still, bankruptcy does stare New York and other cities in the face, and it has to be dealt with. Patch-up grants, bail-out loans, and other short-term palliatives may stave off the day of reckoning, but they will not save a single city unless, during the additional time they allow, more permanent reforms are put in motion. Among the longer term measures required are these: stringent cost containment in which public employee unions cooperate, more federal government help with welfare, further resort to user charges for certain public services, taxes on industries that pollute the air and water, financing of regional functions such as transit on a regionwide basis, greater state assistance for education and health programs, and encouragement of voluntary private efforts where possible as a substitute for governmental activities.

As an example of this last, I would cite several efforts I sponsored when I was a member of the governing board of Arlington County in Northern Virginia. A modest neighborhood conservation program was developed through which the County put up funds to build sidewalks, curbs, and gutters and improve streets in a neighborhood if the residents developed a general improvement plan for the houses, yards, and play areas and agreed to do these elements themselves. Some thirty neighborhoods have completed their programs so far. A similar effort has been launched for business areas. In ways like this a little government encouragement and money, when matched many times over by citizen participation, can go a long way toward remaking neighborhoods which are, after all, the vital components of a city. In the course of improving their neighborhoods, the neighbors invariably find satisfaction in the espirit of getting together to help one another to work on a project together.

This brings me finally to the spiritual and religious aspect of cities and people—really the most important aspect. What makes a city great? Jobs? Clean air? Sound finance? Efficient administration? These all help, for sure, but it takes more to make a city great. It takes a sense of community purpose, a devotion to ideals for the city's future. It takes a willingness to share the burdens, especially of those most in need. It takes a feeling of solidarity on the part of all citizens, a binding together that is both mystical and practical. A true city is a statement to the world that its inhabitants can live together in a finite space peacefully and happily, respectful and caring of one another, engaged constructively in common endeavors, nourishing and being nourished by the culture they create.

What makes a city strong and great?
Not strength nor brick nor wood.
But justice, love, and brotherhood,
And men who see the civic wrong
And give their lives to make it right.

Building St. Augustine's City of God in New York or London or Washington is probably beyond our capacity. But we can aspire to right some civic wrongs and, as we see opportunities, promote justice, love, and brotherhood. Especially the churches, I believe, can do these things as part of their mission to minister to the needs of people and lift up their spirits. Religious groups are credible and can be effective in reducing complaisance with corruption; they can reach out to welcome newcomers and to comfort the distraught and the dispossessed; they can help make fractured individuals whole again.

After surveying the immense complexities of new York City E.B. White once wrote: "The miracle is that the city works at all." Cities now need a second miracle: To make the city work humanely, compassionately, and religiously so as to restore dignity and joy and hope to the lives of its inhabitants. This should be the nation's urban policy for the future.

Universal Architect and Builder:
Instruct us how to make our city great;
to give it —
        Pleasing form,
        Efficient function,
        Graceful style,
        A caring heart;
That it may be restored to health
And we, its citizens, as well.

A House of Cards

Though I have wealth and worldly goods,
  if I ignore the plight of those in poverty,
  I am myself impoverished.
For if I close my eyes to homelessness,
  to nakedness and hunger,
  to illness and to suffering,
My wealth is then diminished. It is meaningless.

Though I have education, knowledge, and acuity,
  if I neglect the plight of ignorance
  and mental disability,
My own potential is not realized.
For if I fail to use the benefits
  of education for those whose lives
  are threatened with destruction,
Then I myself shall live in ignorance.

Though I enjoy acceptance in society,
  if I ignore the lonely and the insecure,
  my own security is tenuous.
For if I am insensitive to fear,
  to prejudice and isolation,
  to suffering and humiliation,
Then I have built myself a house of cards
  with poverty of body, mind, and soul.

Poverty in an Affluent Society:
A Religious Challenge

Surely one of the profound ironies of recent times in the United States is the continued widespread poverty in the midst of affluence. Evidence of this is everywhere to be seen. Walk about in our central cities, and you will see urban poverty in row houses, and tenements. Drive through our backwater rural areas and you will see country poverty in tarpaper shacks and trailers. You will also see penthouses and luxury apartments in the city and mansions in the country. Even in the comfortable suburbs you can find pockets of poverty.

The income spread between the top five or ten percent and the lowest twenty or thirty percent is wide, matching the disparity in housing. The gap has not been narrowing significantly. Even hunger continues to be the daily condition of millions of Americans and of many Virginians as a recent General Assembly committee report on hunger will attest.

Our own Commonwealth of Virginia is no exception. We have plenty of poverty. In fact, in the 1980s it began to increase again after a 20-year decline. The increase during the past four years has been around 25 percent. I am referring here to those below the official poverty line. Some 825,000 Virginians are below the poverty line, more than one out of every seven.

Here are some profiles of poverty:

- a middle aged man, laid off from his job in a declining industry five years ago, unable to find work, unemployment insurance run out, afraid to enter a retraining program, unwilling to stick to a lower paid job, broken family, started drinking, gradually lost interest in work and finally in just about everything;

- a young man, or woman, low IQ, mildly retarded, never got into any proper treatment or training program somehow; left school special education too soon, drifting on the edge of society, no visible means of support;

- a young woman, raised in poverty, no stable family herself, victim of child abuse and neglect, drugs always on the scene and a user herself, pregnant and a mother at age 16, minimum schooling;

- an old man, or more likely a woman, since women outlive men by five years on the average, somehow never qualified for retirement insurance, unable to work at all because of severe arthritis, children scattered and unconcerned;

- a young person, most likely a Black or Hispanic, never able to land that first job, lost in the drug culture, unemployable without rehabilitation, depressed, criminal record; and

- a woman, or a man, anywhere between 30 and 50, with a lowpaying but steady job, making just enough to bar qualifying for welfare, spouse at home but unemployed, several children, unable to quite make it to decent self-sufficiency, one of the working poor.

Poverty in America and in Virginia more and more seems to be concentrated in single parent families headed by women. Almost half the poor people live in such families the number of which has doubled in the past 20 years with the increase in divorce, desertion, and women having children without marrying. This phenomenon is called the "feminization of poverty." Fortunately, and contrary to the general impression, only about one in six families on Aid For Dependent Children programs is locked into the poverty syndrome. They are likely to be Black or Hispanic, to have children outside of marriage, to have a large number of children, to lack a high school degree, and to have had no previous earnings. But the other five do make it back into the regular system; half of them were on welfare for less than two years and another third from three to eight years. There is some recidivism, of course, but we can take heart in the success most welfare recipients have in finding and holding jobs.

Enough of statistics and case histories, for the moment anyway. The matter is clear: poverty continues to afflict our society even as our society grows in affluence. Nothing new in this, you say. Been going on for a long time, perhaps forever. But not with such a productive economy as ours. Not with the most productive agriculture of any country in all history. In short, not with the real possibility of eliminating poverty. But enough of the basics—food, shelter, health care—for everyone in this country seems to remain just beyond our reach, perhaps only by inches.

The most determined, conscious effort to master the poverty problem came during the Kennedy-Johnson-Nixon period. Building on the spurt of welfare and employment efforts of the New Deal in the depression-ridden 1930s, the Great Society period of the 1960s and early 1970s saw Medicare for the elderly, Medicaid for the poor, cost of living adjustments in Social

Security, the Elderly Americans Act, expansion of food stamps, federal aid to elementary and secondary education, community action programs, extension of unemployment insurance to nearly everyone, not to mention WIC, WIN, CETA, and lots more alphabetical efforts—many of these part of the Anti-Poverty Program. Many of these were entitlement programs available to any qualified person who stepped forward.

I watched and took a leading part in establishing the Community Action Agency in Arlington County while I was on the Board of Supervisors. And then a group of us pioneered in establishing an anti-poverty program and agency for the Washington Metropolitan area, before the federal Economic Opportunity Act initiated a national effort. These were heady times, full of idealism and trying new things. Legal assistance, prevention programs in health and social services, assistance in personal financial planning, job training—all of these were brought together in the attack on poverty. Representatives of poverty groups made up a majority of the United Planning Organization as it was, and still is, called.

A monumental and noble national and local effort was put under way. Subsequently it ran into trouble. Beginning around 1973 the economy stopped growing and inflation set in. The pie wasn't getting any bigger and each piece cost more. Later in the 1970s and more so in the 1980s, military expenditures increased. Place these factors against a voters' determination not to raise taxes and the problems on the anti-poverty programs become clear—not enough money to sustain the expansion built into the systems and built into the expectations of recipients.

Furthermore, a case can be made that we bit off more than we could chew. I remember vividly an evening in the White House with President Johnson, with a group who had chaired advisory committees at the start or the term he had just been elected to by an overwhelming vote. During the course of a long evening the President banged his fist on the table and said, "I'm going to put so much social legislation on the books that it will take the country a generation to adjust." Talk about prophetic words!

There are limits to how much government can do in a hurry without outstripping administrative and financial capacity and, more important, without outstripping the willingness of voters to continue their support.

Interestingly, the main elements of the Democratic Great Society Program were endorsed by President Nixon. At another White House session on a similar occasion four years later I heard President Nixon say, "Let me be perfectly clear: I do not intend to dismantle the social legislation recently enacted." In this case he was as good as his word.

During the Carter presidency efforts to deal with poverty weakened. He launched a welfare reform effort that fizzled and advocated larger job-training programs with limited success. Carter had the misfortune to be President during the energy crisis and the years of stagnation and, as he put it, malaise.

Ronald Reagan came riding into Washington in January, 1981, carrying the banner emblazoned with one of the most effective political one-liners in our national history, "Get Government Off Our Backs." This is accomplished, he has communicated to us, by cutting or limiting taxes and by restraining social and other non-defense programs. He said, "One area we will not touch, however, is the safety net for needy Americans." But the Social Security program he agreed to would place 650,000 additional persons below the poverty line, according to the Congressional Budget Office.

We must not be too hard on President Reagan. However we got into the deficit mess, the problem of getting out of it is proving to be excruciatingly difficult without touching the human resource programs. More careful administration, continual review of standards of eligibility, collection of child support payments that are due, extension of food banks, more job training targeted on job opportunities—these, not a meat axe approach to poverty programs, are the ways to go. Incidentally, this story is very well told in Herbert Stein's book, *Presidential Economics*. He is a professor at the University of Virginia.

Our difficulty has been that some of our welfare programs have been stretched so as to include persons well above the poverty line or include services that are not entirely necessary for meeting realistic standards of need. But most of the programs such as Aid For Dependent Children, Food Stamps, and Medicaid, Supplemental Security Income, are means tested and confined to poor, needy persons. Unfortunately there is the lady in Chicago who drove in her Cadillac to the supermarket to spend her food stamps. Her story lives on even though she may never have existed, and it contributes to the disrepute with which many people view welfare.

In this regard an ugly psychology is at work, now as before. Lots of people want to put welfare out of mind, sweep it under the rug. They are uncomfortable with the existence of the problem of those 36 million Americans below the poverty line. They are uneasy about their own relative affluence and like to think that most of the poor would be OK if only they would buckle down to work. Why should my taxes go to provide food stamps for that Chicago lady, they ask over and over again. These poverty moralists are taking a psychological cop-out in my judgment. For whatever reason they fail to face the issue that society and they are unwilling to face the issue head-on.

Having been concerned with these matters before I became Secretary of Human Resources for Virginia, I have come to the view that military expenditures, deficit projections, and the incidence of taxes, are not central to the problem or poverty. As a nation we can afford to do what we need to do to eliminate, or largely eliminate, poverty. So it comes down to what's more important to us as a society and what's less important. I am convinced that as Americans we should trust in our ideals of generosity, of helping those in need, of lifting the yoke of poverty from the backs of all who are poor. And we should act accordingly.

Of course, our federal, state, and local governments should require that those receiving public assistance—with obvious exceptions such as mothers with babies or young children, persons with extreme disabilities, and the elderly—should take suitable jobs if jobs are available and should enroll in training programs. Of course, absent parents earning money should contribute to the support of their children. Of course, welfare cheaters should be rooted out. Of course, no one genuinely in need should fall through the cracks. None of these is easy, but each must be done if citizens are to have confidence in the programs.

But I'm driving at something deeper than administering poverty programs efficiently. Correcting poverty, that age-old problem, is a matter of will and determination, individual and collective. A moral force, a religious impulse, is needed to get the job done. Without this public programs will never be accorded high enough priority. The military, or road builders, or tax cutters will always win out. So in the end we can do what our best values require us to do; we can afford what we want to afford. It's as simple as that and as difficult. That's why I speak of poverty as a religious challenge.

Poverty is not confined to not having enough income to live on decently, or to have acceptable housing or even enough food. The ultimate poverty is poorness in spirit, depression, hopelessness. These characterize the lost souls in our society who need ministry, not administration. I see these persons in mental hospitals, soup lines, and prisons. But the poor in spirit also inhabit offices, workshops, regular homes, even country clubs. They all need help. Even more than for economic poverty, the private and non-profit sectors will have to carry a large share of the responsibility. Frequently a joint government/non-profit effort can be arranged.

In Virginia many examples of such joint effort can be found: the Better Beginnings Program for dealing with teenage pregnancy, the sheltered workshops for physically and mentally retarded persons, other organizations to deal with child abuse, foster parenting, head injuries, developmentally disabled youth, ex-offenders, retired persons, and on and on. All of these groups contribute one way or another to healing the sick at heart, restoring the poor in spirit.

A prescription for curing, or at least alleviating, poverty in this country would include:

- A national program with federal, state, and local components to raise basic welfare payments (ADC, Medicaid, Food Stamps, SSI) to meet minimum needs as defined by poverty standards. An additional program to catch those not covered by the categorical programs might take a number of years to achieve.

- An increase in the earned income tax credit, graduated so as to help the working poor.

- Strict enforcement of support from absent parents.

- Job training programs in cooperation with the private sector for all who can benefit from them.

- A healthy, growing economy that provides jobs for all persons able and willing to work.

- Progressive elimination of barriers to employment and discrimination against minorities, handicapped, women, youth, elderly.

- Imaginative use of incentives (such as taxes, matching grants, subsidized loans, bonuses, public recognition, promotions, special services, and technical aid) to stimulate private anti-poverty efforts.

- Willingness to support good programs with additional taxes.

Finally, what I call the religious challenge must be taken up if people, acting through democratic processes, are to force poverty to the top of the national agenda. I'm with the Catholic bishops who wrote in a recent economics pastoral letter: "Dealing with poverty is not a luxury to which our nation can attend when it finds the time and resources. It represents a strong moral claim on all or us." No great and good deeds are ever accomplished without moral fervor and religious inspiration. Without such a driving force America will not make the headway against poverty that its affluence now makes possible. With it the goal of a decent life for everyone can be achieved.

Keeper of the conscience
  Of those of us with plenty
  Or at least enough:
Remind us of the condition
  Of those who are poor
  In worldly goods or in spirit
That we will offer to help
  In a generous and sustaining way
  As befits a religious community.

The Words of Gandhi

His wiry, wizened body clad
    in plainest doti, feet unshod
        the prophet Gandhi spoke to us
            of good and evil ways.

What good is wealth, he asked the world,
    if unaccompanied by works?
        What pleasure can there be
            when conscience is denied?

What good is commerce when
    morality is set aside?
        What is the worth of knowledge to
            a people lacking character?

What good is science if it lacks
    humanity, if it destroys?
        How can we worship when we fail
            to give—to sacrifice some selfish want?

What good is there in politics
    that function without principle?
        What good is life and work and prayer
            if we deny humanity?

And so the prophet Gandhi spoke,
    his deathless words engraved upon
        the conscience of us all. They killed
            the body, but his soul lives on.

The Evil That Men Do

Criminal behavior and wickedness, to use a vivid but somewhat old-fashioned term, seem to persist in human affairs from one generation to the next, changing only in their outer manifestations. The effort to understand the nature and causes of evil has occupied, frequently preoccupied, the attention of religious leaders from the beginning; similarly, the effort to improve the criminal justice system has been the concern of judges, prosecutors and defense attorneys, and legal scholars. To date their success has not been outstanding. Why should this be so?

One theory has it that men and women have a darker side prone to evil doing, against which they must struggle, never winning entirely and never losing. Redemption is always a possibility but not likely to be realized fully in this world; the forbidden fruit has been eaten, and we have to live with our fall from grace. Confession of sins, repentance, new resolve to sin no more can head us in the right direction and make us feel better about ourselves, but temptation can always take us off the path of virtue. Mephistopheles, the Devil, hangs around with a tempting bargain: power, money, security, revenge, advancement, even love in exchange for our souls. Everyone, I suppose, at some time or other is tempted by a Faustian bargain, though on a less awesome and dramatic scale than that portrayed by Marlowe, Goethe, Gounod, or Thomas Mann.

The dualism of good and evil runs through several religious-philosophical systems and is epitomized by the light and the dark of Zoroastrianism and the yin and yang of the early Chinese. The forces are pitted against each other—the good guys and the bad guys with a shoot-out at high noon every day. Neither side ever quite wins, and the world—this world anyway—is condemned to a permanent draw. Those who fight hardest on the side of goodness have the best chance in heaven or any next world there may be, or in the lottery of reincarnation. And so it goes, as Kurt Vonnegut would say, age after age.

Goethe's way out of this dilemma is to encompass the struggle between good and evil in the mind of God who, in a sense, arranges the whole drama. Faust gains in wisdom and character as a result of experiences during his 24-year pact with the Devil and in the end is saved. Job suffers through another kind of testing and finally is found worthy. Captain Ahab, a tormented, though righteous personality himself, finally destroys the forces of evil represented by Moby Dick, the killer whale, but loses his own sanity and then his life in the process. I think Melville, as well as Goethe, may be saying that the white-black, good-bad dualism is neither a useful nor a truth revealing way of looking at life.

The struggle against sin seems to be a continuing preoccupation of people, although many sins of former years seem quaint and unimportant to us nowadays. My Puritan ancestor, Parson Jonathan Fisher of Bluehill, Maine, never relaxed a minute in concern for his sinning parishioners. His extensive diaries, written in the late 1700s and early 1800s in a mysterious shorthand of his own devising, record that Brother Andrew Wood was charged not only with neglecting family prayer but also with "yoking his oxen on the Sabbath and loading hay between three o'clock and sunset." He escaped excommunication, Mary Ellen Chase wrote in her biography of Reverend Fisher, by his alacrity to make amends. In the year 1800 Benjamin Clough was accused of breaking the Sabbath by "singing a dancing tune" and "speaking reproachfully of church members." In a spirited defense Brother Clough argued that he could "glorify God in a dancing tune as well as by any other" and that the church was only "hardening him in sin" and was "in the same ditch" from which it was vainly trying to haul him. Upon this torrent of language, Mrs. Chase wrote, the Brethren unanimously voted for excommunication. Of course, other breaches of church law that so troubled Reverend Fisher's early Congregationalist soul have a completely modern ring.

Surely there are evil tendencies in the nature of things, and any person may succumb to the temptation to do evil. But the notion that life consists mainly of a battle against the forces of evil with the odds heavily against winning is unacceptable to me. I see good and evil, and all the gradations in between, as parts of one fabric: the fabric of reality, the fabric of life. Each individual, each group, each nation through thought, discipline, and action can, if the will is strong, move to higher, more satisfying levels of morality. Sympathy, patience, and love rather than punishment and damnation are the appropriate means for achieving improvement. Embraces of friendship work better than chains of hate.

Religion, as I see it, should encompass the full spectrum of thoughts and deeds—good, bad, and indifferent—and the full range of people—the bad actors and the good plus those in between—in a single concept, and then build a faith in the ethical superiority of the good, or at least the better, in human terms. People may not be perfectible, but they are improvable. Evildoers can be rehabilitated, made sound and whole again, if the right approach is found.

Admission of guilt and feeling sorry—confession and repentance frequently are the first steps in the restoration process—the return to grace. That such rehabilitation—it has also been called habilitation since evil ways frequently begin in childhood—is possible, I do not doubt. It is a matter of faith in human beings, a divine faith.

This may be heavy and philosophical, but I have a notion that Americans make little headway against evil and crime because we haven't come to terms with them yet at the ethical and religious level. We blink at or turn our backs on wrong-doing. We don't know whether to punish or excuse. We oscillate between a utilitarian idea of justice and punishment—if it works, it's OK—and retribution, in the sense that trespassers should get what they deserve, regardless. We want to see those convicted of crimes dealt with promptly and sternly, but we are unwilling to face up to the costs of modern prisons, more judges and judicial administrators, adequate half-way houses and crime prevention programs. Let's consider some of the issues of criminal justice facing this country at the present time and then, at the end, come back to the religious perspective.

A recent report from the Congressional Research Service of the Library of Congress characterized the situation.

A Gallup Poll conducted in June 1975 indicated that almost half the population of this country fears walking alone at night in their own neighborhood. A more recent poll showed that Americans view crime and lawlessness as the fourth most important problem facing this country today. A look at a few statistics may indicate why there is such widespread public concern about crime.

First, there's more crime in the United States than in any other Western nation, more this year than last year, and much more than in 1965 when the Gallup Poll reported that for the first time Americans viewed crime as one of the most important problems facing the nation. From 1960 to 1975, the number of serious crimes reported to the FBI increased by an alarming 232 percent and the crime rate nearly tripled.

Second, crimes of violence—those that most terrify people—had an even sharper increase, leaping 256 percent from 1960 to 1975. Murder jumped 125 percent; forcible rape went up 226 percent; and robbery more than quadrupled.

Third, statistics have shown that, given the rate at which homicide is increasing in our major cities, an urban American boy born today is more likely to die by murder than an American soldier in World War II was to die in combat.

Fourth, although the cities remain the major centers of crime, the rate of increase is now actually greater in the suburbs and rural areas.

And fifth, the total crime bill in this country is estimated at nearly $90 billion per year—an average of about $420 for every man, woman and child in the United States.

In 1967, the President's Commission on Law Enforcement and Administration of Justice noted that "there is probably no subject of comparable concern to which the nation is devoting so many resources and so much effort with so little knowledge of what it is doing." Since that Commission report, innumerable experts have studied the crime problem, a host of remedies has been suggested and tried, and expenditures for the criminal justice system have tripled. Yet today the situation remains much the same. Officials still see no end to the frightening rise in crime.

There has been little progress in devising solutions because there is little agreement about the causes of crime. The blame has variously been assigned to unjust social conditions, to the permissiveness of society, to unemployment and inflation, to leniency by the courts, and to moral depravity of a few chronic offenders. But whatever the causes of crime, there is general agreement that new methods must be found to deal with it, and that the whole criminal justice system—from criminal codes to prisons to parole procedures—needs re-evaluation.

My approach would be to view the whole criminal justice process as it applies to an individual as a line or as a loop made up of a number of segments. First are the events leading up to the commission of a crime. Then comes the crime itself, followed by arrest, trial, probation perhaps, or prison, parole in some cases, efforts at rehabilitation, and finally release. Problems and opportunities are present all along the line.

The pretrial phase is troublesome: on the one hand we presume people to be innocent until proven guilty, and on the other hand there is the risk to the individual and to society if the offender is let out on bail or personal recognizance. If the individual is detained, suitable facilities have to be available. Even if bail is to be permitted, it is unfair to the poor. They cannot afford bail, nor can they afford to miss work or caring for their families. In either case the individual should be assured a speedy trial. Unfortunately many court dockets are so crowded that months pass before cases are brought to trial. Costly jail space is taken up by persons awaiting trial. And the aphorism, "Justice delayed is justice denied," has much truth in it. In addition is the problem of making sure the poor and less worldly wise are represented adequately by legal counsel. My own experience, as a founder and trustee of the United Planning Organization—the anti-poverty agency in the Washington region—convinced me of the need for competent legal advice and of the importance of fairness and consideration during the pretrial period.

At this pretrial phase plea bargaining frequently takes place. The person under indictment may decide, or be induced, to plead guilty to a lesser crime carrying a lesser sentence or none at all in exchange for avoiding the wear-and-tear of a trial. The plea bargain may also involve revealing names and information the prosecution can use to apprehend or convict accessories or principals in the crime. I think that plea bargaining, in the Watergate trials or any others, is immoral. A person should be tried for the crimes he or she is charged with committing, and not be let off for the convenience of the court. Unfortunately, plea bargaining as commonly practiced is a way the clever and unprincipled can escape full justice.

Thereafter, the trial should be conducted impartially and with dignity according to established rules. Unless there is an acquittal, sentencing follows. Here practice seems to vary, especially in states like Virginia where peer juries with little knowledge of either sentencing standards or the personal history of convicted persons pass the sentences. The comprehensive overhauling of the Federal criminal code, passed recently in the Senate, would establish a new Federal Sentencing Commission to prepare sentencing guidelines for felonies and misdemeanors. Penalties would be permitted to vary by no more than 25 percent. The Attorney General of Virginia has recently put forward a similar proposal covering sentencing under the State's criminal code, but it has not met with much favor in the General Assembly.

The Senate bill clearly subordinates rehabilitation as a purpose in sentencing to deterrence, protection of the public and punishment of the criminal. And it would eliminate parole unless requested by the judge. All in all, the Senate action is a decisive turning away from discretion in sentencing and toward re-educating prisoners. Whether the new, more rigid approach will bring better results remains to be seen. Personally, I doubt that it will.

Probation before jailing continues to be viewed more favorably than parole after jailing. It is still the best way to deal with first offenders who are not dangerous to others. But it has to be monitored closely. Work reliability and performance have to be competently directed, half-way houses are often necessary, and professional guidance has to be continuous. Too often prisons are schools for criminals, thus carefully planned probation can prevent future crime. It is also cheaper. It costs more to send a criminal to San Quentin let alone to a community vocational rehabilitation program, than it does to send a young person to Harvard.

Next is the prison experience which ought to be made as effective as possible protecting society by preventing escape, protecting prisoners from one another, providing them with experiences which will help in eventually restoring them to useful places in society, and keeping them physically and mentally healthy. None of this is easy, and it isn't cheap.

Parole, or partial parole, has long been justified as a way of reintroducing prisoners to ordinary living. Too frequently it has merely been a way of relieving pressure in crowded jails. By all accounts, parole has not been working well; the recidivism rate has been high, and the parole system has been viewed by large numbers of citizens as a threat to personal safety and civil order. An old political campaigner like me knows what a numbing experience it is to knock on an apartment door to speak for a favorite candidate and to have to talk through a closed door or a door ajar on the night latch because the person inside is afraid you are a criminal or a parolee. Yet despite its problems, many criminal justice officials have not given up on parole. A recent 50-state survey of correction officers showed that 63 percent still believe that rehabilitation programs can change inmate behavior for the better. An American Corrections Association statement says that indeterminate sentencing and parole are needed to motivate inmates to take advantage of rehabilitation programs.

Finally, ending the long loop that started with events leading up to a crime comes the release from prison and the reabsorption into the community. Obviously a shirt, a pair of pants, and ten dollars handed out at the prison gate will not be enough of a grubstake to get the freed person started. Help will be needed in job placement, family rebuilding, education, recreation, and general counseling. My impression is that these needs are well tended to in only a few places. Offender Aid and Restoration (OAR) programs deserve community and individual support. The stationery of the Fairfax County OAR carries a quote from Dostoevski, the great Russian novelist who wrote *Crime and Punishment:* "The degree to which a society is civilized can be judged by entering its prisons." We may add: It is judged also by its success in restoring criminals fully to society.

So the loop closes. Will the criminal who has paid his debt truly rejoin his family, his fellow workers, and his community or will he repeat the loop? That depends on the individual and on how successful we are in shoring up, and improving, the criminal justice process.

Many other controversial criminal justice issues could be considered here. Capital punishment has received support lately. However, I find it an unacceptable, admission that a human being is totally beyond redemption. In addition, I find no convincing evidence that capital punishment will deter future murderers.

Gun control is another gut issue of our times. A large fraction of the major crimes such as rape, robbery, and of course, murder involve guns. I would advocate a three-part program to reduce gun-connected crime: enforcement of existing laws with prompt, severe sentencing of those convicted; more effective educational programs in the proper use of firearms; and a ban on concealable hand weapons of the "Saturday night special" type which are the ones most used in gun connected crimes. I am convinced that licenses and permits would be almost impossible to administer effectively and would be unacceptable to a large number of people. As one who has owned guns, enjoyed hunting and target shooting, and as a World War II rifle soldier, I can assure pro-gun enthusiasts that Saturday night specials are no good at all for hunting or hitting bulls eyes. They don't shoot straight.

Street crime is endemic in large American cities. Young male minorities and poor people show a high incidence of such crime. The need for corrective action is urgent. Success will require getting at the root causes: family and neighborhood breakdown, lack of job opportunities, inadequate schools and recreation facilities, and poor leadership. Unemployment among minority high school drop-outs in central city runs up to 50 percent—small wonder that a disproportionate number of them become involved in breaking and entering and robbery. Juveniles or adults who transgress the law have to be dealt with to prevent recurrence.

But crime in city streets is matched by crime in office suites. The U.S. Chamber of Commerce estimates that white-collar crime, sometimes called upper-world crime, costs the nation some $40 billion dollars annually. Bank embezzlers steal more than bank robbers. Violent street crimes cause immediate injury; illegal air pollution works quietly but may cause thousands of casualties. Businesses that overcharge only a penny or two steal more from the public than all the purse snatchers put together. Violations of the anti-trust laws and income taxes, and marketing defective or dangerous products are also crimes. No class, has a monopoly on crime, but the street criminals are sent to prison more frequently than the white collar types. This is grossly unfair.

The litany of deficiencies in the criminal justice process is long and sad. But it pales compared with crimes beyond the reach of the law that we call evil or sin. Jealousy, ambition, lust for power, faithlessness, perpetrating psychological damage, withholding love, excessive pride—each of us can make up our own seven deadly sins. O'Neill has dealt with them one after another in his marvelous but depressing plays.

I see good and evil and all gradations between as part of the fabric of life; religion should encompass the full range and build a faith in human improvability. There are not good persons or bad persons, with the good ones either incarcerating or rehabilitating the bad ones. Each of us has better moments and worse moments; each of us is generous and mean, caring and ignoring, constructive and damaging. None of us is born either with horns or with wings. The hymn says, "What we choose is what we are, and what we love we yet shall be." The role of religion is to encourage making right choices as the way to move toward worthy goals. It is like the role of the parent or teacher or friend but at the most profound level.

For my purposes in this essay-sermon on religion and justice, I want to reverse the words, evil and good, at the opening of Mark Anthony's funeral oration for Julius Caesar: "The *good* that men do lives after them; the *evil* is oft interred with their bones."

Religion, therefore, must include the evil-doers and criminals just as life includes them. Religion owes an example motivation, and a helping hand to the ones who stray from justice and righteousness, even while civil punishment is meted out. Religion must never condone evil or injustice, but it must always recognize atonement, must always forgive transgression, must always welcome a fresh start, must always assist in rehabilitation. In this way the frayed and broken threads in the fabric of life can be mended and the cloth made whole and strong again.

> Let the divine concept —
> God, Cosmos, Life —
> Include the evil-doers also,
> That they may never
> Become disconnected from the whole,
> That they may one day
> Resume their roles
> In the drama of living.

Morality

I must suspect the honeyed voice
    that boasts its own morality,
    that claims to cherish unborn cells of life
    yet turns to gall and vinegar
    when faced with human need and want.

I must suspect self-righteousness
    that boasts religiosity,
    that finds its strength in prejudice
    and feeds upon intolerance
    and sanctimonious bigotry.

I must suspect those patriots
    who tout the ownership of guns,
    who hide themselves behind the flag
    yet show no genuine concern
    for life and freedoms they proclaim.

This sham they call morality,
    this sanctimonious bigotry,
    this pseudopatriotic talk
    must be revealed for what it is:
    myopic immorality!

Blurring the Edge:
Politics and Religion in the 1980s

There seem to be two views: one is that the edge between politics and religion should be sharp and clear; the other is that the line should be blurred and that we learn to live with it that way.

Unitarian Universalists believe profoundly in the separation of church and state. At the same time, our tradition, temperament, and passion for social reform propel us into political action. We agitate politically for keeping government out of abortion decisions and school prayer that we regard as personal. At the same time, we advocate expanded government programs in health, social services, children, aging, housing, and education. To spin the wheel half way around again, many Unitarian Universalists oppose drafting young men and women into the military services, and we march against U.S. intervention in Nicaragua and El Salvador, unless perhaps the intervention helps the faction we favor.

The edge between politics and religion appears blurred. Is our devotion to freedom of religion such that we can rush to political action when it suits our purpose and yet lambaste others when they do the same thing when it suits a purpose different from ours?

Unitarians and Universalists have been into political and social action for 150 years at least, certainly since Theodore Parker in Massachusetts and Starr King in California. They were in the vanguard of the abolition movement, universal free education, prison reform, mental health, voting rights, environmental protection, peace—you name it.

During the last couple of decades, the fundamentalists have caught the fever. Reverend Jerry Falwell of Lynchburg, Virginia, has activated a self-styled Moral Majority, recently renamed the Liberty Federation. Some would say it is neither moral nor a majority, but none would deny that it is a religious and a political force. Many of the political objectives and ethical values proclaimed by Jerry Falwell, Pat Robertson, Oral Roberts, Jimmy Swaggert, and others, were adopted by the Reagan Administration. These religious fundamentalists have mastered the techniques of motivating the masses to offer up money as well as their souls, of using the best in radio and television. They are not hampered by intellectual or moral scruples about invoking religious authority for political action. They believe that the guarantee of freedom of worship in the First Amendment to the Constitution needs drastic changing.

For sure, they are different from us. They rant and rave; we reason and lecture. They invoke God, the Bible, and Jesus; we invoke science, sociology, the Constitution, and Thomas Jefferson. They let themselves go when they sing; we hum along without knowing the tune. So it goes. Our icons are different but they serve the same purpose; they reinforce our convictions.

For both fundamentalists and Unitarian Universalists, the edge between politics and religion is blurred, although our side is uneasy with the ambiguity. Furthermore, we Unitarian Universalists regard the Moral Majority appeals to God and the Bible as unfair, unwarranted, almost immoral. They regard our appeal to science and sweet reason as trivial and unimpressive, just what you would expect from secular humanists.

Rather than flail the fundamentalists, it is more important to look to our own beliefs, as religious liberals. How we bridge the gap between politics and religion is much more important than taking out after other church groups.

Let me interrupt the flow here to cite several examples from my experience in government with issues that involve conflicting considerations of a political and religious nature.

Five experiences in government: one local, one state, one national, one regional, one international.

Local: Problem of locating homes for mentally retarded, drug addicts, alcoholics, teenage runaways, and others against the zoning laws and the wishes of the people who live nearby.

State: My four-year struggle to reconcile human needs for public assistance with budget stringency and deficits.

National: For example, whether to allow less than minimum wage for six months in first jobs for unemployed youth despite labor objections that such a move would undermine the minimum wage principle.

Regional: Special advantages to minority contractors to help them get started even though lowest responsible bid awards might have to be set aside.

International: High-tech U.S. aid in Iran while the Shah was still in power when it was obvious that this would produce major social problems, even revolution. The same thing is being done in Saudi Arabia at the present time.

In each of these cases a cause or an objective that religious liberals believe in comes up against a practical or a political difficulty. Solutions or reconciliations have to be found if progress is to be made.

It is important for religious activists to keep the pressure on. For example, recently in Arlington several churches, including the Unitarian Church of Arlington, decided to take homeless persons into their church buildings for overnight lodging. This was done despite county ordinances and liability. The action put pressure on public authorities and led quickly to the county's purchase of a suitable overnight house for the homeless. This is religious activism at its best.

Religious fundamentalists and the religious liberals are clearly at issue in the matter of prayer in the public schools. The first group seeks an interpretation or a change in the First Amendment to the U.S. Constitution to permit prayer in the schools. The second group opposes this position. Ironically, religious liberals are often strict constructionists, the conservatives opposing change.

Until the early 1960s, a prayer at the beginning of each school day was common. Then the Supreme Court ruled this practice to be in conflict with the Establishment Clause of the First Amendment, made applicable to the states by the Fourteenth Amendment. Quite a few states have laws permitting a "moment of silence" during which students may voluntarily pray, meditate, or daydream. The constitutionality of this has not been tested. Numerous constitutional amendments have been proposed during the last 25 years. The Reagan Administration—along with the National Association of Evangelicals representing 45 denominations, the Moral Majority, the Christian Voice, the Christian Broadcast Network, the Union of Orthodox Rabbis, the U.S. Catholic Conference, and the Southern Baptists Convention—favors spoken voluntary prayer in public schools. Arrayed on the other side are mainline Protestant and Jewish groups—the Episcopal Church, Lutheran groups, the American Baptist Churches, the United Church of Christ, the United Methodist Church, the Seventh Day Adventists, the Union of American Hebrew Congregations, the National Council of Churches, and the Unitarian Universalist Association.

A Gallup poll in 1983 indicated that over 80 percent of the American people supported a constitutional amendment to allow voluntary group prayer in public schools. Other polls show less support if the prayer is mandatory.

I got hold of the Issue Brief prepared by the Congressional Research Service of the Library of Congress prepared for Members of Congress looking for background material on the issue.

Intriguing issues include the "silent prayer" approach and the "equal access" to school rooms for voluntary religious exercises during extracurricular times. Do voluntary silent prayer or meditation conflict with the First Amendment? It's hard to say what the Justices might decide. Students, if they wish, can pray or think things over during any slack moments in the day. No doubt, going into an exam many students offer up silent prayers.

It seems clear that compulsory, prescribed prayer, as the Court has said, is inconsistent with the Constitution. If the politics work out so as to change the First Amendment to permit formal prayer, I would certainly be upset, as would other religious liberals. I would regard prayer in public schools as totally at odds with our traditions. Jefferson's "wall of separation" would have been breached and our defense of religious freedom, seriously weakened. Silent prayer I could live with, albeit a bit nervously. I would be apprehensive lest some kind of prayer, sanctioned by the teacher, the local school board, or the prevailing religious group in the community would seep in. What could begin as no more than a whispered prayer could grow louder as time passed. Better to leave prayer to families, churches, and especially to individuals.

It is much more important to bring politics and religion into better alignment, to make sure that political decisions are based on ethical principles, religious values, and the best of our traditions. In matters of first-rate importance, the politician-legislator is driven back to a set of values, a sense of ethics, or feel for religion. The Golden Rule, Kant's categorical imperative, the mystical revelation of God's will, or utilitarianism may be instructive.

For Unitarian Universalists it makes sense to ask what our own leaders and prophets would have done. What would Theodore Parker or Dorothea Dix have thought about the voting rights bill? How would Jefferson have advised us on freedom of information? Or Horace Mann on equal opportunities in education? How would the great women of our denomination have voted on the proposition to deny federal funds to a welfare recipient for an abortion? Or on the anti-abortion amendment? What would any of these leaders have said about prayer in the public schools?

So where are we on the issue we started with: the sharpening of the edge or the blurring of the edge between politics and religion? For Unitarian Universalists, clarifying the relationship between religion and politics also means stripping away prejudice, our own included, insisting that positions be supported by facts and analysis, taking a positive approach. It means double-checking our actions making sure that our advocacy is rooted in our deepest beliefs as religious liberals. Also, it means finding a continuum from political action to religious principle, with action emerging from principle. The blurring of the edge between politics and religion becomes complete.

With the blurring of politics and religion, have we lost the First Amendment, which says Congress shall make no laws respecting the establishment of religion or in the free exercise thereof? No, of course not. The First Amendment must remain a pillar of our society. I accept it and I glory in it. Religion should and must give moral quality to politics, while at the same time the stage must not prescribe particular religious requirements of its citizens, children included. I am insisting that politics pay attention to religious and ethical principles and that the two be connected and made harmonious.

> Mentor of us all:
> God, tradition, profoundest human impulse —
> Help each of us to see the wisdom of basing
> action on thought, politics on religion,
> So that the line between
> Connects, not separates, the two.

Permanence

I'd like to think that there's a permanence
To life and love and creativity.
I like to think on generations past
Who loved the places I have learned to love,
Who walked along this rocky shore and marked
Each stone and boulder with the changing tides
And fondly gathered flowers, herbs, and grasses,
Shells and driftwood, brightly colored pebbles.

I like to watch the creatures of the sea,
Themselves creations of the generations
Past who taught them patterns of the sea.
The stately heron mounts his guard upon the shore,
And seagulls cry and soar in search of prey
As ebbing tides reveal their secrets.
By outer ledges seals cavort and splash
And clamber up to bask on ageless rocks.

And now I watch a little child who finds
Identity with sea and shore, and stakes
His claim upon a rock or underneath
A grove of spruce — a claim well known to all
Who from the distant past have learned
To love this land and water and to hope
That there is permanence of life and love,
An endless world of creativity.

৵

Reflections on a Wasteful Society

For my text I draw from a little booklet, a recent best seller, entitled *50 Simple Things You Can Do to Save the Earth,* prepared by the Earth Works Group in Berkeley, California—where else? Some of the things to do are simple, some take a little effort, and a few are for the committed only. For example:

- One is called "The Great Escape." Every winter, the energy equivalent of all the oil that flows through the Alaska pipeline in a year leaks through American windows. Things to do include having energy audits to find the leaks, then insulate better.

- Another: "Use Cloth Diapers." Americans throw away 18 billion disposable diapers a year—enough to stretch to the moon and back seven times.

- "Rinse Old News." It takes a forest of half a million trees to supply Americans with their Sunday newspapers every week. What to do? Recycle.

- "Make It a Royal Flush." Forty percent of the pure water you use in your house is flushed down the toilet. One answer: put a capped plastic bottle weighted with a few stones in your toilet tank.

- "The Twilight Ozone." According to the National Resources Defense Council, leaky air conditioners are the largest single source of chlorofluorocarbon emissions to the atmosphere in the United States. CFC's are a major culprit in depletion of the ozone layer which protects us from skin cancer. Therefore, make sure your air conditioners work properly and use them only when necessary.

These few lively examples from the Earth Works Group may overstate the case, but they make their point. We Americans are a careless, untidy, wasteful bunch.

This was brought home to me a few years ago when my wife and I and two or three of our children took a picnic lunch to a beach in Denmark. After eating we gathered up our food scraps, paper, bottles and the rest and walked over to a large receptacle. I was amazed to look inside and see only tightly wrapped little packages tied neatly with string, one for each family's refuse.

No mess, no slop, nothing on the ground, an almost antiseptic appearance. I wondered how many generations it takes to develop this discipline, not only for picnickers, but for every consumer, producer, shipper and handler, even trash collector.

Most jurisdictions have a problem with solid waste. Present landfills can't accommodate much more. New sites must be found. Nobody wants them in the neighborhood. The waste has to go somewhere, but NIMBY—Not In My Back Yard. Much of the land is in someone's back yard. No sooner is a site proposed than a small army of neighbors protests to the Planning Commission or the Board of Supervisors. Just the kind of problem that gives elected and appointed public officials fits! Just the kind of problem that exposes a major weakness in our governmental processes, a character weakness we all share!

We can take some consolation in knowing that we are not alone. Many, perhaps most, U.S. cities, towns, and villages have the same unpleasant flaw. The NIMBY syndrome has become ubiquitous. Western Europeans coal emissions blow eastward to fall as acid rain on Eastern Europe. Dealing with waste has become a bloody headache for which quick fixes, like aspirin tablets, don't last.

Being a materialistic people with a deep faith in technology, we Americans tend to look for technical solutions to our problems. So it is with our waste problem. Can we bury it deeper, disinfect it, burn it up, compress it, chlorinate it, recycle it, convert it into other products, or perhaps make electricity out of it? Each possibility has to be examined and, where feasible, used.

Frequently, however, behavioral changes have to go along with technical solutions. Behavioral changes are more difficult. The technology for recycling newsprint or aluminum cans is well established, but people have to be willing to separate their trash or support laws and regulations requiring them to do it. So too, industrial firms know how to deal with waste products but say they will lose out to competition if they spend money to prevent, treat, or reclaim the waste. Incentives have to be found to induce changes in industrial behavior.

Politics may become [entangled] in waste issues. When I was Chairman of the Board of Directors of the Metropolitan Washington Council of Governments, we were seeking a large solid waste disposal site. We looked everywhere—abandoned mines in West Virginia, off-shore possibilities, nearby public and privately owned sites. NIMBY kept blocking us. Finally we found a site outside the Washington region in a rural county. COG was willing to arrange handsome payments for each ton placed there. COG would also compress, dry, disinfect, remove unpleasant odors, and even grade the land into playing fields and a golf course after the disposal site was filled. We softened up the local county commissioners who agreed to the proposition if we would wait until after the upcoming election. We thought we had a deal. But even though our commissioners were re-elected, they backed out at the last minute. The NIMBY people raised such a ruckus that the commissioners couldn't take the heat. They caved in. Moral: politics are more difficult than technology and planning. Einstein had it right: politics are more difficult than science.

Until recently the Americans have been concerned exclusively with the economic benefits of organizing raw materials, capital, and labor to produce efficiently and massively the goods and services people want to consume. No one cared too much about the remains of the industrial process. The law of conservation of matter says that what we in our self-centered way call consumption is not the end of the matter. The food we eat, the water we drink, the clothes we wear, the newspapers we read, the cars we drive, the gasoline that fuels them, and the spent nuclear fuel don't disappear from the face of the earth. They change their form and go elsewhere. Only now are we beginning to worry about what happens [elsewhere] with the sewage, the auto emissions, the worn out cars, and the ordinary junk. I predict that from now on as much attention will be paid to dealing with after-consumption wastes and residues as has been paid in the past to fight before-consumption activities. Already public policy is addressing disposal of radioactive substances, CO emissions, toxic chemicals, and household and industrial waste. The voluminous Clean Air Act amendments testify to this.

At the bottom of most of the problems are people, you and I, and what we do with our wastes and left-overs. What we do day by day, what regulations we will abide by, what taxes and penalties we will live with, what incentives we will respond to will determine whether we'll change our wasteful habits.

These changes will not come easy in a development-oriented society such as ours is. A major theme in our economic history has been the development and improvement in living standards. Cut the forests, develop the land, extract the minerals, expand the cities, grow, grow, grow. Development lies deep in the American psyche and tradition as well as in its economy and institutions. Sinclair Lewis, a major American novelist of the 1920s and '30s, not much read in recent years, expounded on this theme in a series of novels capturing the boosterism of the American Midwest.

Now in the late 20th Century environmental limits are constraining economic development. We are running out of backyards in which to dump things. And backyards include streams, lakes, the ocean, the atmosphere, and underground aquifers in addition to the land. Ecology has a noose around the economy's neck and it is tightening.

In Northern Virginia the biggest political issue is development. How fast should it proceed? What should be the cost to the community and the developer? The political pendulum swings back and forth between rapid growth and slow growth. The two sides contest in public hearings, in the media, in the market place, in elections. Neither side can win. Both sides need to recognize the validity of the other's case. A wise old professor used to talk about "the ecology of man (and woman) and the economy of nature." The advocates of fast growth must recognize the limits to what the environment can tolerate; the advocates of slow growth must concede that economic development accommodates a larger population and its desire to live better. Either way, the waste problem will be with us for a long time.

The more I reflect on our wasteful society, the more certain I am that behavioral changes will not be enough. A moral imperative based on ethical principles will be necessary if we are to turn the corner. The new ethic that draws together ecologic preservation and economic development in a society that wastes little is usually called sustainable development nowadays. The moral imperative forces us to plan and act to support sustainable development. I call it the ecologic-economic approach—the eco-eco approach. And don't forget: the Greek root of both words is household, where the moral imperative for sustainable development has to take firm hold.

This moral imperative should govern equally on the local level and world scale. Locally it means thinking through the problems of landfills, stream pollution, tract development, air quality, and open space. And then it means acting on these problems to promote sustainable development and minimize waste. In global terms it means supporting international measures to restore clean air, reduce acid rain, check carbon emissions, and control ocean dumping.

Finally, a religious foundation supports these ethical principles and moral imperatives. The physician, Albert Schweitzer, called it reverence for life. The ecologist, Aldo Leopold, called it the sacredness of the land. My friend and theologian, Ronald Engel at Meadville/Lombard Theological School puts it this way:

> No amount of attention to new moral ideas of sustainable development
> and no amount of new moral resolve can by themselves put the world

on a sustainable development path. . . . This can only be done with the help of spiritual disciplines that restore the proper relationship of human beings to the ground of being, disciplines that depend upon religious insight and ultimately upon faith.

My reflections on our wasteful society end where reflections on most subjects end, on a religious note. Grandma was right: cleanliness is next to Godliness. The eco-eco approach to sustainable development and waste reduction won't take us toward a better life in a better world unless the power of religious conviction and moral values is there to guarantee the worth of both the goal and the approach. Our home community is as good a place as any to put this to the test.

Part Four

Living and Loving

Our Heritage—This Earth

When will the devastation stop?
    The great trees crash to earth.
    We tremble with the land
    As deer and rabbits scatter
    Seeking shelter in their shrinking habitat.
When will the devastation stop?
    Hawks and osprey arc into the sky
    as tons of twigs and clay, ancestral homes
    For generations crumble in the holocaust.
When will the devastation stop?
    The great blue heron and the little blue
    Cry out, and frightened ducks and geese
    Abandon nesting grounds along the shores
    As wetlands are destroyed
    By asphalt, concrete, chemicals, and silt.
When will the devastation stop?
    Tearing down the growth of centuries
    Machinery rumbles on denuded earth,
    Hauling off the once proud trees,
    Changing contours of the land and waterways.
When will the devastation stop?
When will the blind ambition of
Despoilers of the earth awaken
To the deadly cost the search for profit will incur?
When will we see before it is too late?
Our heritage — this Earth — is all we have.

People, Nature, Culture:
The New Trigonometry

Many of us took trigonometry in high school and learned something about how triangles work. A few of us have had the opportunity to apply the rules of right triangle trigonometry to the navigation of ships or aircraft. The heart of it all lies in the way the three sides and three angles—sine, cosine, and tangent—are inter-related. You need only simple instruments for taking measurements and confidence in the rules to reach your destination.

To leap from the predictable world of ordinary trigonometry to the real world of people, nature, and culture we live in, we need a new trigonometry to guide us on our course. With human population increasing worldwide at an alarming rate, with the natural environment being degraded and worn thin, and with control and guidance systems not working well, we need a new trigonometry to navigate into the twenty-first century and beyond.

Nearly 200 years ago the Reverend Thomas Malthus postulated that population tends to increase geometrically while the means of subsistence increases only arithmetically. Ultimately war, disease, and starvation check the increase in population unless the birthrate could be sufficiently restrained. In the western world, ever since, science, technology, and economic development have staved off the Malthusian day of reckoning.

In recent years the rise in the standard of living in our country has slowed. In much of Africa, Asia, and Latin America people are worse off than they were 20 years ago. Nearly 25 percent of the world's population, about a billion and a quarter people, live in absolute poverty with not enough to eat. By the year 2000 another billion people will be added, nearly all in the less developed countries. Producing enough of the basics—grain, oil, wood products—to keep up with the population increase, never mind to get ahead of it, will be difficult, perhaps impossible.

In addition to the problem of providing a decent life for the world's people is the problem of severe pollution. Toxic wastes, both chemical and nuclear, air pollution from automobiles and coal-fired electric-generating plants, and degradation of surface and ground water have become major threats that we are only beginning to deal with. The prospects for global warming and depletion of the protective ozone layer add to the lugubrious litany. Even Perrier isn't foolproof!

How can we avoid this future trap of too many people, too little food, and too much pollution? Whatever policies we pursue, whatever actions we take, it won't be easy and it won't be cheap. It will take changes in the third element of my trigonometry, that is, in the cultures of the world. Possibly a grand bargain can be struck, a social compact by which the developed countries like ours will reduce their pollution, while the less developed countries will cut down their birth rates.

The most comforting approach would be to let things roll on and trust that technology, economics, the peace dividend due to arms reduction will bail us out in time. Such a course would be risky in the extreme, it seems to me. We can and must do better. We need a new trigonometry to chart a new course.

First of all we need a new perspective. Recently I was in a small group talking with Admiral Richard Truly, a former astronaut and now director of the National Aeronautics and Space Administration. We were discussing the Earth Observing System by which NASA is learning more about the land, oceans, and atmosphere and the linkages among them. Truly began by saying, "If you have any doubts that this earth is precious, you ought to look at it from outer space as I have. It is beautiful but so fragile. It and we depend totally on such a thin envelope of air." This is the first time in history, he added, that humans can deliberately affect the global system and all life in it by changing the earth's climate.

This power opens opportunities; it also demands farsightedness and a high sense of responsibility. "Whatever we do to the web," Chief Seattle of the Snoquamish tribe wrote to President Lincoln in a remarkable letter, "we do to ourselves." Information and knowledge gathered by sophisticated instruments placed in orbiting satellites will not be enough without the will to use what we learn wisely. T.S. Eliot wrote:

> Where is the wisdom we have lost in knowledge,
> Where is the knowledge we have lost in information?

So we need perspective not only on our world but on our place in it as custodians as well as users. The lines of May Swenson give us pause:

> And what
> if the universe
> is *not about*
> us? Then what?

> What
> is it about
> And what
> about
> *us?*

The Biblical perspective set forth in the first chapter of Genesis hardly squares with modern ecological principles:

> . . . and God said to them, "Be fruitful and multiply, and fill the earth and subdue it; and have dominion over the fish of the sea and over the birds of the air and over every living thing that moves upon the earth."

It comes down to this. To navigate our space ship earth, as Adlai Stevenson once put it, will require a new trigonometry composed of population planning, environmental protection, and cultural adjustment. None of the three will be easy to accomplish.

Population planning, though expanding in most parts of the world, still leaves major countries and many persons outside the reach of effective programs. Traditions, religious tabus, ignorance, and cost are among the obstacles the poorer countries face. Without family planning it seems unlikely that population growth will be checked in time to avoid even more serious difficulties in feeding and sheltering people, for example in Ethiopia. Our own country is shielded from the worst aspects of over-population by space, plentiful natural resources and institutions that support smooth adjustments of policy and action.

But even here the fight for more family planning, democratic style, is far from won. Local communities in Virginia are in the throes of establishing under state law family-life education programs centered on the well-being of children. At the heart of the controversy is the so-called right-to-life versus right-to-choose issue. The free choice approach appears to maintain wider support; it is more consistent with the deep-seated American preference for keeping government laws and regulations out of intimate personal and family matters.

At the national level the issue boils down to whether this country should provide aid to international population and family planning programs and under what circumstances abortions should be allowed here at home. The fact that 1.5 million or so abortions have been performed each year, both before and since the 1973 Roe v. Wade decision, indicates that in practical terms the issue already should have been settled.

On the second side of my triangle, the environmental front, the situation is deteriorating. Deserts are advancing southward from the Sahara in Africa, and acid rain is diminishing the fish in lakes in the Northeastern United States and adjoining parts of Canada. What to do with nuclear wastes has not been resolved, and the burning of fossil fuels in autos and power plants continues to worsen the quality of the air. The disposal of ordinary solid waste constitutes a divisive problem in virtually all of our local communities. The modern ballad puts it this way:

> Of just two things you must beware:
> Don't drink the water and don't breathe the air.

Environmental protection has to be approached as an all-pervading strategy at all levels of government and society. Education, prohibition, economic incentives, international conventions, and changes in personal behavior will all have roles to play. New compromises that sustain both the economy and the environment must be arranged. Fortunately there are examples of progress: the recent Montreal Protocol on emissions of chlorofluorocarbons into the atmosphere, the air quality legislation now emerging from the U.S. Congress, and close-to-home agreement to improve the Chesapeake Bay. All is by no means lost, but time is running short.

And this brings me to the third element in my new trigonometry, the cultural side: the range of institutions—like government, family, school, church—and mind-sets—like choice of having children, ecological responsibility, one's view of the long-range future, motivating values. It is in the cultural sphere that we find both the sources for understanding problems and the capacity for action. One of our favorite hymns proclaims:

> Fair are the verdant trees,
> Fair are the flashing seas
> Glorious the earth and resplendent skies!

How can this vision inspire us to act and to support actions to restore our planet?

If human life is as precious as we believe it to be, how do we find the discipline to look far ahead and plan now for the welfare of our children's children? How is a greater sensitivity for the welfare of all world citizens—young and old, present and future—to be developed in each of us? How can a respect for nature become a part of us?

In these matters, I am sure, we must involve more than science, demography, ecology, economics, and government. We must turn to religion as the deepest source of inspiration and the surest guide to action. The kind of religion I have in mind is a religion of man and woman, a religion of nature, and a religion of the culture that brings the first two together in a seamless web in which, as Chief Seattle said, "All things are connected."

On this religious foundation my new trigonometry can chart our course through the perilous seas to a safe harbor ahead.

To Be a Woman

To be a woman is to be attuned
    to life and time, to dreams and fantasies,
        to pride and trust, to restlessness,
            to ego trips and empty vacillation.

To be a woman is to know the pull
    between the love of man and personal
        ambition to be recognized for her
            own worthiness, ability and skill.

Between the love of man and yearning for
    his children, she reaches bravely to achieve
        success in everything and in the seeking
            wonders why frustration takes its toll.

The challenge then is not to settle for
    an empty dream but rather build on strength.
        Those skills which she possesses must become
            the cornerstone on which her life will stand.

Where there is knowledge, skill, and competence,
    where there is love, respect, and compromise,
        where life is rich and varied she will be
            a woman who can meet the test of life.

The Bond That Broke Too Suddenly

Oh weary world that has no faith, no time for understanding —
It pains my heart that years of love, of hopes and dreams
Have come to this embattlement of spirit
Where generations find no meeting-ground
But seek their vengeance in their bitter words.

Oh God! Why should this happen to so great a love?
I do recall that precious child who first did suck my breast
When love flowed freely as the miracle of life was shared.
That little child, his hand in mine would give me strength and utter joy,

On through the years a growing intellect soon passed my own,
And I was proud and gladly let him go into the world.
But something snapped — the bond that held us broke too suddenly.
It threw us both so hard we lost our reasoning.

Oh God, dear God, I know somehow, some time that awful chasm
Will close. Bridges will be built, and once again
My son will take my hand and give me strength,
And I will look to him to lead the way.

The Home Base of Religion

Much of the living people do is still in their homes. Eating, sleeping, conversing, cleaning, laughing, crying, arguing, being sick, writing letters: all these are mainly home activities done within a family group, large or small. Of course, the family is not the tightly-knit group of our idylls and memories. Gone is the turn-of the-century daguerreotype family posed before the fire as father in stiff collar reads to the child on his lap while mother instructs her daughter in the domestic art of sewing with the sleeping dog or cat nearby. Grandma and grandpa, not to mention the faithful housemaid, are also gone from this picture. From remembered pictures to today, much has happened to the American family. But fractured as it has been, it remains in the scene, pre-eminent among society's primary groups. It is hard to imagine how things would be without the family.

Changes in the American family can be portrayed by telling about cases and by citing statistics. Cases of family deterioration abound; we have seen them: the southern male who went north for an industrial job and who may not have sent for his family; the older person who moved to a retirement community or nursing home rather than "burden" the children; the teenager who rebelled against the home that provided neither love nor security; the working mother and father who thought the day care center and the sitter could substitute for parental care; the workaholic husband and/or the working wife whose preoccupation with career left no time or energy for cultivating their marriage and home.

Statistics show how many changes in the family have weakened that institution. Since around 1950 the percentage of women working outside the home has almost doubled. Fifty years ago half the family households included at least one adult other than the parents; now they rarely do. The number of children living with only one parent has almost doubled in the past 25 years. The divorce rate has shot up, with over a million divorces recorded in 1975. Nearly 40 percent of all marriages now end in divorce and more couples separate. In the past quarter century illegitimate births have more than doubled, from four to ten per 100 live births.

Ambition and economic and social conditions seem to conspire against family stability. Tensions mount as people strive to fulfill their individuality, and yet deep inside feel uneasy about the consequences to their families.

They think that the family as an institution and their own personal families can absorb the shocks, but they are not so sure. This is a prescription for psychological and social disruption. Unless preventive and remedial measures are taken all, especially the children, will suffer. Urie Bronfenbrenner, professor of human development and family studies at Cornell and a national authority on families describes the situation:

> At a time when our nation more than ever needs public spirited and enlightened young, and when the best new research is pointing to the critical role of the family, our nation pays little attention to the family as a key social unit, and there are mounting indications that the American family as we know it is falling apart.

Some trace the problem to an over-emphasis on individualism in this country; the civil rights and equal legal protection for individuals, non-discrimination, equal employment opportunities for minorities and women. We are devoted to individual rights. "All men (and women) are created equal . . . are endowed by their Creator with certain inalienable rights. . . ." The great American epic is the struggle of colonists against English tyranny, of the pioneers against the wilderness, of African Americans against slavery and bondage, of working men against the bosses. In each case the individual was the chief agent of change.

Our own increasing affluence and sense of social responsibility is another disintegrative factor. By national policy social security entitles most people to old age retirement benefits. Business firms, labor unions, professional groups, and the federal civil service provide additional annuity payments. The financial independence of the elderly has effectively removed grandparents from most family units and eliminated the experience and wisdom available to children. One response to this change has been the extended family, which offers a broader contact for part of the time as well as a kind of insurance for emergency situations, but it also acknowledges the loosening of conventional family ties.

Others trace family decay to our national obsession with mobility. As a people we came from Europe, Africa, and most recently from Latin America and Asia. For three hundred years we pushed our way westward. In the last century many of us left farms and small towns for the cities of the industrial North; then from the cities to the suburbs. More recently we have followed the sun to Florida, California, and Arizona. Even locally, people move to a different house, or apartment, or neighborhood. The average Arlingtonian stays only about four years in the same dwelling. Such frequent uprootings are hard on children and families, as anyone who has had to move with teenage youngsters knows.

Another profound impact on the family is the increasing employment of women outside the home. Last year more than half the married women with children between the ages of six and seventeen, and two-fifths of those with children under six were either working or looking for work, twice as many as 25 years ago. Two-thirds of the women were working full time. The recent growth of unemployment, along with the substantial increase in the number with jobs can be explained by the flood of women into the work force. This change for so many women has increased the number of latch-key children, diminished the time mothers have to be with children, and has provided higher family income. Typically, grandma is far away. The supervision of young children often is entrusted to older siblings or neighborhood teenagers who otherwise would go home after school to empty houses.

Robert Frost wrote: "Home is a place where, when you have to go there, they have to take you in." The modern version would say: "Home is a place where, when you have to go there, you'd better have the key."

Social, economic, and psychological forces have always tended to pull families apart. Some years ago in an old attic trunk, I ran across a heart-rending exchange of letters between the brother of my great-great grandfather and his mother. He was trying to explain why in 1849 he had shipped on a sailing schooner from a Maine coastal town bound around the Horn for San Francisco, and she was trying to persuade him to come home.

Sometimes family and home ties were strong enough to hold the young ones; other times a whole family could move together. In the film of Alex Haley's *Roots,* the matriarch held the family together by sheer force of character and will. Shortly before the Civil war when conditions on the Virginia plantation became almost unbearable and the younger ones were threatening to leave, she said, "Just remember, we is a family and we's going to stay a family." (The singular verb *is* was correct in this instance when you stop to think about it. She meant "we" as a collective calling for a singular verb.)

But more and more frequently, the family seems to be losing out. The search is on to find substitutes for the security, and affection, that a family provides.

The Advisory Committee on Child Development associated with the National Research Council recently published a report, *Toward A National Policy for Children and Families,* recommending a "program to insure that families have the minimum income necessary to provide adequate food, shelter, and care for children. . . . No child should be deprived of access to a family living standard lower than half of the median family income level (after tax) for a substantial period of his or her childhood and thus income should not fall below the government defined poverty level even for shorter periods. . .(or the only) parent should remain in direct and full-time care of a child under six without being deprived of the income level specified above." This is a brave and good goal. The distinguished Advisory Committee proposes to achieve it by drawing more family members into the labor force and providing work training programs for them. This prescription, if followed, could make the ultimate cure for family decay even more difficult. It implies the need for better child care, better family health care, and a variety of additional services. In fact, the Committee's recommendations which would cost a good deal of money, but none gets to the heart of the matter, which is to restore the security and interpersonal bonds of the intimate family group.

Day care is a case in point. More than six million children under six have working mothers and very few have grandmothers in the house. Outside day care is absolutely essential and increasingly available. A well-run program with trained, warmly understanding teachers or supervisors can go a long way toward providing a home substitute. In some cases the day care experience may be better than home. But even extended day care cannot do the whole job. Our study of programs in the United States, the Soviet Union, and Israel concludes that group upbringing can also lead to delinquency and violence at one extreme, to unquestioning conformity at the other. In this country, economic and psychological forces are propelling us toward more government subsidies to support day care centers. I have a sinking feeling that many of the so-called remedies to problems modern families face, however necessary, carry the family even faster toward deterioration.

The best hope is to simulate in the day care program a genuine primary group situation in which the individuals relate to one another in a sustained way as whole persons. Government financial aid, technical training, and volunteer aid should be deployed with this in mind.

Some stresses families face are traumatic. Recently I was told of a family in which the wife and mother decided to have an abortion. The husband, devoutly believing that abortion is murder, was torn in two. Personal desire, women's rights, even practical wisdom collided with moral and religious conviction, about the sanctity of potential life. Honorable, workable compromise, evidently, was not possible. The family was wrecked. No community resources or inner resources of the man and woman could repair the damages.

Situations like this convince many people that we need a national law or an amendment to the Constitution to help the government chart a course on abortion. Others see only an unwarranted intrusion by the state into private matters, a usurpation of individual rights.

All parties to the dispute seem to agree that removing the conditions giving rise to the need for abortion would be highly desirable. Measures to achieve this could include instruction in contraception and family planning, marriage counseling and family therapy, reduction of the stigma and shame that accompanies illegal births, and provision of medical, psychological, child care, and employment assistance. Improving adoption procedures will open alternatives for pregnant women who can't care for children. I have become interested in a bill to establish comprehensive family support centers and to furnish financial and technical assistance to existing centers.

To help cope with the family consequences of unwanted pregnancy and other family problems, government and private programs should be pursued intelligently, aggressively, and hopefully. But no program can check the forces that fracture and diminish the family as the primary institution within which individuals find their way through life. To meet this more fundamental challenge a psychological, moral, spiritual reawakening is needed. Without it, the hundred practical programs for restoring families and shoring them up with community services will not succeed. To a critical extent, churches and religion can help.

For example, churches can educate children in church schools about family problems in a more intimate and morally directed way than can public schools. Churches and ministers can make their marriage, family, and youth counseling services, more professional while retaining an ease hard to find in a more formal setting. Churches can plunge into community efforts to improve housing and neighborhoods and can work for more effective welfare, day care, and foster homes. Churches can cut through bureaucratic red tape and reach people directly to motivate them to deal with their own problems. Our own church in Arlington has been an effective agent. As churches strengthen families, so too will families strengthen churches.

The yearning for home and family remains strong. "Home is a place where, when you have to go there, they have to take you in." "Home is the sailor, home from the sea." "Home, home on the range, where the deer and the antelope play." "Be it ever so humble, there's no place like home."

Neither nostalgia nor promising programs will suffice against the disruptions of home and family. To reestablish a modern family spirit, to recreate the belonging each of us craves, to restore small group security within which each person's individuality can take root—this is a task for religion because its completion will require faith in a beneficent outcome and dedication to a continuing effort. As religion is the undergirding of the family, so is the family the home-base of religion.

God of our forebears, God of our children,
Teach us to understand, to feel
The precious qualities of family, homes, and
       neighborhood;
And give us wisdom and determination
To treasure these qualities, and thereby
Enrich our very soul.

Let There Be Time

Let there be time unhurried
    before it is too late.
Let there be seeing of life's beauty
    before it slips away.
Let there be gentle understanding.
    while there's a chance to help.
Let there be sharing
    while we have a gift to share.

Too often in the harried pace of living
    no time is saved for beauty.
Too often conversation is aborted
    and understanding lost.
Too often noise replaces quiet,
    and the heart beats not with love but stress.
Too often the race to win
    turns into bitter loss.

The time is ours if we but pause to see
    the loveliness of life on earth.
The time is ours if we but pause to listen and respond,
    to share our thoughts as we would share a gift.
Time is ours to shape the bonds
    with family and friends
And find the strength and inner peace
    that comes with understanding love.

Learning to Live

Everyone goes to school, not only when he or she is young but throughout life. Factory, office, home, wherever you happen to be can be a place to learn just as much as a schoolroom. Some of the best teachers aren't called teachers and don't think of themselves as teachers. Of course, not everyone learns in any of these places or from any of their teachers. One can learn or not learn on the journey through life depending on desire to do so, need for knowledge, skill of the teacher, and the way others regard learning.

The purpose of education, formal or otherwise, is to learn how to live—to live happily with oneself, helpfully to others, and hopefully about the future. The purpose is not to learn how to avoid the problems of life, but how to solve them; not how to climb over others, but how to cooperate with them; not how to take unfair advantage of the future, but how to realize its possibilities; not how to fight life but how to live constructively with life.

Normal children are eager to find their way in the world. They have a natural curiosity about how things work. They like to experiment to see if they can make things work better. Sometimes they like to be shown; other times they like to try for themselves. For the most part they are sensitive toward the things and the ideas that come their way and toward the teachers and others around them. Whether such an open, receiving attitude will continue through adolescence and the adult years will hinge on the quality of the educational experiences that come along.

Each of us can look back and pick out critical moments in school experience, turning points that led one way or another: success with a science project, ridicule of an essay or a drawing, an original idea put forward so tentatively and then encouraged by a teacher, the same kind of idea rejected or not even heard, the satisfaction of helping another student having even more difficulty with the assignment than oneself, the thrill of thinking a new thought no one has ever had before, the satisfaction of knowing more about some tiny crevice of the universe than anyone else, failure to complete the assignment one knows should have been completed. Experiences like these are the high, or low, points in one's education which turn a person on or turn a person off. Similar educational turning points are encountered out of school as well as in school—in the home, on the playing field, on the street corner.

Adults are not essentially different from children in these matters, although perhaps not quite so impressionable and easily encouraged or discouraged. Unless we adults become totally beat down, most of us retain a good deal of resilience against lack of rewards and appreciation, even against failure. Curiosity about things, though more constrained, remains high, and we continue to be open to new educational experiences.

I remember as a boy going fishing with an older man in our town. He taught me something about the art of fishing. I showed him where the best pool was. But later a raccoon—it might have been a bear—gave us both a lesson. We put the forked stick of trout down on the bank while my friend took a nap and I went swimming, and the raccoon made off with the fish. Herm and I vowed revenge on the raccoon. Each of the three parties to this story learned something and taught something as well. I suppose the moral is that a trout on the bank is worth two in the stream to a raccoon.

Frequently we find our best teachers in unexpected places, not in the classroom or the home or the shop. One of my best teachers was in the rifle squad I had charge of in infantry training camp years ago. He was a roly-poly, soft spoken, Mexican-American from Bakersfield in the San Joaquin Valley. The Army had taught him to read and write. He had been a migrant farm worker and occasionally a construction laborer. His given name was Jesus. Pronounced in American style his name gave rise to such remarks as: "Jesus, Jesus, what are you doing there?" which he bore with good natured resignation. I always addressed him as Jesus for which he was deeply grateful.

Jesus taught me many things: how to use a shovel properly for digging slit trenches, what kind of local plant leaves make a passable tea to drink, a few useful swear words in Spanish. But he also gave me some understanding of what it was like to be brought up in a poor, migrant farm worker family in California. He was marvelously patient and tolerant, a kind person with no sham about him. His integrity was absolute, instilled in him by his parents, I am sure. The most hard-bitten of drill sergeants sensed Jesus was different, on a higher plane and not to be barked at in the usual way.

One day while we were in a live training exercise, one of our men went where he shouldn't have and was wounded. Jesus crawled over to him and pulled him back to safety. That night Jesus and I were boiling up some of his tea over a soldier's fire and fell to talking. I asked him what he wanted to do with his life after the war. He said he thought he'd like to study to be a nurse. I asked him why? He said his goal was to help other people to the extent of his ability. Then he said simply and straight-forwardly, "My mother and father gave to me the name, Jesus. I must try to be like the one I am named for as much as I can."

So, insights and learning are found in many places; I am almost prepared to say in every place if one's eye is quick and one's hearing sharp. This isn't to say that teaching and learning don't occur in regular classrooms. They do, of course, and in great abundance.

In our own community here in Arlington, the public education in the last three decades has progressed from tradition-bound, not too well supported schools, to a modern diversified program with per pupil expenditures approaching $2000 per year and a highly trained faculty more than half of whom have master's degrees. Many new schools have been built and others modernized. Racial desegregation under the law has been achieved and a certain amount of desegregation-busing is carried on routinely without audible objection. Free kindergartens have been added for all, special programs for handicapped and gifted youth added, and new programs launched for students for whom English is the second language. In addition, the years since the Second World War have seen the establishment of the Northern Virginia Community College System with several campuses and the founding and rapid expansion of George Mason University.

The opportunities for rich, varied, and exciting learning experiences have multiplied rapidly around here. We should be grateful for these gains even while we complain that our schools should be better—which, of course, they should be. After all, the drop-out rate is still too high, drugs too prevalent, petty theft too common, teaching too often uninspired, students disrespectful and insufficiently motivated, administrators overly rigid and pompous, parents uncooperative, and on and on. In improving the education of the young there will always be much to do, in school and out. And the same thing goes for the education of even the oldest adults.

My title is "Learning to Live" because it seems to me that the reason for learning—the purpose of education—is to assist persons to have more happy, useful, fulfilling lives. I would not prescribe what a happy, useful, fulfilling life should be (although I know certain things it should not be), but I would want individuals to work that out according to their own talents, objectives, and style. The challenge to educators is to help people find the life which, at their best, they most want to have. One of my old teachers used to say he only wanted to help his students become more nearly what they really are. Given the multifarious goals and modes of life, given the multiplicity of genetic endowments and environmental influences, given the marvelously rich and varied culture from which all may draw, the task of teaching has to be endlessly fascinating—exceeded only by the even more fascinating prospect of learning.

I have not talked much of the content of learning or of the methods of teaching. This is mainly because I don't know exactly what to say even though I have studied these matters in a graduate school of education and been a teacher off and on most of my life. I know a little about the classical, humanistic content the ancient Greek philosophers emphasized in their writing about education and the inquiring methods espoused by the Sophists. And the same for Luther, Calvin, Comenius, Locke, Rousseau, and others who in the periods of the Reformation and later, the Enlightenment, broke the mold of church education that had held firm for a thousand years. And for Pestalozzi, Froebel, Elizabeth Peabody in Boston, and Montessori whose adherents are still to be found here in Arlington as elsewhere—all with their concern for the free, happy, uninhibited development of the child. And on to Horace Mann, the so-called father of the American public school system, to Henry Barnard, the first U. S. Commissioner of Education, and to John Dewey, whose complicated writings emphasized "learning by doing" and "education is life, not a preparation for life." In a more scholarly treatment of my subject "Learning To Live," I would have combed through the records of these and other great figures in the history of education for insights that bear on my theme. I am sure I would have found many insights.

Exposure to education helps a person to live the best he or she can according to his or her lights, necessarily within reasonable social and, of course, legal constraints. As for educational methods, I say let a hundred flowers bloom, each in its own season. But let the methods be those of kindness, patience, and understanding. The child, I believe, is much more likely to be spoiled by using the rod than by sparing it. I would expect the content and curriculum to change slowly over time, and the principles and pedagogy to change also as the world of education turns around. But a few things won't change: the effort to help students learn about themselves, other people, and their earth; the importance of a good teacher like Mark Hopkins at the other end of the log.

Having tried to set a tone on education and living rather than to establish a position, I want to consider briefly several current issues to be found near the intersection of education and religion. The matter of an amendment to the U. S. Constitution to permit prayers in the public schools is still on the national agenda. A fair number of Americans believe the provision of the First Amendment stating that "Congress shall make no law respecting an establishment of religion, or prohibiting the free exercise thereof . . ." should be altered so as to permit school prayers. They argue that it is sacrilegious and Godless, as well as somewhat silly, not to let public school children say a prayer. Even Congress opens its sessions with a prayer, they point out. On the other side are those who think that any prayer, however bland and neutral in its phrases, will necessarily convey the denominational theology and style most prevalent in the community and thereby will be found unacceptable by students and their parents with different religious orientation. This group notes that many immigrants came to these shores seeking religious freedom in a secular state. Unitarians and Universalists unequivocally have been in the second camp.

There seems to be a simple way out of this bind: add at suitable grade levels, a course or series of units on ethics in which individual and social problems (which some think prayers would ameliorate) are examined to see how they can best be dealt with. Needed changes in behavior could be indicated and the views of various religious groups considered. I believe the curriculum makers are skillful enough to arrange this in ways suitable to various ages. Problems could be approached in a direct, action-oriented manner that undoubtedly would mean more to students than the stilted recitation of traditional prayers or even the listening to or the giving of original prayers. This approach could help students in learning to live with the Constitution of this country while learning also how to apply ethical principles to their problems.

A second issue concerns equality of educational opportunity regardless of place of residence, wealth and income, race, sex, or national origin. This too has Constitutional as well as ethical aspects. Not only the "equal protection of the laws" feature of the Constitution, but its whole spirit goes to ensuring equal opportunity for all. In education this has to mean an equal chance for African Americans, Vietnamese and Hispanic children, now lawfully residing in our country, an equal chance for women in colleges and universities, an equal chance for those who live far from college towns, and for those who are poor to go to public educational institutions. No doubt it is not feasible to make educational opportunities precisely equal for all of these within reasonable limits of cost, but the thrust and movement should clearly be in that direction. The means chosen for moving to greater equality will have to vary according to the situation. Busing of students, for example, can be employed when it is acceptable and makes sense. In other situations other means should be found for complying with the laws, with busing then only a last and poor resort. It is my belief that, given reasonable time, various means for achieving equality of educational opportunity can be brought together by local school authorities into a workable program.   Magnet schools of excellence, locating new schools on the borders of ethnic neighborhoods, redistricting, and consolidation are among the techniques available.   Each generation has to learn to live with the principles and traditions of our country, to adapt to them constructively, and occasionally to alter them.   In Bergson's marvelous words we "need to think like men of action and act like men of thought," in this matter as in so many others.   As a final issue, how can our education—our teaching and learning—be improved so as to make us sounder, healthier persons and our community a better place in which to live? Plato put the question just right: "How shall we arrange the education of our citizens so that each of them may be one person, and not many persons, and that through them our city also may be one and not many?"

I believe such an integrating kind of education will have as its aim learning to live—learning to live, happily with oneself, helpfully to others, and hopefully about the future.   Learning to live in this way is a life-long, cradle to grave occupation, to be pursued diligently and enthusiastically.   It can make the difference between a dull life and a sparkling life.   The values underlying this kind of education will be religious values.   The motivation for this kind of learning will be religious motivation.   The dedication for this kind of teaching will be religious dedication.   As with the other great enterprises of life, so in education, in learning and teaching, religion enters in—or rather was there all the time.

> Help us, great Teacher,
> To learn to live,
> And in turn to teach others to live,
> So that our living and their living
> Will advance the human enterprise
> Toward its divine destiny.

Reaching Out

I shall pray for you in my own way,
Reaching out with heart aching,
Tears welling in my throat,

Pain and agony I feel
As I try to share your suffering,
Hope against hope and disillusionment,
I pray that through the mist and fog of your fear,
Through the shadows of uncertainty and pain,
That through all of this my prayer
Shall reach you and give you peace and strength.

I shall pray for you in my own way,
Reaching out to a force greater than my own —
Unfathomed, incalculable, undefinable.

You know that force is there,
Reach out and touch it with your finger tips,
Try to feel its gentle strength,
Listen to the sounds of nature's vital pulse,
Take my hand, and let us share the quest.
This is my prayer, the longing of my love for you.

Taking Care

In our family when two members part, we frequently say to each other, "Take care." We even end our letters to one another with the same words. Perhaps this began as a maternal or paternal admonition. Perhaps it was a way of saying, "With love," without embarrassment. Perhaps the message was literally, take care of yourself and all else that comes within your compass. It's not a bad piece of advice to offer for close relatives or friends.

Taking care of yourself and of others—protecting, encouraging, occasionally disciplining—is required for a good life. It implies responsibility for one's own health and for that of others. Without this, the ideal of a sound mind in a sound body or a sound person in a sound community will not be achieved no matter how many doctors, hospitals, or health insurance plans there are.

Taking responsibility for one's own health and, that of others is desirable from a practical standpoint, but it is also a moral imperative with religious dimensions. If the essence of living a good life is religion, then health, as an integral element of the good life, is also a part of religion.

This doesn't mean that everyone has to be healthy. But it does mean that a deeply committed and sustained effort toward health at the individual and community levels is necessary if we are to live religiously.

I hope my position does not seem stern or uncompromising or even unattainable. A person in good health has an obligation to try to maintain it. A person in poor health should try to improve it. A person with an incurable illness should do his best to cope. And the first two, especially the one who is in good health, have the duty of helping the third right to the end.

For these things to happen requires a religious basis. Otherwise, experience shows that the effort toward health I am calling for will be forthcoming from neither individual nor the community.

I know this sounds like a throwback to the shaman and the witch doctor. But consider that the physician nowadays fulfills the functions formerly performed by priests, ministers, and rabbis. The doctor may be the figure to whom a patient unburdens problems in a kind of confessional, who takes responsibility for a patient's major decisions, or who may be asked to validate a decision already made. The physician provides sympathy and moral support in time of deep trouble.

The difference between the psychiatrist and the pastor is a thin line. Someone has said that people now find a white coat more reassuring than a black one. It has been argued that the decline of religion in this century has been a factor in rising medical costs, as doctors and nurses do religious counseling formerly done by the clergy.

If you think the connection between religion and health is tenuous, I remind you of the abortion conflict, of treatment for alcohol and drug addiction, or of the ethical conundrums posed by organ transplants. Health is a part of all religions in all cultures.

I have been stressing the individual's responsibility for health: for self and for the community. Both are important.

Evidence has been accumulating that additional spending on medical personnel and equipment is not yielding significant improvements in health. Victor R. Fuchs, an expert on health economics, writing in the Summer 1979 issue of *The Public Interest,* comments:

> The most important, and perhaps the most surprising, finding of health economics is that the marginal contribution of medical care to health is very small in modern nations. Those who advocate ever more physicians, nurses, hospitals, and the like are either mistaken or have in mind objectives (political, for example) other than the improvement of the health of the population.

Stanford Professor Fuchs refers to a Rand study which showed little gain in recent years from applying additional health resources, in lowering mortality rates or in improving heart-related illness. Keep in mind that Fuchs is an economist and measures medical care in dollars. But he's essentially correct: it costs a great deal to obtain even modest improvements in health.

Many of the most effective, low-cost interventions, such as vaccination and antibiotics for bacterial infections, are already well established while the long-term benefits of many expensive procedures, such as renal dialysis and organ transplants, are in doubt. Furthermore, illnesses that arise as a result of medical care are on the upswing. Finally, Fuchs concludes, "It is becoming abundantly clear that factors other than medical care (for example, genes, environment, life styles) play crucial roles in many of the most important health problems."

A distinguished task force reported several years ago to the National Conference on Preventive Medicine that a number of simple, basic health habits affect life expectancy:

- three meals a day at regular times instead of snacking
- breakfast every day
- moderate exercise (long walks, bike riding, swimming, gardening) two or three times a week
- moderate weight
- seven or eight hours sleep each night
- no smoking
- no alcohol or only in moderation

A 45-year-old man practicing less than four of these habits can expect to live to age 67; practicing all seven adds 11 years to expected life. Women and men following all seven have a health status about the same as those 20 to 30 years younger who follow none of them.

Voltaire wrote: "Regimen is better than physic." Franklin put it in his usual straight-forward manner: "Be sober and temperate, and you will be healthy." Continued progress toward better health will require each individual to assume personal responsibility for health, to take care. It's as simple and as difficult as that.

Information about the effects of tobacco smoking, overeating or irregular eating, and failure to exercise are widely available. No diet or exercise books, or classes at the local Y or spa, or health foods or diet drinks, U.S. Department of Agriculture bulletins will help unless the individual makes the effort toward health and adopts good health practices. Changing behavior patterns, establishing new habits of living, is hard work. I claim the individual is much more likely to make the effort to regain or maintain good health habits if he or she has self-respect and self-control which are part and parcel of living.

Of course, I recognize the necessity of advanced medical diagnosis and treatment for biological and psychological disorders, from skillful open-heart surgery to deep probing psychotherapy. But new medical technology and practice is often extremely costly, and, naturally, every hospital and every community wants the latest and the best. Just as naturally, consumers dislike paying the high costs whether it is through insurance premiums, taxes, or direct payments. Where and how to apply restraints on advanced medical techniques is one of the most vexing problems of our times.

The individual's responsibility for the health of the community, especially the national community, can be expressed in several ways: by supporting governmental and private health insurance programs; by insisting on adequate standards of occupational safety and health, air and water quality, food and drugs, and dangerous chemicals; by making sure poor and elderly people and others with special needs are not left out; by containing costs in every reasonable way; and by arranging incentives—even penalties—to achieve health objectives. This is a large order taking time, patience, and a willingness to experiment, compromise with competing interests and approaches. It is not easy even for a determined person to figure out what should be done.

How can health be improved without costing too much? One recent magazine article carried the title, "Health In the Future: In the Pink or In the Red?" Nearly everyone would like to moderate the rise in hospital and other health costs, which have, been going up more rapidly than consumer prices. Those in the health professions are trying with some success to contain hospital costs through coordinated voluntary efforts. The Ways and Means Committee of the House of Representatives, of which I am a member, has reported a bill that would establish a voluntary increase limit plus a standby mandatory containment program. The Commerce Committee, which shares jurisdiction over health with Ways and Means, has reported another similar bill.

I know how perplexing and difficult it is to translate worthy objectives into effective legislation. My own preference is to approach comprehensive health insurance one step at a time, with each step moving toward the goal of quality health care for all, but justifiable on its own even if nothing more is done. The constraints on moving more rapidly are high health costs and inflation, the federal budget deficit, and our limited capability for administering the programs fairly and efficiently. I would also like to improve Medicare for the elderly and the Medicaid program for those with low incomes. We urgently need insurance protection against the cost of catastrophic illness. Finally, I would like to increase the individual's responsibility, especially for health insurance by requiring first dollar financial participation in meeting hospital and other health costs to hold down costs and allocate scarce health resources. Whatever steps we take, members of the health professions should be closely involved in setting and enforcing treatment standards. Consumers also must participate.

The citizen's role is crucial, far more so than used to be thought appropriate. Citizens should inform themselves on the issues so as to play a part in determining what is to be done. This can be through all of the ways in which citizens bring their views to bear: letters to legislative and executive officials, resolutions by citizen organizations, and votes in elections. Like legislators, the citizens should aim to move the system toward handling health problems more responsibly. A person's tenacity, sense of what is practical and feel for what is fair and compassionate will be greater if the objectives are consistent with his or her ethical and religious values. Without this religious base, motivation for action is likely to be weak and insufficient.

My friend, Walsh McDermott, M.D., professor emeritus of public health and medicine at Cornell with long experience in developing countries and a health statesman has written:

> Medicine is . . . not a science but a learned profession that attempts to blend affairs of the spirit and the cold objectivity of science. Everything the physician does, therefore, is a blend of technology and Samaritanism. By Samaritanism is meant that collection of acts, big and little, that lends reassurance or at least gives support to someone troubled by disease or illness.

To put the matter in a Buddhist and holistic mold, good health is a right relation with oneself and with others. Pope John Paul II, who has been preaching in this country this past week, is a fascinating and powerful priest who combines conservative dogma with liberal humanism. Meeting him yesterday at the White House, I saw in him a visible example of the good health that comes from right relation with himself, with others, and with God. This kind of good health should be sought by everyone. It can be found by everyone, the sooner if real effort is put to the search. Significantly, right relation with oneself and with others, good health in this sense, is also available to those with incurable ailments who rise above them.

Health, then, is a matter of the spirit as well as the flesh, Samaritanism as well as technology. It is fundamentally a religious matter.

Good friends, take care.
   Take care of yourself, each one,
   That you may breathe long and deep
     Of life's challenge,

   Take care of each other
   That love may flow strong and swift
     In life's river,

   Take care of your world
   That the harmony of good health may prevail
     In yourself and in all,

   Good friends, Take Care.

The Drudge and the Drone

How dreary is the household drudge
Who sees a prison in the home,
Who finds the children quite a bore
And feels a slave to every chore.

How weary is the office drone
Who wishes that the work were done
And lacks imagination to
Do more than one's required to do.

The sad lament, the endless gripe,
The aching back, the nasty snipe,
The lonely soul who feels abused
Is sure he/she is being used.

In home or shop where there is one
Who'd like to see the work undone,
Who'd like to chuck the enterprise
And find a pie in outer skies,
The chances are this sky will fall.
The place may go to one more tall
Who sees in labor greater stakes
And with devotion gets the breaks.

Press On

To you who labor for some greater good,
    I say, press on! Don't underestimate
        your power to make your mark upon the course
           of human enterprise. Press on!
To you, the engineer or architect
    or carpenter, who by your fine design
        enhance the quality of human life,
           press on, for quality can be your mark.
To you, who work the soil, who nurture life,
    who work with flowers for beauty and for love,
        or harvest crops to feed a hungry world,
           press on, for by the land your soul is fed.
To you who govern or who seek to lead,
    and you who serve in business enterprise,
        integrity of purpose be your guide.
           Your true fulfillment is the greater good.
To you, the doctor, nurse, or minister,
    who work to guide and comfort those in need;
        to you, the judge and lawyer, who defend
        the civil liberties of rich and poor,
I say, press on, for human need is here
    and present. Health of mind and body and
        society depend upon your skill
           to rectify the wrong and light the way.
And you, the artist, with your brush and pen,
    who seek to capture beauty to be shared;
        and you, the dancer, move with strength and grace
        exalting feelings words cannot express.

And you, the writer, reaching out from deep within
   to find those words to illustrate your thoughts;
      and you, musician, find expression with
         your composition, instrument, or voice —
Press on, for as you cultivate your skill,
   perfecting each expression of your art,
      the joy of confidence will overcome
         frustration. You will know the soul's release.
To you, the teacher, sharing knowledge you
   possess, awakening minds to new ideas
   and new horizons only dimly seen,
      press on, for your horizons, too, shall grow.
And you, the parent, who with patient love
   exemplify respect and trust, and guide
     young minds and bodies to maturity,
     press on, for this is your posterity.
To you, who make a house a loving home,
   and you, who freely give your time to serve
    some human cause, I say, take pride!
     Press on! Humanity is at your side.

The Work Whistle

During most of my early boyhood our family lived in a small Rhode Island mill town. Life there was regulated by the work whistle. At 7:30 or so in the morning a loud whistle sounded at the textile plant signaling the beginning of the work day. At 5:22 in the late afternoon it sounded again for quitting time. The afternoon work whistle also meant that small boys should head for home. I don't remember why it blew at 5:22; probably I never knew. But it was a significant punctuation point in the day: the end of work for the men and many women, the end of play for the youngsters. The boy who failed to heed the 5:22 was headed for trouble.

Work has to be an important part of life if only to sustain life. But it should also be much more: an opportunity for creativity, for both physical and mental exercise, a chance to experience the satisfactions of competition and cooperation, the sense of providing for one's family and one's self, a way of fulfilling some of life's purposes. Work also can be dangerous, boring, frustrating, unappreciated, and demeaning. Whether we regard work in positive or negative terms depends not so much on the work itself as on the perspective we bring to it. One man's meat is another man's poison. Work for one is fun for another. Perspective and attitude toward work are wrapped up in a personal and social work ethic, even in the religious values that underlie it.

On the basis of a 40-hour work week, a little over one-third of the waking hours of an employed person is spent at work—close to 40 percent for urban workers including commuting time. Ironically homemakers who don't count in the statistics of the labor force unless they are paid and whose work output is not included in the gross national product, frequently work longer hours and at socially more significant tasks. My wife has taken pains to point this out to me from time to time; she's right, of course.

Forty years ago or so Harry Wallace, then Secretary of Agriculture, I think, wrote a book called *Sixty Million Jobs*. The goal seemed an impossible one to reach in those depression days. Now the number of jobs is fast approaching 100 million. If the homemakers and others whose work is not counted in the statistics are included, the number would exceed 100 million for this country. Despite seven million unemployed and more underemployed, an enormous amount of work is done each work day and each year in the United States.

How effectively all this work is done—nearly two trillion dollars worth a year—is another matter also of great importance. Productivity-output worker-year—is one measure of work effectiveness. In recent years, apparently, it has decreased somewhat, and much thought is being given to increasing the productivity of the economy. How productively people work depends on how skillful they are, their educational level, how good their tools are, how efficiently their activities are managed, the kinds of incentives and penalties that may be applied, and frankly how hard they work. This last factor is the telling factor for many jobs and depends largely on the motivation that arises out of the way people view work—work in general and their own jobs in particular. This applies to those counted in the official labor force and those who work outside that labor force.

A widely held opinion today is that the discipline and morale of the work ethic have deteriorated. Things come too easy, it is said. Welfare payments are not confined to those who need them and are too high anyway. Unemployment compensation encourages many people to avoid looking for work. The food stamp program is a mess. Young people don't get out and hustle. You've heard the recital. Practically everyone's grandfather and grandmother seems convinced the good old American work ethic with its emphasis on thrift and hard work has gone down the drain. The younger generation, as usual, is going to the dogs, and the future of the republic is threatened if not already lost. It is easy to caricature this view and to overlook the possibility that there may be some truth in it.

It may be that the material standard of living for large numbers of Americans is now such that the necessity for back-breaking, or mindbreaking, work is no longer present. The rewards of working harder or longer, given the general degree of affluence and the high rates of a progressive income tax, no longer outweigh the effort and cost of climbing up the corporate ladder and may well have lost their appeal. Perhaps the youth rebellion of a few years ago has left a lasting impression; perhaps blue jeans and a sweater will continue to be preferred over a gray flannel suit—update that to a pin-stripe suit—by many of the rebels of the late 60s and early 70s as they move past 30 years of age. We shall see.

The trade-off points between work and leisure, or more work and less work, are hard to predict both for an individual and for society. To work or not to work is an easier choice for most of us than to work a little more or work a little less. Obviously a person requires leisure and recreation not only to get ready to work again but also for the independent values they yield. All work and no play may make Jack a dull boy; all play and no work would probably make him duller. How to strike the balance between work and leisure: the answer to that question would be worth a lot more than $64 even adjusted for inflation. No magic will give an answer for everyone. One thing seems certain: leisure is more satisfying after work, and work is more inviting after leisure. In the oscillation between work and leisure, I suppose each of us has his own amplitude and periodicity, some swinging wildly back and forth and others gently.

Of course, a few workaholics seem to work all the time. I once had an insufferable colleague who arranged his life so as to arrive at the office before anyone else and leave later. From this superior position he smirked at the rest of us with evident disdain. He made us even more uncomfortable by working hard all day.

Others work very little on the job, preferably not at all. There are many techniques for accomplishing this. The most direct way is simply not to show up for work. The problem with this approach is that the pay will soon stop. There are more subtle ways of avoiding work without losing pay; some have developed work avoidance to the level of an art form. The techniques include making simple tasks appear difficult, convincing the boss that work results that don't need checking should be double and triple checked, taking long coffee breaks or preferably a sequential coffee break, and so on. Years ago when I was a private in the infantry I knew a few real artists in work avoidance who no doubt were descended from those who invented the term. The rules were fairly simple: in the field, get behind a bush or squat and keep a low profile; in a group stay near the middle neither at the front nor the rear; study carefully the habits and routes of movement of all sergeants so as to avoid them. One wag said, "Work fascinates me; I can sit and look at it all day!"

I have often thought that the lucky ones are those who enjoy their work so much that they scarcely know when leisure stops and work begins, or vice versa. For them the work whistle doesn't make much difference. Prizes should be awarded to people who can figure out how to make work enjoyable, how to lessen the significance of the work whistle. Careful placement of employees in suitable jobs, close attention to training and retraining programs, improvement of working conditions, good tools, fair wages, challenging jobs—all of these can help. But the real measure of the success of these efforts will consist of enlarging the perspective people have of work. Now and in the future in this country and other economically developed countries, challenge, enjoyment, diversity of experiences, appropriate participation in policy making and even management, stock ownership, genuine and responsible collective bargaining, and in-depth information about the outlook for the plant or office are likely to be increasingly important to workers morale and effort.

You remember the story of the common laborer who replied, when asked why he was digging a hole in the ground, "I'm not digging a hole in the ground; I'm building a cathedral." Perspective and attitude transform common labor into uncommon opportunity.

Last evening a friend of Italian background asked what I was going to talk about this morning. I said, "Work." He said, "Ah, work; how wonderful it is. If a person has work, though little else, he has life and dignity and achievement. Il bello lavoro—beautiful work," he concluded. Again, perspective and attitude make the difference. If beauty is in the eye of the beholder, then true value is in the mind and heart.

In my role as a legislator a number of issues have come up recently that have caused me to re-examine my views of work. As a member of a special energy committee in the House of Representatives, I have been involved in trying to bring together a compromise program to meet critical energy supply and price problems. Our country needs to proceed along two lines: to encourage conservation of oil and other forms of energy and to stimulate additional production of coal, nuclear, and solar energy, as well as oil and natural gas. We must try to use less and produce more—at least use energy less wastefully and produce it more efficiently. The latter requires harder, more effective work especially in the higher levels of research and technology—in geology, offshore drilling, development of safe nuclear breeder reactors, oil shale and coal gasification demonstration plants, solar energy experiments, and so on. Much of this work is exciting and soul-satisfying. A worker installing a solar energy collector on a roof is engaged in building a cathedral for the future. The scientist who figures out how to safely contain the immense heat in a fusion reactor at reasonable low cost will be working close to the heart of the universe.

But others working on energy will have to perform less glamorous tasks some of which are downright dangerous. The largest work requirement will be for coal miners in both underground and stripping operations. In the former, cave-ins still occur and black lung is endemic. In the latter, the ripping up of vast areas of landscape is necessary with consequent damage to the ecology of agriculture, water supply, and wildlife not to mention scenic attractiveness. In these efforts to produce more coal, the challenge will have be to find out how to do the work with minimum risk to health, safety, and environment. Government incentives and regulations can help if they are not overdone, but a genuine and lasting solution will depend on the determination of each worker and manager to do his job differently with more attention to conservation, efficiency, health, and environmental protection. In short, perspectives and attitudes will have to change.

To make progress in energy conservation, everyone will have to take a responsibility. The prescription is obvious: smaller cars, 55-miles-per-hour speed limit, thermostats down five degrees in winter and up five in summer, better insulated homes and buildings, time-of-day pricing of electricity, perhaps even long woolen underwear. These measures, obvious and down-to-earth as they are, will require rather profound behavioral changes if they are to succeed. They won't be achieved easily, especially in view of the fact that the energy crunch appears to be five to ten years off while actions to meet it must be begun right away. A new energy ethic consultant with Aldo Leopold's and Henry Moreau's land ethic is urgently needed. All who will be working in conservation themselves or in instructing others the new perspective should take pride in being part of a movement of great historic significance.

A week or two ago the House of Representatives voted to increase the minimum wage from $2.30 an hour to $2.65 next year with additional 20 cents an hour raises in each of the following two years. Those increases were substituted for an automatic escalation based on average wages in manufacturing that would have continued indefinitely. Most everyone would concede that not only is a good hour's work worth at least the new wage levels, but it would hardly be enough to support a person, much less a family, above the poverty level. The problem is to set the minimums high enough to prevent exploitatively low wages but not so high as to lead to unemployment. The problem is especially acute for unskilled teenagers seeking their first jobs. Because unemployment recently has been concentrated among young workers, especially urban minority groups reaching as high as 40 to 50 percent for black city youths who have not finished high school, I favored a six-month relaxing of the minimum wage for them. Labor union opposition pointing out that this might only result in jobs being taken away from older employees helped to defeat this provision by one scant vote. Like other proposed legislation having to do with workers and wages, the vote on this one was close and not easy to cast. I finally came down on the side of giving an extra break to young people trying to get started in a job.

Recently I have been concerned with other employment matters, such as a youth job corps and public service jobs, with social security financing, and

with welfare reform. Each of these has brought me up against problems of
work from a young persons first job to the retired person's benefit payments,
to the level at which society should help those who cannot find work despite
their efforts to do so and those who are handicapped to the extent they cannot
be expected to work. The goal of economic policy is employment for all
whom society believes should work, employment at the highest level of skill,
and wages, social contribution, and personal satisfaction that can be achieved.
This is not an easy task in view of budget constraints and the strong, widely
accepted preference for individual job choice in a predominantly private
enterprise economy. Government's mandatory jobs for all unemployed—the
idea that the government should guarantee jobs as the employer of last resort
if all else fails, is an attractive policy to many persons. But as a program it has
problems: should competitive or less than going wages be paid for such jobs?
How inflationary would such a jobs program be? Will the federal
government budget stand the likely expenditure? Can it be administered
effectively? Perhaps the will-of-the wisp but highly desirable goal of full
employment can be approached by other less rigid and more practical routes.
Thinking back to my own experiences as an economist on the staff of the
President's Council of Economic Advisors during the first six and a half years
of its existence, I am inclined now to look for a further development of a
full-employment-with-stable-prices policy along the lines of the basic
Employment Act of 1946, emphasizing both short and long range
economic-analysis and program formulation. I would favor eclectic and
flexible use of fiscal, monetary, wage-price-profit guidelines, and anti-trust,
incentive, and regulatory measures—along with more basic reforms in tax,
welfare, international trade, environment, energy, and some other fields.

I could go on with further examples to illustrate my theme that work can
continue to occupy a central and honored role in the life of individuals and
society, and that much will depend on the perspective and attitude with which
work is regarded. Tax incentives to encourage saving and investment, raising
or lowering employment taxes, enacting work tax credits, various budget
decisions setting priorities among competing programs some of which are
labor intensive and some not, occupational safety and health regulation,
procedural changes in bargaining and labor relations, job stimulation efforts,
vocational education—these and many others constitute the specific ways by
which legislation can affect the amount and conditions of work and of more
lasting importance.

Most would agree that the inherited Puritan work ethic has been hard
pressed in recent times. One wonders if it has fulfilled its historic role and is

now shuffling off the scene. The British historian, R. H. Tawney, 50 years ago in his book, *Religion and the Rise of Capitalism,* convincingly demonstrated that capitalism, enterprise, thrift, hard work, individual economic advancement, and all the rest of that syndrome known as the Puritan ethic emerged directly from religious reformation in northern Europe. This whole development reached the level of caricature 75 or 100 years ago in this country with industrial barons in steel, oil, and railroads who were moralistic about the virtues of hard, honest toil as the route to salvation as long as they were based on a 12-hour day at survival wages. If the day of the Puritan work ethic has run its course, what work ethic is to take its place?

The outlines of a new work ethic, which would be a significant modification of the old Puritan work ethic, are apparent in the points I have been trying to make: more emphasis on challenging work assignments, well designed educational and training programs, careful job placement, appropriate but not irresponsible participation by employees in policy formulation, a balancing of leisure with work such that the line between them becomes less sharp. The relentless drudgery of the Puritan work ethic should give way to an ethic that embraces newer elements. The sheer quantity of goods and services produced, and the resulting monetary income, should be accompanied by an increasing concern for quality of both the work experience and the products. A revised accounting of national income and product is needed to reflect quality. The key words for economic growth in the future ought to be quality, social equity, sustainability, fairness, and deep inner satisfaction as much as quantity of output, highest possible wages and profits, and relentless competition.

The necessity of a religious dimension to any new work ethic becomes obvious. Religion provides the psychological, emotional underpinning for any ethic which otherwise tends to be too intellectual and dry to sustain itself. We need another Tawney or Max Weber to explore the religious foundations for a new work ethic and perhaps a new economics. One thing seems sure to me: the work whistle that signals the beginning and the end of the work day dividing work and leisure into airtight compartments, needs to be replaced by a symbol which signifies that work and other activities are parts of continuum of a useful, satisfying life for individuals and of an integrated, purposeful society.

Give us, Teacher, the wisdom
to place work in a new context
That embraces refreshing leisure
    and rewarding labor
To form whole persons
    in a whole society.

Remembered

Born of beauty, love and hope
New life begins. Forgotten soon
Are pain and little pangs of fear.
Remembered are the tiny hands
And searching lips and searching eyes.
Remembered is the sacred pledge
To help this child to grow
In stature and in love secure.

The span of years from birth to death
Is temporal. We cannot know
Its length or consequence or strength.
This much is certain: we will be
Remembered for the good we bring,
The joy we give, the love we share.
Forgotten soon will be the pain
And suffering, for life goes on.

Forgotten is the withered frame
And fading flesh and fading sight.
Forgotten are the lonely hours
When death approached to take its toll.
The gentle graciousness of time
Replaces grief with memories.
Remembered is a lifetime gladly
Shared to make a better world.

The Cycle of the Years

Hope is borne with springtime,
New life growing from the old.
Each blade of grass, each infant
Newly born and loved,
Each flower to unfold
Contains the precious germ of life.
The cycle of the years:
The rhythm of the seasons told.

The joys of summer like
The playful joys and passions of
Our youth appear unending
As with beauty, health and love
We while away the days
Unheeding of the past or future
As distant as the stars above.

The cooler days of autumn
Like our milder middle years
Find us settled into patterns,
Secure in our experience
And easy with our peers.
Of storms there are aplenty,
But cooler are the passions,
And more reasoned are the fears.

The graying skies of winter
When trees have shed their leaves
Remind us time is passing.
Those we love become more precious.
On each passing someone grieves,

Yet there's a peace of understanding
As quiet as the snow.
Each day we live must be worthwhile,
For none the past retrieves.

Hope is born with springtime,
new life growing from the old.
Each blade of grass,
each infant newly born and loved,
Each flower to unfold contains
the precious germ of life.
The cycle of the years:
the rhythm of the seasons told.

Endings and Beginnings

Sooner or later one has to think about birth and death, beginnings and endings. There is no escape from this obligation. The brackets that enclose life are birth and death in a hard, practical, real sense. Within the brackets life's experiences are packed of work and play, pain and joy, achievement and failure, time used wisely and time wasted. Outside the brackets on the one side is the inheritance each of us receives from the past and on the other side the effect each of us has on the future. What lies within the brackets, our lives, is all we can know for sure; the rest is history or prophecy.

Everyone has to cope with birth and death, both in concept and reality, personally, and for others around him. Some seem to be able to do this easily and naturally, accepting both birth and death as parts of the total experience of living, as events in the continuum of life. Others, perhaps most, have difficulty coming to terms with the birth-life-death process, especially with death. They fight it; they fear it; they concoct elaborate theories so as to avoid it. But escape is impossible; once birth has occurred, death must follow. If this inevitability is accepted, then the full focus of attention can be directed on living, where it belongs, on the objectives and principles of the good and worthy life. Helping us as individuals to accomplish this focus is, I believe, a major task of religion.

The other day I reread Wordsworth's magnificent poem, "Intimations of Immortality from Recollections of Early Childhood."

> There was a time when meadow, grave, and stream,
> The earth and every common sight,
>   To me did seem
>   Appareled in celestial light,
> The glory and the freshness of a dream.
>
> Our birth is but a sleep and a forgetting:
> The Soul that rises with us, our life's Star,
>   Hath had elsewhere its setting,
>   And cometh from afar:
>   Not in entire forgetfulness,
>   And not in utter nakedness,
> But trailing clouds of glory do we come

From God who is our home:
Heaven lies about us in our infancy!

In contrast to this beautiful, romantic vision some of my own most vivid recollections of early childhood would more accurately be thought of as intimations of mortality, rather than immortality. Each of us can look back and recall the early experiences of birth and death. Regarding birth, we think of the baby sister or brother; we remember the new puppy or rabbit; if we were brought up on a farm, the recollection of a calf being dropped or litter of pigs or an egg hatching will never be forgotten.

But the more poignant memories for most of us will be the death of plants, animals, and persons. As nearly as I can recollect, my first observation of dying and death came when, as a small boy, I watched bug-eyed as two older boys clubbed a porcupine to death in a gory and horrible scene. Then they cut off a paw which could be turned in to the local game warden for a twenty-five cents bounty.

I remember bending birches in early spring with some other boys. This is done by selecting a birch tree of just the right size, shinnying up into its branches, and then grasping the main stem firmly, swinging one's legs out and down. As the supple birch bends, one lowers slowly to the ground. Then one springs upward off the ground, then up and over to the ground on the other side, with the birch again bending with one's weight. The trouble was that on this occasion the slender birch snapped as it bent toward the ground, a long green-splint break. But what I really remember is the sight of the birch when I returned a couple of weeks later. The fresh green spring leaves had already dried and turned brown. The moist soft wood under the brown bark had dried and hardened. I lifted the tree, half expecting it to spring upright again, but it fell lifeless to the ground as soon as I let it go. The birch was dead.

We all remember our first encounter with human dying and death—the strangeness, the unreality, the impossibility of it. Someone who was and then is no more—a grandparent, a neighbor, a friend. These experiences, however long ago, are too sharp and poignant to focus on even now more than momentarily. Whether person, tree, or animal, their dying is among the child's first intimations of mortality. Later on the intimations become more frequent and insistent and have somehow to be enveloped in an explaining and protecting philosophy.

Of course I am not thinking about birth and death in biochemical terms relating to conception, growth, decay and death. This aspect can be largely explained by scientists who understand these matters. Nor am I thinking of the ordinary economic and other practical functions a person performs during his life, valuable though they are. Or, carried to a ludicrous extreme, I am not thinking of the few cents the chemicals that make up a new baby are worth increased to a dollar or two for an adult, plus an allowance for inflation. Rather, I am thinking of all the things that can be done between birth and death: the beauty to be seen, the music to be heard, the work to be accomplished, the fun to be had, the love to be given and received; and also the disappointments to be endured, the pain to be suffered, the self-doubts to be overcome, the niche to be found and filled. Between the promise at the beginning and the reckoning at the end are the years of living. In the living, I maintain, is to be found both the justification of birth and the justification of death.

It may be argued that this is too stern a way of looking at life and puts too heavy an obligation on us all to achieve. It is much too hard, it may also be pointed out, on the low-level achievers, the unambitious, the handicapped, and the disadvantaged. Perhaps this is so, but the pressure is surely no greater than that applied to avoid reincarnation as a low and despicable form of life or to avoid eternal damnation in a fiery place. Furthermore, acceptance of the importance of life on earth and living it well does not mandate that everyone try to be superman or superwoman. The most that could reasonably be asked for is that each individual give life a good go and choose something useful and considerate to be made of it. Those who wish to try for true and absolute excellence should be encouraged. Achievement in relation to one's potential is a fairer measurer. Those who can't aspire to compose or play great music can listen to it respectfully and with enjoyment, or they can turn their attention elsewhere. My point is: if we only go around once, as the beer ad says, we'd better make a try and not be afraid of failure; we'd better not take a cop-out here with the idea we'll have another chance in the happy hunting grounds. Human dignity requires no less, whatever the odds against us. Intimations of mortality should spur us on because there isn't all that much time. The message of death is life, even though the end of life is death.

This is all very well, some may say, this assertion that life is the thing and all else is trivial. There has to be more, they continue, than the here and now, peopled largely by the young, the bright, and the active. If the proverbial three score years and ten are all we have, then life is really a hoax, a great expectation that for most will never be fulfilled. Even if the existential now is stretched to cover a lifetime, they say further, its spectrum is still too narrow for all the colors to show. There still is death out there somewhere ahead of us like a great wall. Will it stop us cold? Or is there a way to get over it or around it? And if there is, what lies on the other side?

I think the imagery is wrong. Death is not a wall at which one arrives frustrated and defeated, wondering how to get over or past it into new, lush fields. Rather it is a slowing down, a loss of momentum, a fading out like a road in the woods that gradually stops being a road or even a trail. The end, death, creeping in like the silent fog, is usually a gradual loss of separate identity, a merging back again with nature just as our forebears have done. There is nothing to get past or over, it is ending by absorption: the forest, the earth, the air, the universe simply gathering in their own. When death is sudden, as it sometimes is, the same gathering in takes place, only more quickly; what is gathered in is not so much the death and the last moments of life but the whole life itself from its beginning in the cradle through its growing up and its maturity—a gathering in of the whole life and its total effect.

But what about those who are left—wives, husbands, sons, daughters, fathers, mothers, friends? What of them? How are they to accustom themselves to the passing of the one they love—to reconcile their hurt with the finality of what has happened? Of course, no easy adjustment for them is possible, no swift and easy passage back to life as usual. But no one should ever think that life is easy, it is not; it is full of difficult passages. Surely those who remain after will be comforted if the one they loved lived life with dignity, truth, consideration, and love. Surely they will be encouraged if their departed friend predicated his life on generous thoughts and good deeds for all. Surely they will also regain composure if they think of death as a natural, essentially uncomplicated and inevitable event to be mourned for a time and then placed gently into memory. It is sound advice regarding the passing of a loved one or a friend: we shall never forget the death, and we shall always remember the life.

In the long cycle of life from birth to death, special care needs to be exercised near the beginning and near the end. Parents, neighbors and friends, and society generally have to pay particular attention to the rearing and education of children and to the encouragement and support of the elderly. The quality of a society—a city, a state, a country—can be gauged quite accurately by the care it devotes to its children and its senior adults. I am not thinking here so much of government funds and private programs as of the total concern by individual persons. In our own country, progress has been quite good in recent years, but never good enough. The regular schools are well established with competent faculties, but problems of drop outs, disorderly conduct, unappealing curriculums, and clumsy administration remain. Kindergartens, child care centers, and special programs have multiplied, but increasing divorce rates, more working mothers, and perhaps less paternal concern for children have taken a toll. The exhaustion of readily available tax sources will make further public efforts to improve education. The main issues of life and death can be considered in church schools to good advantage and in other educational experiences. I am pleased that our church school curriculum deepens children's understanding of the whole life process from beginning to end.

I wish our county did as well with programs for older citizens as for school pupils. Good county programs, like those offered in Culpepper Garden, the retirement home sponsored by our church, fall far short of meeting the rapidly growing need. There is not enough suitable housing for the elderly. Transportation, though slightly subsidized for them, is still too expensive. Food stamps are available for some, but the program is not well administered. Property tax and rent relief for low income people over 65 helps but only a little. Medical costs are still troublesome despite the boon of Medicare. But the most serious problem of the elderly, I think, is the need for friends, relatives, and the whole community to care more in hundreds of little personal ways. This attention, so much needed and so deeply appreciated, fortunately requires no tax dollars, no elaborate administration, only some human sympathy and willingness to help.

Recently Ira Lechner brought forward a "death with dignity" bill to Virginia's General Assembly. Delegate Lechner proposes that persons who wish to avoid prolongation of their lives when members of their families and competent medical doctors agree that hope of recovery no longer exists, may so specify and have this honored in law. The safeguards have been thought through carefully and there appears to be widespread support of the measure among all age groups. Those who favor this approach argue that it not only will save large and futile medical expenses but will avoid unnecessary suffering and anguish as well. So far the General Assembly has been unwilling to take this step. It seems to me to be a more natural and sensible alternative consistent with my emphasis on living with death as the natural termination of human life.

A sentiment about old age that has always appealed deeply to me is beautifully expressed in the last stanzas of Longfellow's poem, "Morituri Salutamus" (We Who Are About to Die Salute You). Incidentally Longfellow read his poem, named after the Roman gladiator's cry, at the fiftieth reunion of his graduating class at Bowdoin College in Maine, my college also.

> The night hath not yet come; we are not quite
> Cut off from labors by the failing light;
> Something remains for us to do or dare;
> Even the oldest tree some fruit may bear.
>
> For age is opportunity no less
> Than youth itself, though in another dress,
> And as the evening twilight fades away
> The sky is filled with stars, invisible by day.

Analysis and cerebration by themselves are not adequate for understanding birth and death. Religion must be brought to the task. Especially this is so if mature men and women are to find the support necessary for a view of birth and death, in their deepest meaning, as natural, integral parts of living without the psychological props of miraculous birth or heavenly hereafter. The natural birth-life-death process is miracle enough.

What we experience during the span of our lives, then, is all we can know about ourselves, our companions, and our world. What we do with the years between birth and death will tell the story. If there is a heaven, it is in us and in the earth, imagined as potentiality, waiting to be born. It is not a condition that comes automatically or as a reward after death; rather it is a vision of a better life, a better world, to be created here, now, by us as our legacy to the future. This is the intimation of the only immortality we can count on; the immortality of the good and worthy life whose influence lives on in the hearts and minds of those whom it touches.

Religion, guiding each of us through our years, can help to transform the reality of our time into the vision of what it can become. Such a religion gives meaning to birth and death, and the living in between, and can truly make beginnings out of endings.

O God, give us the insight to see
That death is only the end of the beginning;
That the life-work of a person
    Who has contributed something of worth,
    Something good, or something beautiful
Lives on in the hearts of men and women
And in the structure of the universe.

Part Five

Faith and Freedom

Freedom Is the Means

Freedom lies not in the absence
of restraint, nor in chaotic
anarchy, nor does it come with
irresponsibility or
lonely, blind indifference.

Freedom is the means and not the
end for which we strive. It is the
possibility of growth, the
gateway to a larger world of
mutual respect and purpose.

Freedom should be meaningful and
add dimension to our lives and
to lives which touch our own.
Our time on Earth is limited.
God help us learn to use it well.

Freedom for Responsibility

America has aimed, still aims, to be the country of freedom. From the Pilgrims in 1620 to the Cubans and Vietnamese of recent years, immigrants have come here to be free. Our national poets like Walt Whitman have sung of freedom. Our greatest political leaders like George Washington, Abraham Lincoln, Woodrow Wilson, and Franklin Roosevelt have led us in fighting for freedom. Our pioneer ancestors crossed the continent in search of freedom. One of our favorite hymns speaks of "freedom's holy light." Our national anthem proclaims ours to be "the land of the free and the home of the brave."

Emancipation, then, has been the dominant theme in American history—the culmination of intellectual, social, and emotional forces set in motion in Europe by Copernicus and Galileo, by Locke and Rousseau, by John Milton, by the framers of the Magna Carta. But despite magnificent progress toward freedom, its full realization continues to elude us, as does the sense of national well-being and individual happiness that are supposed to go with freedom. Having reached a degree of political, economic, and personal freedom hitherto unknown, we are dismayed to find that freedom alone is not enough, that one person's freedom frequently is another's constraint, that the end result of freedom frequently is unsatisfying.

I believe the missing element is responsibility in the use of freedom so that freedom is employed for purposes beyond itself: for helping others, for example, or for artistic creation, or for discovering scientific truth, or for working with skill, effectiveness and pride. We yearn for freedom *from* responsibility only to discover that what we really want and need is freedom *for* responsibility.

This linkage between freedom and responsibility is not a new idea. But lack of novelty must not be confused with lack of significance. Thinkers through the centuries have known that both moral and political freedom implies responsibility in its exercise. "No man is free who is not master of himself," Epictetus's aphorism reminds us.

John Stuart Mill, reflecting on liberty, wrote: "The only freedom which deserves the name is that of pursuing our own good, in our own way, so long as we do not attempt to deprive others of theirs, or impede their efforts to obtain it." As he grew older, Mill emphasized social responsibility in the exercise of individual freedom if that freedom were to have wider utility and value. In fact, Mill, having started out as an individualistic liberal, died a socialist.

I think the immigrants who have been coming to America, for over 400 years, understood as well as the philosophers that freedom is only the first step to a good life. Emma Lazarus's poem at the base of the Statue of Liberty says: "Give me your tired, your poor, your huddled masses yearning to breathe free." But after they arrived and settled here, the immigrants began the long task of achieving other goals: education, a prosperous farm or business, the building of a town, the establishment of a church.

Roots, which so many of us have watched on television, is the saga of a family struggling for freedom, not for itself alone but to achieve greater economic security and personal fulfillment. During dramatic moments when one or another of the central characters is about to strike out blindly to prevent an act of repression, he or she is restrained by a cooler and wiser person demanding, "What is you going to do with your freedom after that, if you gets it?"

Two kinds of freedom can be distinguished: political freedom in the sense of laws, the secret ballot, and constitutional protection of individual rights; and moral freedom of a personal nature based on free will and free choice. The latter, I would argue, is more fundamental than the former, although the relationship between the two is complex and subtle. Without genuine choice there is no way individuals can erect and maintain free social institutions and political processes. And without free institutions and political processes, personal freedom to choose is impossible or meaningless in the public realm.

Philosophical opponents of free will argue that a person's decisions and actions are entirely determined by environment, heredity, chance, or fate. Those on the other side, while conceding the relevance of these factors, insist there is room for the exercise of choice, either deriving from God or within the nature and destiny of humans. I have some sympathy for Dr. Johnson who closed a debate on this point by thundering, "Why, sir, we know the will is free, and there's an end to it."

"We hold these truths to be self-evident, that all men are created equal, that they are endowed by their Creator with certain inalienable rights, that among these are life, liberty and the pursuit of happiness." The lineage of these precious words of Jefferson, inscribed in the hearts of Americans as well as written in their Declaration of Independence, is distinguished. It runs back to George Mason, who drafted the Virginia Declaration of Rights shortly before, to Voltaire and other philosophers of the French revolution, to John Locke in England, and more remotely to Greek thinkers of the Golden Age of Athens. The lineage has also run forward from Jefferson to Lincoln and the emancipation leaders, to Susan B. Anthony and the suffragettes, to Horace Mann and others who established free public schools, to Martin Luther King, Jr. and other leaders in the civil rights movement. The sincere but somewhat fumbling effort of President Carter to reassert this country's devotion to human rights in the world, the preeminent right being freedom, is part and parcel of this tradition.

Political freedom requires a confidence that such freedom will be exercised responsibly. If it is not used responsibly, it will not be sustained, nor perhaps should it be. Freedom without responsibility is freedom run amok, guaranteed to "loose mere anarchy upon the world."

The classic example occurred in revolutionary France during the Reign of Terror. Marat was murdered in his bathtub; Robespierre was executed by the guillotine along with several thousand others found by kangaroo courts to be guilty of treason against whatever Jacobin or other political club held the power of state. Reaction to this excess was inevitable, and Napoleon took over. Lest you think this example is far-fetched, recall what happened in 1917 to the short-lived Kerensky government in Russia and observe the events unfolding in Iran at the present time, the outcome of which cannot yet be seen.

If a sense of responsibility is essential to the proper exercise of freedom, and ultimately to its existence, then what can undergird this sense of responsibility? What can assure its presence? Here, I believe, we must look to religion. Religion has to supply the cement that binds, in this case the cement that binds individual commitment to freedom to an outlook and mode of action for freedom in the political and social spheres.

Two 19th century American Unitarian ministers preached eloquently on this matter. William Ellery Channing wrote:

> Political liberty is of but little worth but as it springs from, expresses and invigorates spiritual freedom. . . . Civil freedom is a blessing chiefly as it reverences the human soul and ministers to its growth and power. . . . The only freedom worth possessing is that which gives enlargement to a people's energy, intellect, and virtues.

And Theodore Parker wrote:

> It is because I've seen in him [man] a great nature, the divine image, and vast capacities, that I demand for him means of self-development, spheres for free action—that I call society not to fetter, but to aid his growth.

Religion asks the question: freedom for what?—and then searches for an answer that represents men and women at their best. This gets to the heart of the issue, freedom for responsibility.

In his essay, "Science and Religion," Albert Einstein, the centennial of whose birth we are celebrating this year, stated the goal correctly in both its religious and human forms: "Free and responsible development of the individual, so that he may place his powers freely and gladly in the service of all mankind." What could be a more responsible way to use freedom?

Freedom, it turns out, can be misunderstood, misdirected, and misused. It can even be perverted into an evil thing if its link to responsibility is broken.

In the spring of 1936, during the long holidays students in England used to enjoy, I was headed for Bavaria to practice my German and do some hiking. I took a night train from Brussels. We stopped in Cologne about midnight and then proceeded south through the Rhineland, then part of France, it having been annexed after the first World War. I slept fitfully on the wooden bench in a third class compartment. Toward dawn the train seemed to stop frequently and then start forward again, interrupting my sleep and that of my fellow travelers. As daylight came on, we became aware that things were not as they should be. Train conductors kept scurrying through the corridor; outside groups of people waited at village stations and road crossings. The stops became longer and more frequent. The train pulled into one town where a large crowd had gathered in the main square beside the railroad station, including a small, oom-pah German band. The Brown Shirts, Hitler's quasi-militia, were out, as were the Hitler Youth. A company of more organized troops came carrying out-of-date rifles and others armed only with wooden sticks. Uniformed men were shouting orders and directions through hand megaphones. A sense of excitement and danger was everywhere. We weren't allowed off the train. It was difficult to figure out what was happening.

Finally a military officer, a little man with a big voice, marched into our car, followed by several Brown Shirts who commanded us to be silent. I could understand most of what the little man with the big voice said. He said, "The Rhineland is being retaken today by German troops—reunited with the Fatherland—German rights and dignity being regained—nothing to fear, France will do nothing, too weak and irresolute—the train will move on soon, schedules will be resumed—a great day for the German people— *ein Lande, ein Volk, ein Fürer, Freiheit für Alles! Heil Hitler.*" And off he marched.

The Rhineland was being unilaterally reoccupied in the name of freedom. A bold, first step had been taken. No one—not France, not Britain—had the foresight or the will to stop it. The dominoes started to fall: German rearmament on a modern and massive scale forced Anschluss with Austria, the take-over of the Sudetenland on the Czech border, the short-lived nonaggression treaty with the Soviet Union, the invasion of Poland to begin the classic Drang nach Osten, the strike across the Low Countries to outflank Paris, the Battle of Britain . . . and so on to the tragic end five years or so later in a bunker in Berlin. But only after 20 million people, one way or another, had lost their lives.

And so much of it was done in the name of freedom, at least for the self-proclaimed master race—a freedom too narrow, too exclusive, totally lacking in a tolerant and generous outlook, a perversion of freedom beyond belief of persons not there at the time and almost beyond their belief to those who look back on it.

I went on to Munich and then to a small town in the foothills of the magnificent German Alps where I lived with a *gemütlich* German family. One of the sons, with whom I went mountain climbing, had already been drawn into the Hitler Brown Shirt organization and was beginning to revel in the "free spirit" he felt from it. He shared this with me on the trail during our hikes and there seemed to be nothing I could say that had the slightest effect on him. He took me to a meeting of his group and it frightened me.

Several months later when I returned briefly during the summer vacation, he took me to a gigantic rally in Munich in connection with the forthcoming Berlin Olympic Games. The highlight was an impassioned, almost hypnotic speech by the Führer, Hitler himself. What a mindblowing experience it was— with Hitler's screaming, the unison responses screamed back by the crowd, the hundreds of swastika banners, the phalanxes of young Brown Shirts with their hard-set mouths and their eyes alight. The word, *freedom,* was shouted over and over.

My friend, I guess I would still call him that, was killed in the war somewhere on the Russian front.

The ugliest depravity of those hideous years was the extermination of several million Jews, all justified by freeing and purifying the master race. In his book, *The Anatomy of Liberty,* Justice William Douglas, himself a champion of freedom, quotes a few lines from the Russian poet, Yevtushenko, written in 1961 about Babi Yar, a ravine near Kiev where the Nazis massacred 100,000 Jews. The words are immortal:

> There is a rustling of wild grass over Babi Yar.
> The trees look fearsome, like judges,
> Everything here screams in silence. . . .

This has been a long personal and historical account in my philosophical and religious discussion of freedom *for* responsibility. But the frightful Nazi experience, which made such a sharp and deep impression on me and my generation, must be learned from.

One thing lacking in Germany in those years was a strong, secure tradition of legal, political, and human rights—a bill of rights such as ours in the United States, won with blood, sweat, and tears, or an ancient tradition of such rights as evolved in England since the Magna Carta of 1215. Freedom of speech and the press, freedom of assembly, freedom to petition the government for redress of grievances, and especially freedom of religion guaranteed in law—these support a free people. Consider just the first: freedom of speech and of the press. How hard they were to establish and how vigilantly they have to be kept!

Still the most eloquent testimony to the importance of a free press is John Milton's *Areopagitica,* an essay on freedom of the press after the Order of the Long Parliament on the regulating of printing:

> . . . as good almost kill a man as kill a good book; who kills a reasonable creature, God's image; but he who destroys a good book, kills reason itself, kills the image of God, as it were in the eye . . . for books are not absolutely dead things but do contain a potency of life in them to be as active as that soul whose progeny they are. . . .

The story of Elijah P. Lovejoy of Alton, Illinois is precious, especially to journalists. Lovejoy was an abolitionist editor in a town divided on the slavery issue. A public meeting was called on November 3, 1837 to demand that he cease writing and publishing on the subject. His defense is still eloquent:

> If the civil authorities refuse to protect me, I must look to God . . . I have sworn eternal opposition to slavery and by the blessings of God I will never turn back. With God I cheerfully rest my cause. I can die at my post but I can never desert it.

As Justice Douglas tells the story, four nights later a mob destroyed Lovejoy's press and Lovejoy was killed in the fracas.

Notice that both Milton and Lovejoy, in the ultimate sense, relied on God, on religion, to support their belief in freedom of the press. They reached beyond themselves, beyond the immediate situation, beyond temporal power, beyond law to justify their beliefs and actions. Notice also that they did not separate the general principle at stake, freedom of the press, from their own personal commitment. And notice finally that their love of freedom was matched by their devotion to proceeding in a thoughtful, thoroughly responsible way.

These are not academic observations, relevant only as history. Think of Solshenitzen and Pasternak in recent times in the Soviet Union, or of the German novelist, Thomas Mann, only a few decades ago, or of threats against our own denominational press, the Beacon Press, when it published the Pentagon Papers. Among the authors whose books have been banned in the United States, in my lifetime alone, are James Joyce, William Faulkner, John Dos Passos, H.L. Mencken, Erskine Caldwell, Edmund Wilson, Erich Maria Remarque, and many more. Jefferson was right: eternal vigilance is the price of liberty. Equally, Jefferson might have said—and somewhere probably did say: responsibility is the price of freedom.

In our time—the years since the Great Depression and the second World War—we have directed attention toward civil and other rights for minorities which are necessary if Blacks, Indians, Hispanic Americans and others are truly to be free. All of us have our own stories to tell. I recall the soul-searching of the members of the faculty at the University of Mississippi in Oxford, where William Faulkner lived and wrote, when the Supreme Court handed down its unanimous decision on racially segregated schools in Brown v. Board of Education of Topeka. I was teaching there at the time, a Northerner with a Unitarian and abolitionist heritage, observing as sympathetically as possible my new Southern friends as they struggled with the problem of how they, their families, their university, their South could move from where they were in race relations to where they knew they had to go.

I remember also the discrimination I saw directed against the Indians in the villages along the Alaska Coast where I lived and worked when I was younger: their wretched housing, tuberculosis, separate and unequal schools, the low wages and their inability to get out of debt.

I don't forget either our efforts here in northern Virginia for opening restaurants, movie theaters, and public parks to Blacks; our fight for fair housing; our elimination of Jim Crow buses. And I am proud that my own church broke the back of the policy that prohibited integration in Arlington County parks by going through with an integrated church picnic, despite warnings. Several of us got hauled into the police station on that one.

Like many of you, I still thrill to Martin Luther King Jr.'s exultation at the Lincoln Memorial: "Free at last. Thank God Almighty, free at last."

So we continue to make progress toward freedom, though much remains to be done—for women, for the handicapped, for the poor, for minorities, for those lost in the swamps of drugs and alcohol, for the neglected whatever the reason, for the sick at heart—so that all persons may breathe free.

But the hardest part, I think, will be to match every gain in freedom, in equal rights and equal opportunity, with an increase in our willingness fully to accept responsibility for the consequences of that freedom. Only then will the blessings of freedom be realized by individual persons and by society. Only then will the exercise of freedom be a religious experience.

> May the urge for freedom
> And the discipline of responsibility
>   Travel together,
> So that, undergirded by religion,
> Freedom will be *for* responsibility
>   Not *from* it.

To Turn a Dream

That life is meaningful which looks
With level eye at harsh reality
And dares to reach beyond into
A better world, that learns to cope
With loss and inner hurt and seeks
New avenues, new outlets for
Creative skills and ingenuity.

That life is meaningful which meets
With calm determination pain
And suffering and finds new strength,
New wisdom in adversity,
That treats with sensitivity
The frailty, the vulnerability
Of fellow creatures, young and old.

That life is meaningful which faces
Aging as a fact of life,
Which neither pities nor begrudges
Youth nor looks with fear on passing
Time or passing life, but makes
Each day an opportunity
To turn a dream into reality.

Living with Reality and with Dreams

Among the fascinating aspects of life is the way we deal with reality and with dreams. We dream awhile of how things would be at their best, or their worst. Then something happens—a loud noise, a bump—and we are brought back to reality. Or it may go the other way: we are proceeding routinely, dully about our tasks when imperceptibly we drift off into a dream world, as Walter Mitty did.

You remember in James Thurber's story, Mitty was in his car waiting for his wife to return from shopping in a nearby store. A meek, hen-pecked husband, he imagined himself successively to be a cool and fearless flying ace, a take-charge executive, and several other types he dreamed of being. Each time his fantasy would be broken rudely by a policeman rapping on the car window and saying, "Move on, buddy," or by some other outsider. The contrast between dreams and reality, the irony and humor, the profound sadness of it, are touching. Every one of us can identify with poor Mitty even though we are more fortunate in our spouses.

Life, it seems, is an alternation of dreams and reality, visions of how life and the world might be, moving into our consciousness, and then moving out to be replaced by the hard rock of what really exists out there. And then reality again gives way to a shimmering vision of what might be. We have to learn to live with both and, if possible, to extract something from the dreams that leads to improvement of the reality. Equally, we should allow reality to temper and restrain our dreams, at least our wilder dreams.

The dreams I have in mind are not those of persons who have gone entirely round the bend into abnormality. They are the garden variety type that everyone has. Also, I shall have some comments on the shared dreams or hopes of large numbers of people for peace, prosperity, and the good life. Dreams, whether individual or societal, do come up against realities, against what is possible given the situation. This, of course, is no reason not to dream, daytime or nighttime. I do some of my best dreaming in broad daylight while fully awake. I want to deal with the interplay between dreams and hopes on the one side and the realities of life on the other.

At their most useful dreams give the dreamer a glimpse of how he or she might solve a personal problem, realize his or her potential more fully, or relate more satisfactorily to others. Useful also is the dream that makes disasters vivid before they happen, allowing corrective action to be taken in time. Even if we haven't had the experience ourselves, we all know of someone who escaped a disaster because it was foretold in a dream—the ticket canceled at the last minute on the flight that ended in a crash, all because of a premonition in the night. Of course, we forget those secret warnings of catastrophes that don't occur. One author called dreams "children of the night, of indigestion bred."

One is tempted to say that dreams are tricky and unreliable while reality is solid and always there. I'm not so sure. Dreams in the sense of perceptions of what might be frequently overcome reality. Alexander dreamed of conquering the world and very nearly did so. Joan of Arc had a vision and saved her country. I understand that major break-throughs in science occur while the scientist is not paying much attention: Newton day-dreaming under the apple tree; James Watt idly noticing the bouncing of the lid on the kettle of boiling water; Fleming removing the mold from the window sill where he had thoughtlessly placed it. The results were the laws of motion, the steam engine, and penicillin. Reality in each case was given a new dimension. Some of its secrets were pushed into the open by reverie, idleness, carelessness, dreaminess.

But notice that in each case what I loosely call dreaming sparked an insight in the mind of someone who had been puzzling on an aspect of reality he already knew a lot about. In each case there was that "flash upon the inward eye," but also the background of knowledge to understand what the flash meant. Reality, I am arguing, conditions speculations, hypotheses, even dreams, distorted though they may be. And dreams help to unravel the mysteries of reality. The interaction between the two is altogether fascinating.

Many facts of reality are hard to live with: the reality of one's limitations, the steady dripping away of time, the awareness of mistakes made, the facing up to uncertainty and unknowableness, the lack of control over events of immense significance to one's life, the fact of deceit and evil in the world. No amount of wishing these elements of reality would go away will move them so much as an inch. They have to be faced, dealt with, but each has its other side.

Limitations are matched by opportunities. Time can be turned to account and be made to yield a dividend even as it slips away. Mistakes can be learned from. Uncertainties can be insured against. Self-discipline can bring a measure of control over one's life. And evil time and again has been rooted out.

My theme is that reality itself can be bent to our will, at least a little bit, even as we learn to live with it. And flashes of insight, dreams if you wish, frequently give us the clues as to how to do it. Such insights can come at the strangest times and in the strangest places. For me the first moments of wakefulness in the morning when I begin to turn my attention to the problems of the day ahead is the time I am most likely to catch a glimpse of how to meet the on-rushing problems. The inconclusive ruminations of the day and night before come into focus; lights appear at the end of long tunnels. It makes me want to get up and have at the day, problems and all. My wife, tells me, that she has certain places she goes to when she needs to work on a problem: out beside the garage, her studio where she paints, sometimes at the kitchen sink. I think her mind goes into a kind of mystical over-drive, a fourth gear or dimension, which enables her to figure out how to cope with some intractable part of reality.

Just as reality can tear you down, so too can dreams tear you down if you allow them to run wildly beyond the reach of your little portion of reality. In a curious sense dreams can become too unrealistic. This tendency may be relatively harmless, as in Walter Mitty's case; after all, who would blame him for wanting to escape an over-bearing wife and a dull job occasionally? But totally unrealistic dreaming can be tragic, as it was for the poor soul in Tennessee Williams' fragile Glass Menagerie or for Miniver Cheevy in Edwin Arlington Robinson's poem:

> Miniver Cheevy, born too late,
> Scratched his head and kept on thinking,
> Miniver coughed, and called it fate,
> And kept on drinking.

Another Robinson character, Richard Cory, who seemed to have it made, to have life and reality by the tail, "one summer night went home and put a bullet through his head."

One inevitable part of reality for each of us that is particularly hard to face is failure. My friend, Steven Muller, president of Johns Hopkins University, offered a marvelous homily at a university commencement a few years ago on the subject:

> Americans do not understand nor do they live well with failure. Yet it is an inevitable part of the human condition: no one can win them all . . . who can do more than one's best? As a people we try to shut out the realities of failure and death (the ultimate failure). . . . Each of us will die and each of us will fail at things. . . . Failure is no disgrace. He who never fails can never have tried very hard. . . . In fact, those who try most will fail most. . . . To each I wish a successful life of self-respect based on your best efforts exerted without fear of failure.

Sometime later I was talking with a young friend who graduated that day and heard Steve's talk. She said his words had suddenly lifted a great weight from her shoulders, had liberated her from the fear of failure that had petrified her for years.

Failure, for sure, is a reality for all of us. But the insight that failure has its uses and is not the end of the line can take the sharp, cutting edge off it. Even death, which is the ultimate failure only in a certain sense, has its use and meaning, as does the life it brings to a close.

In my present position as Secretary of Human Resources in the Commonwealth of Virginia I have general supervision over rehabilitative services and mental health work. One young woman I have come to know and respect utterly, through a series of accidents and misfortunes lost the use of both of her legs. Further difficulties indicated that her life could be saved only by amputation. She chose to go ahead with this drastic surgery because she had a kind of dream, a vision, a faith that her life could have meaning, use, satisfaction even so, for herself and for others. After unimaginable trials she was fitted into a kind of cone for support, is almost free of pain, and moves about in a battery or hand-driven wheel chair. And slowly she is working out a career as a computer operator. She is intelligent, alert, and cheerful—an absolute inspiration not only to the thousands in our state with physical and mental problems, but also to everyone who in any way touches her life. Talk about turning apparent disaster into success—talk about the power of faith and will, talk about living with reality and with dreams—this is the ultimate!

I said earlier that I would have something to say about the discontinuity between dreams and harsh realities. Take peace. Recent polls show peace to have moved to the number one position among the concerns Americans now have, ahead of inflation, unemployment, the environment, and crime. The dream and yearning for peace go back to St. Francis, the Buddha, Jesus, and in our time to Wilson, Gandhi, King, and others. Right now, yet another cry for arms limitation and peace is being heard loudly in this country and in Europe. It is a reaction partly to the military build-up, partly to the numbing fear of nuclear bombing, partly to the deep distrust of the "peace through strength" policy, partly to the sensing that we are sliding helplessly to the edge of a cliff. Diplomats seem unable to stop the slide. Political leaders seem unwilling to stop it. Moral leaders seem impotent to stop it. The dream of peace appears to many to be in danger of being overwhelmed by the reality of war. How can reality be moved toward the dream? How can the gap between them be narrowed, not by giving up the dream but by altering the reality?

Bullying won't do it. Building ever more effective weapons systems for offense or defense is likely to break national treasuries before it breaks the will of the contestants. Arguments about first-strike vulnerability or invulnerability, about retaliatory capability, about fail-safe detection, and all the rest don't seem to go to the heart of the matter—or to the hearts of the people either. This last may offer the best hope. How can people, be so engaged that the necessity and common sense of peace will sweep over the world in an irresistible flood? Do we all have to go to the brink, and perhaps over it, before the hope of peace will prevail over the present reality of arms build-up and confrontation?

The answers, I believe, are to be found in continued, hard-headed realistic negotiations for arms reductions; in a generous and non-threatening extension of economic cooperation and trade among the countries of the world; in a sharing of cultural, educational, scientific, and technological information and experiences; and in the application of new ways of resolving disputes by means of fact finding, mediation, arbitration, police action, and international law.

More than any of those approaches, useful though they can be, the answer, I believe, is to be found in the realm of dreams, hopes, faith, religion. Edna St, Vincent Millay's reminder about what will happen to the world if faith slackens is to the point:

> Faith it is
> That keeps the world alive. If all at once
> Faith were to slacken—that unconscious faith
> Which must, I know, yet be the cornerstone
> Of all believing,—birds now flying fearless
> Across would drop in terror to the earth,
> Fishes would drown, and the all-governing reins
> Would tangle in the frantic hands of God
> And the world gallop headlong to destruction!

Dreams, are essential at the level of individual living and at the level of national societies. But the dreams of the good life for individuals, as well as for the good life for the world must not so far outstrip the world's realities that the dreams are empty. Let us dream possible dreams, unlike those of the man of La Mancha, lest the dreams become no more than futile efforts to escape reality. Rather, let our dreams show us the way, give us glimpses of a better life and a better world.

We — each of us,
Individually and all together —
Must learn to live with both reality and dreams;
    Dreams prodding reality,
    Reality restraining dreams;
With faith of each in each, and each in all,
Guiding us along the way.

For All We Know

On a clear night we stand in awe, staring into the depths
    of a starlit sky.
Great galaxies and constellations radiate their silent
    light amidst the darkness.
We know that there are galaxies and constellations
    we shall never see.
More will be born, and more will fade away,
    yet we shall never know.

On the shore of the sea we watch the waves
    come rolling in relentlessly.
The tides will turn, and islands will emerge and grow and then
    will be submerged once more beneath the sea.
We know of many shores we cannot see where other
    waves and other shifting tides
Affect configurations of the land. We cannot see
    and yet we know.

Our lives, in their brief span or time,
    like waves and tides, like stars and planets,
Find momentum and direction from the forces of the past.
We know that there are lives and generations yet unborn
    that we shall never see.
The heritage we leave for them, the values which
    we seek to carry on are all we know.

Religion and Doubt

In a book popular a generation ago in college survey courses on western civilization, Vernon Louis Parrington wrote of Abraham Lincoln: "The heart-breaking hesitation of Lincoln, the troublesome doubt and perplexed questioning, reveal as nothing else could the simple integrity of his nature."

There is something appealing about a person who broods over an issue looking at it from all angles, losing sleep over it, searching deep into his very soul to find the answer. It is especially comforting when leaders go through this agony before making decisions. We are reassured to see that the same doubts that bedevil us plague them also. They are cast in human dimensions. We do not fear them.

But we are not of one mind on this subject. We are also attracted to the person of supreme self-confidence one who seems never to be assailed by doubts. Although we may not like this type all that much, we are inclined to respect his or her decisiveness and will-do approach. We are a trifle envious, thinking of ourselves wish-washy, full of self-doubt. If to err is human, then to doubt is even more human. There is quite a bit of Charlie Brown in each of us.

My experience has led me to distrust persons who seem never in doubt, or disturbed by doubts. I remember an infantry lieutenant in the training camp years ago who was always sure of everything: why the weapon wouldn't function properly, what the order really meant, how far it was to the stream, when the rain was going to stop. Our sergeant learned how to undercut the lieutenant. In transmitting the lieutenant's orders to us, he would tag those he didn't think were right with "the lieutenant says." "Fall out at 06:00 in full field equipment, the lieutenant says," and we would know the order would be changed later.

I prefer the leader who is secure enough within himself to share his doubts, ask for suggestions, and then make the decision. Sometimes an action will have to be taken the success of which is doubtful. Occasionally, of course, action will have to be committed too quickly with no time for consultation. Precipitate, unexplained action will more readily be accepted if the usual procedure involves sharing doubts ahead of time.

The sense of timing about doubts has to be exquisite, as does the sense of proportion. Too many doubts can immobilize a person, make resolve difficult and effective action impossible. They can freeze a situation and paralyze motion. "He who hesitates is lost." "Nothing ventured; nothing gained."

On the other hand, not enough doubt, or failure to doubt at the right moment, can lead to foolhardy action. There is an attractive bravado in, "Damn the torpedoes, full steam ahead!" But what if there are too many torpedoes? The trick is to know when to take the risk and when not to. "There is a tide in the affairs of men which taken at the flood leads on to fortune. . . ."

A good place to begin thinking about doubt and its role in human affairs is with the writings of Rene Descartes, the great 17th century mathematician and philosopher, father of the age of modern science. In his *Discourse on Method* he wrote:

> Of philosophy I will say nothing, except that it had been cultivated for many ages by the most distinguished men, and that yet there is not a single matter within its sphere which is not still in dispute, and nothing, therefore, which is beyond doubt. . . .

Descartes subjected everything to the test of doubt, including doubt itself. His doubting, he concluded, was real and it led him directly to his basic proposition: *cogito, ergo sum,* "I think, therefore I am." On this foundation—doubt, thought, existence—he built his physics and his metaphysics, his principles of science and his proof of the existence of God. But it all began with doubting; without that there would have been no Cartesian system.

Doubting, therefore, is a most respectable occupation of the mind, engaged in extensively by some of the world's best thinkers. Anyone who shuts doubts out of his mind and life had better reconsider. Properly employed, doubt can be the stepping-stone to truth and wisdom. Rejected, it can lead to narrowness, prejudice, and intolerance.

We hear a lot these days about the Moral Majority. There is a bumper sticker, "The Moral Majority Is Neither." But there are a good many fine people in this group. They are entitled to speak out and be heard. The part of their credo that bothers me is not their position on prayer in the schools or gun control or busing, but their extinguishing of doubt. Their leaders say they have erased doubt from their minds. It's hard to believe they have done so, but that's what the Reverend Jerry Falwell has said, as reported a number of times in newspapers and magazines. He preaches a religious and secular message which admits of no doubts, no uncertainties, no speculations—and, therefore, no differences, either. You have to be with him or against him, all or nothing, one hundred percent or zero.

In his column, "Virginia—From Both Barrels," my favorite Virginia columnist, the late George Bowles wrote about the training sessions sponsored by Moral Majority Inc. for "preacher-politicians":

> The ultimate goal of Falwell and his apostles is simple and direct. It is to change their fundamentalist perception of reality from a religious persuasion into the law of the land. . . . The Biblical injunction to "render unto Caesar the things which are Caesar's and unto God the things which are God's" has become lost in the arcane shuffle of Falwellian politics. Along with it, the wall between church and state has become a fuzzy blur.

Protestants from major denominations, not only Baptists and Methodists but also Catholics who have joined with the Reverend Falwell, need to be reminded of the struggle their religious forebears fought to gain respect and tolerance for religious practices. It didn't come easy. These new zealots would be well advised to cool it, slow down, recall past struggles, and regain a measure of doubt about their own infallibility.

Bowles concluded his column by recognizing the right of anyone in a free society like ours to preach the religious Word as he or she believes it. "But, for Heaven's sake," he says, "let's keep the Word—as any special group understands it—out of the law books."

In these matters many of the Falwell followers are true innocents. Should they succeed, for example, in having legislation or a Constitutional amendment passed removing the ban on compulsory prayers in public schools, they would soon reap a whirlwind. They would find that the prayers said in many schools would not be to their liking. The prayers would tend to be worded in ways acceptable to the predominant religious group in the local jurisdiction: Catholic in Baltimore and Miami, Jewish in New York City, perhaps even Unitarian in the more affluent Boston suburbs. A group that thinks of itself as the majority, and isn't, is sure to get its comeuppance.

I personally have felt the disapproval of the Moral Majority types in my political life. Often their attack has been unfounded in fact and twisted in presentation. For instance, I have been accused of advocating abortion across the board, which is not true. I have been charged with wanting to take all guns away from those who own them, which is also not true. I have even been labeled as opposed to the family because I voted for a federal aid program for battered spouses. One expects exaggeration in a political campaign; I am resigned to it and even a little amused by it. But with seven children and a growing number of grandchildren, all of them wanted, to be called anti-family is a bit much.

"Right-to-life" is an attractive goal. Waiving the questions of when life starts and whether in the fetal stage it should always, in every case, be protected, I doubt the wisdom and sincerity of those persons who, however solicitous of the unborn they may be, show little interest in programs to help those already born who are hungry, sick, physically or mentally handicapped, dispossessed, or otherwise in need.

Sometimes, when I permit myself a little paranoia, I wonder if my being targeted by the "moral majority" groups is the result of undue influence, of special economic interest groups, groups that oppose me as a tax reformer and a consumer advocate on which matters I really did speak out and had some effect, and who may be using innocent people for their own purposes. Most of their members are probably unaware of this influence.

Be all that as it may, my deeper problem with the "moral majority" groups doesn't have anything directly to do with such issues as prayer in school or gun control. It concerns the elimination of doubt from their scheme of things, their religion. This I find distressing. I said earlier that the rejection of doubt can lead to narrowness, prejudice, and intolerance. Even more damaging at the individual level would be the re-emergence of long-stifled doubts at a time of crisis. When major personal decisions have to be made and courses of action launched, the continued suppression of doubts into the subconscious may require the ugly but strong hand of prejudice and intolerance; suppression prevents the doubts from coming to the surface and getting in the way of the decision and course of action. This, in turn, may threaten loss of face, loss of position in the group, loss of reputation; it may even bring painful psychological trauma.

In short, there seems to be something psychologically wrong with expunging doubts from one's mind and from one's religion. The bravado, the cock-sureness that seems to go with a doubt-free religion, I think, is likely to prove under stress to be thin, brittle, fragile—essentially a defense without depth. Once it is broken through, the religion it aims to protect will shatter like a struck pane of glass. We need something better than a Humpty Dumpty religion on a wall, waiting for a fall.

I am aware that the popular view on this is opposite to mine. The religion with less doubt in it is stronger, most people would say. "Our doubts are traitors," Shakespeare wrote, "and make us lose the good we oft might win by fearing to attempt." Certainly doubt that continually inhibits thought and paralyzes action is no help. It would be the mark, if not of a traitor, then of a coward. But a little bit of doubt frequently can save an awful lot of grief. I remember the chairman of one of my political campaigns used to say, "If you're in doubt, don't do it."

In the end, I'm with Descartes. Don't be afraid of your doubts. Wrestle with them. Apply them to situations, occasionally to your deepest beliefs. It is a way of strengthening and reaffirming them. To be worth its salt, religion must be able to cope with living; doubt is surely a part of living and, therefore, of religion. A religion sturdy enough to handle doubt will be sturdy enough to provide a defense in depth against all onslaughts.

Religion at its best is a search for maturity. Maturity includes a willingness to live with doubt and uncertainty, even with unknowables. Maturity does not seek a quick haven of apparent certainty. A religion that admits and copes constructively with doubt is not thereby a doubtful religion; it is a robust religion with survival power. It has integrity, the Lincolnesque integrity I spoke of at the beginning. It is a quality we in the liberal religious tradition should cherish.

Let me add a few lines of whimsical verse.

> Dear friends:
>> Be unafraid of doubt
>> For it is everywhere about,
>> And there is no redoubt
>> Strong enough to keep it out.
>>
>> Rather, really do get smart
>> And take doubt to your heart,
>> And from the very start
>> Of your life, make it a part.

The Right to Happiness

(dedicated to the memory of Hubert Horatio Humphrey)

Is happiness a frivolity?
Is joy a luxury that life
with all its burdens can deny?

Is there not love enough
to undergird humanity
and foster heart and hope?

Is human decency, with kindness and
respect for humankind
a goal too large for us to set?

Is peace impossible for us to keep?
Is safety only for the few?
Must fear deny serenity?

Is it naive to tender hope
of freedom to pursue
a better life for everyone?

Shall we submit to misery
and loneliness? Is disrespect
a necessary part of life?

Is child neglect to be endured?
　Are families destined to decay
　　with focus turned outside the home?

Is care for health and mental health
　attainable alone to those
　　who can afford the cost?

I dare to hope, to dream, to pray
　that we will somehow find the way
　　to right the wrongs we see today.

Let social justice rule the land.
　Let freedom ring with peace and trust.
　　Let human dignity prevail.

We *have* the right to happiness,
　lift ourselves and to affirm
　　that right for people everywhere.

Yes . . .
　I dare to hope, to dream, to pray
　　that we will somehow find the way.

Politics, Religion and You

Politics, an experienced practitioner of the art once told me, is getting on
with things. Politics usually involves many different people, many objectives and many methods of trying to achieve them. What gives purpose, dignity and meaning to politics, he said, are the values which underlie politics.
How political leaders and citizens view politics and religion, or politics and
ethics, reveals much, very much, about the quality of the whole society.

Politics has been defined variously as the art of the possible, the art of
compromise, the art of government. Many think that politics is, inherently
venal, grasping, mean, and unworthy. This view saddens me.

Woodrow Wilson, in measured cadence, defined politics as the "science
of ordered progress of society along lines of usefulness." The Unitarian,
Theodore Parker, said politics is the "science of exigencies." I doubt if a
politician could define theology that succinctly. Daniel Webster said, "I have
read twenty volumes on politics from Adam Smith on. From the whole, if I
were to pick out with one hand all the mere truisms, and the other all the
doubtful propositions, little would be left." A famous Boston politician once
uttered my favorite definition of politics. "Politics," he said, "is the broth of
me life." I take politics to be that very human activity—part science, part art,
part magic—through which people arrange for their government. Usually
honorable, but too often corrupt. Usually tedious, but sometimes as heady as
champagne. Frequently superficial, but occasionally profound.

The practitioners of politics run the gamut like everyone else, only more
so. Noble ones, like Cato the Elder, or Charlemagne, or George Washington;
inept ones, like George III, or Warren Harding; evil ones, like Hitler; cruel
ones, like Genghis Kahn or Peter the Great. In recent years politics in the
United States has been in disrepute and the politician held in low esteem. A
poll not long ago showed politicians at the bottom of the ladder, below trash
collectors, secondhand car salesmen, and even big businessmen.

Even Walt Whitman, one of the all-time great optimists of America,
wrote in 1870, "Never was there, perhaps, more hollowness at heart than at
present. Genuine belief seems to have left us. . . . We live in an atmosphere
of hypocrisy throughout. . . . The depravity of the business classes of the
country is not less than has been supposed, but infinitely greater. The official

services of America . . . are saturated in corruption, bribery, falsehood, maladministration."

Well, what's the matter? What's wrong? My thesis is that politics have become disconnected from ethics and more profoundly disconnected from religion. Not completely, not everywhere, but enough so that many politicians have lost their bearings and people have lost their confidence. And remember, it only takes the misbehavior of a few prominent individuals to discredit all. What then about the ethics from which politics have become disconnected? I take ethics to be concerned with the goals of life, the standards of conduct: happiness, self-realization, stoical acceptance of faith, service to others, devotion to God, the exercise of power, and the pursuit of excellence. Ethics deals with the rightness and wrongness of actions, the goodness and badness of motives. I take religion to be the underpinning of ethics, the psychological, moral, intuitive, even institutional, support. Politics, many would say, are earthy and real. Ethics and religion are lofty and ideal. Politics can serve many masters and many systems of ethics—bad masters and bad ethics as well as good.

During the recent Nixon period and in some places since, politics were made to do the bidding of bad ethics. This is a sure prescription for trouble and trouble we've had. Instead of serving noble purposes of public enlightenment and public welfare in a confident, generous way, politics, especially during the Nixon years, were bent and distorted to win elections at almost any cost, to serve a misguided notion of national security, to reflect a distrustful view of the democratic process, and in the case of Nixon, to bolster the insecure personality of a morally deficient President. Lest we be too holy or too moralistic in our attitude, we would do well to ponder the words of Bernard Shaw when he heard that a labor candidate named Joseph Burgess refused to compromise on an issue during a general election and thereby lost a seat in Parliament.

> When I think of my own unfortunate character, smirched of compromise, rotted with opportunism, mildewed by expediency . . . dragged through the mud of borough council and Battersea elections, stretched out of shape with wire-pulling, putrefied by permeation, worn out by 25 years pushing to gain an inch here, or straining to stem a backrush, I do think Joe might have put up with just a speck or two on those white robes of his for the sake of millions of poor devils who cannot afford any character at all because they have no friend in Parliament. Oh, those moral dandies, these spiritual toffs, these superior persons. Who is Joe anyhow that he should not risk his soul occasionally like the rest of us?

Let me now focus on the decisions that politicians and citizens have to make. We convert our ethical and religious principles into action through the decisions we make. There are all kinds of decisions including no-decision, which all too frequently is the choice of politicians. I remember the story of the soldier who was assigned to peel potatoes while on k.p. He was given two pots and told to put the big potatoes in one pot and the little potatoes in the other pot. Half an hour later the sergeant came back and the soldier was still looking at the first potato, and the sergeant said, "What's the trouble? Why don't you get going on that job?" And the soldier said, "Oh, it isn't the peeling that bothers me; it's the decisions. I don't know if this is a big potato or a little potato." Well, there are hundreds and hundreds of personal and family decisions as well as public decisions. And we spend time on who will make the decisions, and through what process they will be made, as well as their substance.

The facts, analysis, advice, and values all converge at the point of decision. The important thing is to keep your eye on the decision, the ingredients which make it up, and the consequences which follow.

The hard political decisions that face us as a nation and as individuals require more than facts and analysis. They have to be based on ethical and religious values and sometimes they fly in the face of advice and argument. Examples of such decisions are not difficult to find. In the political world that I now move in, there are the gut issues like amnesty, capital punishment, abortion, gun control, drugs, refugees, and illegal immigrants. In addition, there are the other issues, probably of greater moment in national life, like unemployment, inflation, health, welfare, energy, environmental protection, and foreign aid.

A brief discussion of several of these will bring out my theme. How do we deal with amnesty, for example? Should we be guided by strict interpretation of the laws, or should we distinguish between equity for draft evaders and deserters on the one hand and those who served honorably in the armed forces on the other? How can we deal equitably with draft evaders as compared with deserters? Or should we let bygones be bygones? I believe we should forgive or perhaps forget, recognizing that many Vietnam war draft evaders in a profound sense were right all along. But for draft evaders, I would urge at the same time a degree of humility or even expiation or atonement. How easily one falls into the use of religious terms. You can consult the experts and read the statistics until the cows come home, and you won't find the answer. You have to get the answer from your own ethics and religion.

A few years ago, as a Member of Congress, I issued a statement on the Vietnam War, just as we were disengaging from it. I set forward some principles that I thought should govern thinking in the country and votes in Congress. There should be no increase in military aid to Vietnam except to extract Americans from the country and a certain number of Vietnamese who were committed to our affairs there. We should provide generously for immediate economic and humanitarian relief to the people who needed it. And then finally, we should get on with a long-term program to patch up the damage. Some months later when the House of Representatives met throughout one night trying to resolve these matters, it became abundantly clear as the Members became more tired that arguments crisscrossed with arguments and facts confuted facts. Each one just had to sit and figure out what values were at stake for the country and then vote. It was as simple and difficult as that. The values at stake were peace, relief from suffering and danger, responsibility and justice tempered by practicality and freedom. Before the final vote was taken in that exciting and dangerous moment, it became clear that basic values were at last taking over and members were voting according to them.

Ultimate values should govern the lawmaker as well as the citizen. In matters of profound importance judgment in politics consists of stripping decisions back to the underlying values which support not only those making the decisions, but all of us.

Frequently we have to be circumspect in the practical applications of values, and not forward headlong. Our valuing must be thoughtful, even though at the moment of crisis we must think quickly, hope, perhaps I should say that values are there for us at the critical moment.

Many other less dramatic examples could be cited. We face difficult decisions as to how to respond to needs for health insurance that are felt by millions of people, and at the same time respect the capacity and willingness of us all to pay for a higher level of medical care. As another example, judgments, typically compromises, have to be made on reducing unemployment by Federal spending for jobs, by tax reduction, and by appropriate monetary policy at the risk of further inflation or of heating up the economy again, with all the pain that inflicts on millions of people. Part of the problem is how far to go with such programs as food stamps, unemployment compensation, or help for the disabled. How far and how rapidly should the government go in these worthy directions without losing sight of the goal of a balanced budget and of the necessity for maintaining broad citizen support?

The politician-legislator wades through hearings and analysis; he listens to the lobbyists or tries to shut them off. In the end a solution is not so easily plucked. Time after time I find, that the only way to deal with such issues is in terms of a set of values, ethics, a feeling for religion.

Like you and many citizens, I was depressed by what happened during the Watergate period. At that moment however, Americans came face to face with the kind of value-based decision I'm discussing. We saw the spectacle of top government leaders corrupted. Every citizen needed to reach down deep into a conscience-searching process. Ultimately the President searched it as well and resigned. It was a traumatic, soul-searching moment, but a very important one in the history of our republic; a moment when virtually all citizens thought deeply and felt deeply about the state of their country. And when we did that, the way to proceed suddenly became clear.

Sometimes it's possible, I suppose, to consult the great moral precepts in a self-conscious way and find guidance. You can think deliberately about the Golden Rule, doing unto others as you would have them do unto you. Perhaps that will give a clue as to how to decide the question of more welfare or more fiscal responsibility. Maybe the Biblical injunction, "Judge not, that you be not judged," helps. At least do not judge another's conduct quickly or lightly lest that person judge you. You can try to apply Kant's categorical imperative, "Do only those acts which can be made the general standard or pattern for action." Or the pragmatic test of William James: "Will the act or the practice work out effectively in the sense of contributing to individual well-being and to society?"

These are well established ethical precepts. They are guidelines that can be consulted in a rather deliberate way. I commend this kind of decision process to you. I find it very helpful to check a situation this way.

For us as Unitarian Universalists it makes good sense to ask what our own great religious leaders and prophets would have done. What would Theodore Parker have thought about the voting rights bill of a decade ago? Or Dorothea Dix? How would the great women of our denomination have voted on the proposition to deny federal funds to welfare recipients for abortion, or on the anti-abortion amendment? How would Thomas Jefferson have advised us on freedom of information or Horace Mann on equal education opportunities?

But, it will be said, what if the values from which political decisions are derived are not good ones? What then? This is another, far reaching matter about which I will only assert that most fellow citizens in this country, in many other countries with whom we share traditions, and certainly our fellow Unitarian Universalists, will reach consensus through democratic processes—

at least through mutual understanding. The faith that it can be so is the postulate for any civil and workable society.

In the value-finding, or value-revealing, process I am probing here, I see a danger against which Americans especially must be on guard. In our moral zeal for laudable goals we will permit unseemly, even wicked methods. Jacques Maritain wrote:

> Means must be appropriate to the end, since they are ways to the end and, so to speak, the end itself in its very process of coming into existence.... The doctrine of purification of the means ... asks that an end worthy of man be pursued with means worthy of man.

I have no doubt that Maritain's Catholic-democratic values—or others based on the considerations I have been expounding here—will ultimately prevail. Primarily a matter of faith, there is much-evidence of their practicality. Good political decisions come from values of respect for others, freedom, responsibility, kindness, and justice. I speak of the ethical and religious foundations for political decisions and urge you to test your political leaders and yourselves accordingly.

I think generally the objective should be to lead in the ethical or right direction as fast and as consistently as the majority of the people can follow. Sometimes strategic pauses or a step backward are needed to consolidate before taking the next step forward. The frog, you know, gets out of the well by repeatedly jumping two feet up and falling back one. The important thing is to carry on the politics of progress realistically, but always within a framework of good ethical and religious principles.

Look your politicians over. It is not hard to test them. They are the mirror image of yourselves in most respects. Most difficult political decisions on which the evidence is conflicting and the arguments don't persuade can be made with direct reference to a set of values. Look for the values that underlie a politician's decisions, and see if you like what's there. Beware of the politician who resorts to shoddy politics to attain good and laudable goals. Bad means will corrupt good goals just as surely as bad goals will deface good means. Above all, don't be discouraged by lapses of ethical and political conduct that have occurred lately in high places. Have faith in the goodness of people and their capacity to sort things out. This faith, I believe, is the best and perhaps the only guarantee that good ethics will again prevail and that equally good politics will again take over everywhere. This will not be easy. Jefferson's "eternal vigilance" will be necessary. Politics is much harder than physics, as Einstein pointed out.

It is at the intersections of politics and religion that turns toward social progress or toward its opposite. Making the right decisions requires that religion and politics be coherent and harmonious, in the public and individual sense. Such harmony within the one and between the one and the many offers the best hope for the future we desire for our communities, for our country, and especially for ourselves.

> Give us, God of our conscience,
>> The intuition and the wisdom
> To decide justly and to act courageously,
>> With confidence in the worth of our values
> Without which decision and action
>> Can never lift the human spirit.

Commitment

Not very far away a homeless man and woman wander through
    the streets in lonely desolation.
Not very far away a child is frightened and alone,
    and no one hears his cry.
Not very far away sheer ignorance denies an opportunity
    to build a decent life, and desperation turns to crime.
Not very far away injustice born of prejudice
    results in ethnic epithets and bigotry,
And those who should be friends are polarized
    by pressures from their peers.
Not very far away the fear of violence and wars
    reduces hope to bleak despair.

And from the pulpit and the podium our ministers
    and politicians seek solutions to these ills,
And in our congregations we are in accord
    that something must be done:
The church should be more activist.
The government should do a better job or else stay out.
Indeed, we'll give some time ourselves
    and give some money, too, and hope that it will help.
The test of our commitment, though, in not the words we speak
    or contributions that we make,
But in the way we live our lives, in kindnesses we show,
In understanding and respect we feel for others whom we meet.
Commitment comes from deep within —
    from love and genuine concern.

Commitment is not measured out in hours
    or in money that we spend.
It's not defined in caucuses or creeds,
But our commitment finds its roots in our
    sincerity, integrity and will.
It's not enough to speak, though speak we must —
It's not enough to spend, though spend we must —
It's not enough to pray and work, to legislate and vote —
Though all of these indeed we must. For this is all consistent
    with our cause.

Humanity lies deep within the fiber of our being
    for we are one with humankind.
If there is truly meaning to our words and prayers,
Then reverence for life will guide decisions that we make
That we may find commitment in our lives and work
And help to make our dreams reality.

Religious Liberals and the Public Interest

We religious liberals are concerned with finding the public interest and pursuing it relentlessly, even though it is a will-of-the-wisp that eludes our grasp. The tradition and dynamics of liberal religion force us to seek out and serve the public interest almost compulsively, whatever it is.

I am thinking of the public interest as a concept, as a matter of political and personal philosophy, not as the more ordinary notion of what members of the public happen to be interested in, such as the local baseball team, the latest hit tune, or yesterday's crime in the street. You can think of religious liberals as having two major concerns: a social or public concern, and a personal and individual concern. The two concerns are interrelated in so many obvious and subtle ways that they are one concern. The personal concern must undergird and carry into effect the public concern on a wide scale. In James Luther Adams' formulation, "Every personal problem is a social problem, and every social problem is a personal problem."

We begin to develop a concept of the public interest early in life as we experiment with reconciling personal interest with that of our brothers, sisters, and friends. In our family this is illustrated by the story of "the boy with the fat lip." He took his friend's share of the jelly beans and got a fat lip in return!

Many attempts have been made to define the public interest:

- The greatest good for the greatest number over the longest time, as expounded by Jeremy Bentham and the English utilitarians. One trouble with this, as mathematicians know, is that you can't maximize several things simultaneously.

- National aggrandizement or the glorification of the state. Caesar, Bonaparte, and Hitler come to mind. A modified, more acceptable form of this is seen in the post-World War II drive of many newer countries for national identity. The former president of Ghana, Nkrumah, said, "Seek ye first the political kingdom."

- Preservation of social traditions and stability, a worthy goal but one difficult to achieve in a world of rapid, unpredictable change.

- Protection and advancement of an elite group, whether party, church, class, or whatever.

- Economic growth and social reform, as in most less developed countries.

- Individual freedom in a political and social democracy. Our own Constitution has as guideposts along with a Bill of Rights, an equal protection of the laws clause and a general welfare clause that each generation of Justices reinterprets.

Alexis de Tocqueville wrote: "I have never been more struck by the good sense and the practical judgment of the Americans than in the manner in which they elude the numberless difficulties resulting from their Federal Constitution." But these parts of the Constitution have been pegs on which we in this country have hung many needed reforms.

If I were pressed to characterize the public interest, I would say, for religious liberals, that it consists of a ceaseless search for the fuller liberation of each individual, and hence society, from anything that demeans the human spirit—liberation from prejudice, poverty, pettiness, from the tendency to push other people around, from the fear of war. I regard an action as being in the public interest if it affords people wider and freer choice among alternative courses, each of which is judged to have merit—if it increases the opportunity for "the full exercise of one's powers along lines of excellence," in the words of John F. Kennedy.

I believe further that the search for liberation of the human spirit will not be ceaseless or effective or satisfying unless it is supported by and flows from a quality I can only call religious. By religious I mean a deep respect for the yearning each person has to improve the human lot. I mean the sense of comradeship persons feel for all others when they are at their best. I mean a respect for nature and science and their laws as well as for each and every human being. I mean compassion for human failure and encouragement to those who want to try again. I mean each person helping others to become more nearly what they really are and thereby attaining a higher level of fulfillment for himself or herself.

Among liberals, the search for the public interest, springs from their religion and cannot be separated from it.

The religious liberal's approach to the public interest comes through most clearly in issues of social concern. Personal commitment to social advancement is important in each case. I shall be suggestive here, rather than definitive.

- In education, especially at the lower levels, we are still in arrears. The increased number of children now coming into the elementary schools have to be provided with better basic education. As the youngsters move on to the high schools, many of them will have to receive training for jobs if the 30 percent drop-out rate is to be reduced. The cadre of future leaders will have to be educated through the higher levels, not only in numerous professions—some of them not even known two or three decades ago—but also in a broad and deep appreciation for the humanities. For religious liberals, this poses a special problem. We want to have our primary and secondary schools greatly improved, if need be through additional federal aid, but at the same time we wish to preserve the historic separation between church and state. We shall have to think deeply about this matter and seek a new reconciliation under the First Amendment, which states that "Congress shall make no law with respect to the establishment of religion or the free exercise thereof."

- We want to extend civil rights to all citizens, including the right to economic opportunity, open housing, equal treatment in court, and social services. Ever since the epochal Supreme Court decision for desegregation of the pubic schools, we have made much progress, but more is needed. We shall have to continue to make the Civil Rights Act and the Voting Rights Law fully effective in our own communities. We have yet to breach the immense stratification and segregation in housing by color, by income class, by social grouping, by type of employment, and by national origin, and especially by color. Until Americans are willing to live as neighbors with all citizens, our society will fall short of its destiny.

- Poverty still afflicts 15 or so per cent of our people; even in affluent suburbs and upper class city neighborhoods it is surprisingly high. Poverty is concentrated among Black and other minority families, families headed by a single parent who is typically a woman, the poorly educated, and in particular city and rural areas. Poverty exists stubbornly in social, economic, and regional pockets. The same can be said about youth problems, crime, unemployment, and inefficient welfare programs with which poverty is closely linked. It will be a difficult task of public policy and private effort to reduce these afflictions. What are the full responsibilities of religious

liberals in these matters? How can we give effective expression to
our deep convictions and yet avoid "do-goodism"?

• Should this country require that governments receiving foreign aid
  oppose or at least be neutral toward communism? Or that they
  adopt land or tax reforms? How much local authority should we
  transfer to metropolitan-wide authority to deal with regional
  problems like air pollution, water supply, epidemics, and crime, and
  with what safeguards? Or, for that matter, how much of national
  sovereignty should we give over to the United Nations?

• Where does our country's general interest lie in Latin America? We
  face many dilemmas. We want to observe treaties, yet not be
  strapped into them. We want to avoid war, but probably not at any
  cost. We want to help other countries defend their freedom from
  outside aggression and inside subversion—yet not force our help
  where it is not wanted. We want to support new governments if
  they show promise of being more democratic and more concerned
  with all their citizens, but we find it hard to turn away from
  governments we have supported in the past. And so on.

Finally, a down-to-earth example that I call "The Squirrel of Arlington:
Where Is the Public Interest, Anyway: A Fable of Our Times."

A few years ago when I was the elected head of the government of
Arlington County, Virginia, a large delegation of citizens came to our Board
meeting with a complaint. Squirrels were becoming terrible pests. They
were eating through the roof shingles, nesting in the downspouts, entering the
attics and gnawing on woolens, and stealing sunflower seeds from the bird
feeding stations. Furthermore, they were disease carriers and had been
known to bite babies in their carriages. They were dirty, loathsome rodents
and should be exterminated—at public expense, of course.

Ever solicitous of the public welfare, not to mention the votes of irate
citizens, the Board took the matter under advisement, said we'd investigate it,
then act. We consulted the U.S. Department of Agriculture, that great
storehouse of practical knowledge on everything from growing tomatoes, to
how to protect clothes closets from moths, to preparing French omelettes, to
leading group discussions. USDA said that we could trap the squirrels,
poison them, cut down the oak and walnut trees where they get winter food,
or we could shoot them.

So we tried traps, but for some reason we caught mostly bluejays. We
rejected poison out of consideration for children and dogs and cats.

Removing beautiful trees was unthinkable. That left shooting. So we sent one of our police officers to a special training course for acquiring this skill, from which in due course he received a certificate of accomplishment (the Gospel truth, so help me!) When the next complaint came in, the squirrel shooter was dispatched posthaste to the scene where he fulfilled our highest hopes by killing eight squirrels in the first day.

The next meeting of our Board was packed with protesting citizens. The Society for the Prevention of Cruelty to Animals was represented. The Audubon Society, it seemed, had developed a concern for squirrels as well as birds, perhaps thinking that some of the squirrels might be of the flying variety. Mothers feared their children would be shot, while fathers were concerned that windows would be broken. One wrought-up individual ended his peroration with this: "In Arlington, man's inhumanity to man is exceeded only by his inhumanity to squirrels." And another read a touching passage from a book by Thornton W. Burgess called *The Adventures of Happy Jack, The Gray Squirrel.*

Well, to finish this parable about the public interest, the squirrel shooting officer minus his .22 was returned, much to his disappointment, to his regular beat, and we referred the whole matter to staff for further study. We buried it. So if you know any squirrels who want security, cradle to grave, advise them to go to Arlington, Virginia. The moral of this tale is: The public interest is seldom where you think it is, and may not be anywhere at all, but it is instructive to look for it.

Where choices to determine the public interest have to be made at the practical level, there must always be a balance of judgment, a weighing of factors, a certain amount of intuition, and, where the issue is important, a large ingredient of religious faith in the liberating potential of social and individual action.

In the political arena we rely on a process for determining what is in the public interest, and we hope mature and wise persons make the decisions. Although it can help, we must never rely entirely on a fancy measurement of benefits and costs done by those whom Edmund Burke called "sophists, economists and calculators." Incidentally I am an economist. At the personal level we depend on knowledge and/or values when rational processes fail to give the answer. This latter is the religious and ethical element we need when the chips are down.

Our Unitarian Church in Bloomington, Illinois, where I attended the funeral service for Adlai Stevenson a few years ago, had this quotation from Governor Stevenson posted outside: "Freedom is a plant which grows only from faith. It must be watered by knowledge."

We are concerned, therefore, with more than social programs for the general benefit; we are also concerned with the motivation and the attitudes which underlie and sustain any successful effort to improve the general welfare. We must be concerned with what liberating programs do for the people to whom they are aimed as well as to the people promoting and undertaking the reforms. "What does it profit a man to gain the whole world if he loses his soul?" What gain is there in the achievement of a social program if personality or family life is eroded?

Uncomfortably I recall the devastating answer one of our daughters gave when children in her class were asked what their daddies did for work. She said, "My daddy goes to meetings."

As religious liberals we must be cautious about undertaking activities which are, subconsciously perhaps, only an escape from personal problems into frenetic community and public action. I believe individuals should participate in social action to express their highly personal as well as an outgoing concern. Social action should be "inner directed" as well as "other directed," to use David Reisman's phrases. To the question, "Am I my brother's keeper?" the only answer is, "Yes." This holds for religious liberals or anyone else. But this admonition also holds: "To thine own self be true; and it must follow as the night, the day, thou canst not then be false to any man." What directions do religious liberals look to when they try to find the public interest? Let these tests gauge particular actions:

1. Does the action advance material well-being for the basics of food, shelter, and health care, and especially for those in need?

2. Does it add dignity and meaning to life for all people?

3. Does it extend the area of cooperation and reduce destructive tensions?

4. Do those who are or should be concerned have an opportunity to participate in determining the public interest? Are the significant points of view well represented?

5. Is it anchored in what men and women at their best would regard as good and solid?

6. Especially for religious liberals:
   —Will the action help liberate people from anything that would demean the spirit?
   —Will it enlarge our choices among alternative courses judged to have merit?
   —Will it give scope for a liberal and a religious style of life?

I said at the outset I would talk about the relevance of liberal religion to the public interest, not define it. I end in the same vein. The search for the general good is probably more important than its attainment. The ardor, the humility, and the effectiveness of the searching and the learning are the test, especially for religious liberals—with reach always exceeding grasp, with dreams lighting the way, and with progress counted off in practical achievements.

To Reach Beyond

Is there a way to reach beyond
the tiny space we have in time?
Can mortal men and women find
an earthly immortality?

We'd like to plant some trees and flowers
to grow for others to enjoy.
We'd like to cultivate a brave idea
and nurse it to maturity.

We'd hope to turn this brave idea
to service with the men and women
and the children whom we love
for them to share and pass along.

We yearn to foster beauty with
such skill as we possess. With art
and music we would save
a little of the loveliness we know.

We yearn to find the words to write
in poetry and prose the feelings
deepest in our hearts to speak
with generations yet to come.

Perhaps it's not too much to hope
   that life has deathless qualities
      that reach beyond this finite time,
         this precious time we have on earth.

Religion and the Future

In January, 1976, Peggy and I embarked on an adventure, the two of us, to express in poems and essay-sermons our views of religion. The general theme has been Religion and Living. We have dealt with such elements as religion and nature, religion and people, religion and birth and death, religion and science, religion and education, religion and crime, religion and the family, religion and work, religion and art, religion and peace.

Now we come to the last in the series, Religion and the Future; again with an essay-sermon and poetry. The future is partly discernible through prophetic insight and scientific projection; it is also partly inscrutable, perhaps partly unknowable forever. However this may be, we believe that a liberal religious approach to living and to the future will continue to be necessary for many individuals as it will be for a healthy society.

Such an approach, we believe, carries a respect for the wonderful processes of nature, a love of other human beings with all their diversity, orneriness, and genius, and a religious faith that has the potential for truth, beauty, and goodness that can be realized in a person and in the world. Of the three—humanity, nature, religion—the key to the future, we believe, is religion as we think and feel it to be. Religion provides the purpose and perspective, the meaning and motivation for living. The ultimate satisfaction lies in having lived religiously, to use James Luther Adams's term.

An individual's religious view is largely drawn from personal experience of living. Mine is no exception. My personal interests, concerns, and values have developed along several lines, two of which I stress here: nature and people. As a graduate student in economics I concentrated on labor and welfare problems and on natural resources development. After service in the second World War, I went to work for the Council of Economic Advisers to the President. My job title was Human and Natural Resources Analyst. Even as a member of Congress and as Virginia Secretary of Human Resources I found myself engrossed in legislation relating to social security and unemployment, and to resources and the environment. My avocational activities have been along the same two lines. Small wonder, then, that nature and people are at the heart of my views of religion and living.

Looking toward the future, then, I see the need for coming to terms with the natural world and with the world of people in a sustainable, peaceful, cooperative, yet self-fulfilling way. I am convinced that an open, seeking, liberal approach offers the best chance of success; I believe that both nature and people are suffused with a religious quality that ties them together in a single, magnificent, embracing construct. William Blake expressed this inter-relatedness, this wholeness, most beautifully:

> To see the world in a grain of sand
> And heaven in a wild flower.

Note that it is the human being who alone can see the world in a grain of sand, perhaps as an inspiration resulting from what Wordsworth called "that flash upon the inward eye." Others catch a glimpse of the entirety of the world and its meaning, from origins to destiny, in a single human act of kindness, one person to another. A human being enjoys a favorable vantage point for taking it all in. Religion, I assert, is essential to taking it all in.

Religion is not a formal ritual or an inherited set of beliefs. Nor is it a church or any other kind of institution. Rather, religion is the distillation of life's experiences. It is a man looking at the world and learning to live in it. It is a woman discovering herself, shaping her destiny and coming to terms with it. It is a man or a woman being with other men and women, learning from and teaching one another, paying attention to and caring for one another. More than a result of living or a reason for living, religion, I claim, is living at its most sensitive and profound level. Religion is living fully, generously, thoughtfully, creatively, lovingly, looking outward, looking inward, looking back, looking ahead. Religion, in short, is the essence of human existence.

Having characterized the term *liberal* briefly and the term *religious* at greater length, I shall now turn to the liberal religious approach to living in its inward and outward aspects. First, the outward.

Religious liberals today face a long agenda of social improvements to be accomplished, many of which I have dealt with in these essay-sermons. Let me recall a few of them.

At the top of the list is full equality of civil rights, education, voting, and economic opportunity. In the more than 25 years since the epochal U. S. Supreme Court decision for desegregation of public schools and the nearly 15 years since the Civil Rights Act, much progress has been made, but much more is needed. Full equal economic opportunity, is still lacking for minorities and women. We must work at these in our own home communities as well as at the national level.

Ahead of us and hardly breached at all is the immense stratification and segregation in housing by color, by income class, by social stratum, by employment, by national origin. Until Americans are much more willing to live literally as neighbors with all of their fellow citizens our society will fall short of its destiny.

Poverty, sheer poverty, still afflicts a growing proportion of our people. It is concentrated among black, Indian, and other minority families, among families headed by old people or by women, among the poorly educated, and in certain rural areas and parts of metropolitan centers. Poverty exists stubbornly in certain social, economic, and regional pockets; it will be a difficult and subtle task of public policy and private effort to reduce this affliction.

We are in arrears in regard to education. Not only will children have to be provided with basic education, but many of them in the secondary school level will have to receive better training for jobs. The cadre for future leaders will have to be trained through the higher levels not only in numerous professions, some of them not even known until recently, but they will also have to absorb a broad and deep appreciation for the humanities. This poses a special problem for religious liberals. We want to have our primary and secondary schools greatly improved, if need be through additional federal aid, but at the same time we wish to preserve local control of education.

With our strong tradition for action to improve social welfare and medical care, the future will find religious liberals continuing in the vanguard of such movements as that to extend insured medical care to all persons, not just poor and older persons, to improve the humaneness and in the administration of social welfare programs, and to provide work opportunities for youth.

The improvement of both urban and rural living likewise will concern religious liberals. Our cities are at once the glory and the bane of American civilization. How to improve city life, how to make it urbane as well as urban, constitutes one of the major challenges for the remaining years of the twentieth century. Hardly less important will be the conservation and improvement of the quality of our rural areas and natural resources, from poor farms in the southeast to chronically depressed coal mining towns.

On a world scale population is increasing at an average of two per cent per year, which means population will double in 36 years. Americans along with all other nations must be willing to address this issue on a broad front seeking ways of helping more and more families to plan effectively for their own size.

The promotion of world order and peace will continue to occupy us as it has in the past in Southeast Asia, the Middle East, Africa, or wherever order and peace are threatened. Religious liberals, it seems to me, have a special point of vulnerability in this matter. Thus, we must not fall prey to the "peace at any price" idea, just as we must urge others not to rush too quickly to the barricades. To find the zone between the extremes, where constructive action is possible without overextension of commitment, is a most difficult task, especially in view of the inadequate information most of us have.

But religious liberals must be concerned with more than social action programs; we must also be concerned with the inward side of life, with the approach, attitude, and motivation which underlie and sustain successful social action. We must be concerned with what liberating programs do not only for the people whom they are directed, but also for the people promoting and undertaking the reforms. "What does it profit a man to gain the whole world if he loses his soul?" What gain is there in the achievement of his social program if a person's personality is eroded thereby?

Religious liberals must beware of undertaking activities which are, subconsciously perhaps, no more than an escape from personal problems into frenetic social action. I believe there should be an individual, highly personal basis for participation in social action as well as an outgoing quality. Social action should be "inner-directed" as well as "other-directed," to use Reisman's phrases. To the question "Am I my brother's keeper?" the answer must be yes. It is true that "any man's death diminishes me, for I am involved in mankind." But each of us is also his own keeper, involved also in himself, internally responsible.

Along the way toward accomplishing our agenda for responsible social action we shall find many pitfalls. There are few easy answers. The best is frequently the enemy of the good. Occasionally one must choose the bad simply to avoid the terrible. But with a sense of what is right and good, with determination that is neither pretentious nor overbearing, we can make headway.

Our broad objectives for responsible social action are good: peace, justice, equal opportunity, freedom. But in pursuing these programs let us beware of liberal stereotypes, of placing too much weight on federal government action, of the tendency to load too much on the United Nations. Let us also take care not to become impatient with the complexities of foreign situations and domestic problems. Let us also make certain not to undertake activities that recognize social need in the absence of deep personal motivation.

Above all let us not be negative only, but let our protest always be accompanied by positive, practical programs. Remembering that nothing is as powerful, or as responsible, as a practical program that comes from the joining of deep, personal religious impulse to a worthy social cause, let us choose our lines of activity carefully and then pursue them vigorously.

As always, the problem of free men and women is to exercise their freedom wisely and responsibly. The questions are: when to protest, and when to go along; when to be rigid, when to compromise; when to advance, when to fall back and regroup; when to be self-righteous, when to politic for the possible; how to keep steadily on our general course despite much backing and filling. In short, we must know how to take the tide at its flood.

These are the excruciating choices that test a person's religion and common sense. In these choices and how we make them is the essence of social responsibility.

Here I circle back to the questions I posed at the beginning about new directions for the liberal faith. I believe we must find our new directions, our new purposes, our new emphases, in establishing more firmly the personal, individual, private basis for dealing with great social issues. Social issues, I believe, turn out in the end to be intensely personal issues. The individual, the small group, and the larger society are woven into the same cloth, but the threads first put into the loom are those representing individual personality, individual aspirations, individual motivations, individual morality.

New directions for the liberal faith are really new affirmations, or reaffirmations, of the importance and dignity of each person and the necessity for each one, with such help as she or he can get from others, to order life by discovering personal goals and then moving purposefully toward them. The discovering of goals is usually no more than uncovering what is already there waiting to be discovered; the pursuit of goals is then simply the laying on of programs of thought and action through which persons may become more nearly what they really are.

In this day of power—political power, military power, economic power, the power of advertising and propaganda—I am suggesting that the power of thoughtfulness, concern, dedication, and love at the personal and individual level is stronger, or can be made stronger, than we have dreamed possible. We should have confidence in this kind of power; we should rely on it, we should apply it in our own lives and at all the levels of society and public affairs to the problems and crises of our times.

If the problem and resulting crisis in your family (or in mine) involves youth-parent relations, then try an extra measure of patience, which is a form of power. If the problem relates to race in your community, then how about an extra measure of understanding and sympathy? These also are forms of power. If it is the income, wealth, or poverty gap that needs closing, then we can turn to sharing, for much potential good resides in the practical application of the power of concern. In each case I am proposing that the individual take a personal responsibility for behavior. This will do more good for the person and for society than all our laws, decrees, and institutional forms of social action.

I am pleading here for greater use of power in its benign and personal form, employed early and continuously to the problems of our times whether they are family, community, national, or international in scope. The beginning is inside each individual, and it is to the individual that those of us in the liberal faith must now turn our main attention. Let us retreat a bit from frenetic activity in the public arena and look inside ourselves more deeply to make sure that our hearts and minds are ready to do at the level of individual living those things which, in the absence of personal commitment, governments and denominations seem powerless to do on the larger scale. Perhaps in this way we of the liberal faith can liberate ourselves, and by example others, from the hang-ups and frustrations that plague our times.

An article in a recent issue of the journal of The World Future Society, *The Futurist,* quotes Aureleo Paccei, a benevolent Italian godfather of the futurist movement, as follows: "The shocking discovery we have yet to make is that, for all his science and might and all his plans, structures, systems, and tools, modern man cannot change his fate if he himself does not change."

What is most needed is a new statement of a liberal religious theology as our world crosses the 2000 mark and enters the third millennium after Jesus of Nazareth. Building a new theology will provide intellectual excitement and philosophical depth to liberal religion. I have been discussing some of the elements of such a theology, not as a theologian, to which role I can make no claim, but as one whose working life has been taken up with searching for scientific truth and trying to advance human welfare in the economic and political spheres. Like most people I am unable to philosophize without a strong bias derived from my own particular thoughts and experiences. The principal ingredients of this theology, I think, are these:

- Recognition of the overall cosmic unity which contains almost infinite diversity within its compass, plus a confidence that slowly, painstakingly, its mysteries can be unravelled. On the smaller scale in which we live this means respect for nature and natural processes, for ecological imperatives in which humans are viewed as integral parts of larger systems.

- Belief in humanistic values of personal dignity and worth on the basis of which both individual improvement and social progress become more achievable. This, plus a devotion to cooperative, peaceful, generous, and democratic ways of dealing with one another.

- Faith in creative and evolutionary processes of thought and action as revealed through inspiration and insight, as well as through scientific reasoning and experiment. This, along with a willingness, however restless and reluctant, to accept many unknowns, some perhaps unknowable.

- Devotion to a liberal and religious approach through which freedom must be balanced with responsibility, individualism with a concern for others, idealism with pragmatism, and self-respect with respect for all else in the universe.

A theology for the future will have to be flexible enough to enable us and those who follow us to meet a range of situations, none of which can be predicted with any degree of certainty. The population of the world may increase by five times in the next century or two above the four billion people now living. Instantaneous communication from everyplace in the world to every other place is clearly in sight. Interplanetary travel is not far off and the possibility of linking up with cognitive species elsewhere in the universe is not far-fetched. Genetic engineering of human beings has entered the sphere of legal concern. Abundant cheap energy from nuclear fusion or the sun is the object of research and development. Who knows what lies just over the horizon beyond our view?

But not all eventualities are pleasant to contemplate. Also possible is the holocaust of nuclear warfare, or the grotesque genetic consequences of ingestion by humans and animals of chemical or radioactive pollutants, or the destruction of major life-supporting ecosystems. Most insidious of all would be a progressive loss of will to live that might result from repeated technological and psychological shocks. The only adequate defense against devastating future shock, to use Alvin Toffler's term, or against the equal devastation of unbridled, cancerous growth, is to be found in an embracing theology that emphasizes the capacity of humans to cope with whatever the future brings, and to cope in a creative way. I think a liberal religious faith offers the best chance.

Therefore, whatever else religious liberals set out to do in the years ahead. I hope some will undertake the reshaping of a liberal religious theology for the years beyond 2000—a reformation for the future. I believe it can be done and must be done, as the years of the twenty-first century approach and then unfold, if the spiral of our future is to be upward.

The search for religion, therefore, is the most challenging and rewarding of all the human adventures. If you like, religion in the sense I have been using the term can be called God and the search for it can be thought of as divine.

> O, Past —
> Heavy laden with both grief and joy,
> Accomplishment and frustration,
> > Gain and loss.
>
> O, Future —
> Bursting with promise like a spring bud,
> Trembling with imagined danger,
> > Inscrutable.
>
> O, Man
> O, Woman —
> Cut into the unknown waiting to be known,
> Respect the world of nature and all its life,
> Act with caring and with love for all humanity,
> Link Past to Future, Soul with World.
> > Stand on this ground
> > And touch the sky.